CZECHOSLOVAKIA'S
Blueprint for "FREEDOM"

ALEXANDER DUBCEK

ZECHOSLOVAKIA'S

lueprint for "FREEDOM"

STATEMENTS -

**The Original
and
Official Documents
Leading to the Conflict
of August, 1968**

roduction & Analysis by PAUL ELLO, Ph. D.

orgetown University School of Foreign Service

LISHED BY ACROPOLIS BOOKS, WASHINGTON, D.C. 20009

The documents themselves are photographically reproduced from the original papers as translated by Czech linguists in Prague without changes to retain their full original authenticity, including the various imperfections present in the original copy.

ACROPOLIS BOOKS

Colortone Building, 2400 17th St., N. W.
Washington, D. C. 20009

FIRST PRINTING, September 1968

SECOND PRINTING, October 1968

Printed in the United States of America by
Colortone Creative Printing, *Washington, D. C. 20009*

Type set in Baskerville
by Colortone Typographic Division, Inc.

Design by Design and Art Studio 2400, Inc.

Library of Congress Catalog Number 68-58075

A Chronology of Events

1967

June 27-29	The Czechoslovak Writers' Union criticizes openly the domestic and foreign policies of the regime.
October 30	First open student demonstrations caused by bad conditions in student hostels.
December 8	Visit of the First Secretary of the CPSU, Leonid Brezhnev, in Prague.

1968

January 5	Antonin Novotny replaced as First Secretary of the CCP by Alexander Dubcek, who attempts a party-purge.
March 5	First steps towards a relaxation of censorship.
March 22	Novotny is forced to resign as head of the state. General Ludvik Svoboda is appointed as his successor on March 28.
April 3	Government promises investigation of the death of former Foreign Minister Jan Masaryk, said to have been murdered by Stalin's agents.
April 4	Oldrich Cernik appointed Prime Minister. New Cabinet formed.
April 5	Action Program published. Extensive civil rights and reforms promised.
May 4	Dubcek visits Moscow.
May 8	Conference of East German, Polish, Hungarian and Bulgarian Party leaders in Moscow.
May 10	Soviet military maneuvers commence in Poland near the Czechoslovakian border.
May 17	Alexei Kosygin, Premier of the Soviet Union and Marshal Andrei Grechko, Minister of Defense and former commander of the Warsaw Pact armed forces, visits Prague. Czechoslovakia agrees to Warsaw Pact maneuvers on Czechoslovakian territory.
May 30	Antonin Novotny ousted from the Party.
July 9	Prague denies necessity of convening a Warsaw Pact summit meeting because of its reforms.
July 10	Concern voiced about the stay of Russian troops in Czechoslovakia after the end of the Warsaw Pact maneuvers.
July 15	Warsaw Pact structure criticized by Czech General Vaclav Prchlik. New leaders ignore criticism.
July 17	Letter of the other Warsaw Pact members criticizing Czechoslovakian reforms published.
July 29-31	Talks between the Czechoslovakian leadership with members of the Soviet politburo at Cierna and Tisou.
August 3	Meeting of Warsaw Pact members and Czechoslovakian leaders in Bratislava. Soviet troops withdrawn.
August 9	Yugoslavian President, Marshal Tito, visits Prague.
August 10	Soviets resume maneuvers in the Ukraine, along the Czechoslovakian border.
August 11	East German leader Walter Ulbricht is given a cool reception in Prague.
August 14	Soviet press violently attacks Czech reforms.
August 15	Nicolae Ceaucescu, President of Rumania, is given a hearty welcome in Prague.
August 20	Soviet and Warsaw Pact forces invade Czechoslovakia after a secret meeting of Soviet leaders. Dubcek arrested.

A Chronology of Events

PREFACE

This volume is published for scholars and laymen alike.

In the case of the former, the significance of the documents presented here will be obvious. Outside of their intrinsic importance as basic source material, these documents offer what amounts to a blueprint for the further development of a Socialist political order.

As such, not only do they shed considerable light on the present state of affairs in Czechoslovakia, but, more importantly, they provide some indication of the direction which Communist Party State Systems will have to move if they are to survive. The layman will also find much in these documents which is of value.

When read in conjunction with the accompanying introduction and analysis, the documents help to explain a good deal of what has recently occurred in Eastern Europe. In particular, they offer a perspective heretofore unavailable for viewing the Soviet decision to intervene militarily in Czechoslovakia.

The documents are arranged in chronological order. To preserve their value for the research scholar, we have reproduced them in their entirety in their original form.

Students of the Soviet Bloc are likely to experience no difficulty in ascertaining the substance of these documents. The average reader, who, either because he is unfamiliar with the current state of affairs in Eastern Europe, or because he is unaccustomed to the style employed in these documents, is likely to find the going a bit more difficult. Hopefully, the burden will be eased somewhat by the commentary which accompanies each of the documents.

P. E.

ACKNOWLEDGEMENT

This book was prepared with the assistance of Messrs. Joseph Pelton, Henry Kenski, and Miss Cathy Pearson. I also owe a debt of gratitude to Mr. F. Kratochwil, who prepared the Index. I am especially indebted to my wife for her patience and encouragement. As usual, errors of fact and judgment are my own.

P. E.

CONTENTS

CONTENTS

INTRODUCTION

In the evolution of the Soviet Bloc there are those events which, for one reason or another, stand out more vividly than others. The dispute between Stalin and Tito, for example, followed in February of 1948 by the coup in Czechoslovakia, set the stage for five years of rigid Soviet domination of Eastern Europe. Similarly, Stalin's death in 1953, followed by the adoption of the so-called "New Course" and Khrushchev's speech to the XXth Party Congress ushered in a period of transition which, although temporarily halted by Soviet intervention in Hungary, has continued up to the present time.

Although separated in time, these and other events such as the split between Moscow and Peking, the ouster of Albania from the bloc, and now, Soviet intervention in Czechoslovakia, are not unrelated. Taken together, they attest to an ongoing, if somewhat disjointed and not always predictable, process of change and accommodation.

It is in the context of this process that the documents presented here must be read. For it is this process, and not the struggle between freedom and slavery, or the contest between nationalism and internationalism, which thus far has dominated the evolution of the bloc.

THE STALINIST ERA

From the time the Red Army first arrived in Eastern Europe until Stalin's death in March, 1953, the process appears to have worked rather smoothly. In a system organized around the twin principles of Soviet primacy and the universal applicability of Soviet experience, there was never really any question as to who was responsible for initiating change. Nor, for that matter, was there ever any doubt as to where the obligation for accommodation lay. Decisions made in Moscow were by and large simply implemented throughout Eastern Europe.

That the process worked so smoothly can be attributed to a number of factors. There was, in the first instance, the visible presence of the Red Army in Eastern Europe. In addition, there was the fact that those responsible for implementing the policies laid down by Moscow had been handpicked, for the most part, by Stalin. Lacking any substantial basis of popular support, they were hardly in a position to emulate the independent posture of Tito. Then, there was, of course, Stalin himself. As Lenin's successor, he had a legitimacy second to none. Moreover, there was the "Cold War," with its attendant rigid division of the world into opposing camps. Finally, there was the fact that the system, although favoring the Soviet Union, did not work to the total disadvantage of the other members. This is neither the time nor the place to undertake an accounting of the benefits which accrued to the countries of Eastern Europe during the Stalinist era. Suffice it to say that the material advantages of membership in the bloc were not entirely one-sided.

THE TRANSITIONAL PHASE

With the death of Stalin in 1953, the process of change and accommodation began to show signs of breaking down. Although the Red Army was still in Eastern Europe, the death of the Soviet dictator confronted his successors with the difficult choice of either continuing the policies of the past or, barring that, of working out a different sort of arrangement for holding the bloc together. That they opted for the latter is hardly surprising. Five years of rigid Soviet domination, coupled with Stalin's insistence on slavish emulation of Soviet economic and political experience had produced mounting political unrest and growing economic stagnation throughout most of Eastern Europe— a situation which, it should be noted, was not only recognized by Stalin the year before he died, but which was vividly confirmed by the uprising that occurred in East Germany during 1953.

The necessity for developing a new arrangement was, in part at least, also a function of the situation that obtained within the Soviet Union following Stalin's death. In the ensuing struggle for power, elements wedded to the policies of the former dictator were defeated by those whose commitment to economic reform and, in a more limited sense, political liberalization, appears to have extended not only to the Soviet Union but to Eastern Europe as well. For the victors in this struggle the prospect of working through individuals whose loyalty to Stalin was exceeded only by their close identification with his policies could not have been very appealing.

In addition, there was the problem of China. As long as Stalin was alive, his personal stature insured that the process of change and accommodation which characterized the relationships between the Soviet Union and the countries of Eastern Europe would also operate, if in a less effective fashion, in the dealings between Moscow and Peking. The men who followed Stalin to power had no such guarantee. As men of lesser stature, they would, moreover, have to deal with a China which in 1954-55 was considerably more capable of independent action than had been the case in 1949. Confronted with the prospect of being responsible for behavior over which they would be able to exercise only limited control, they undoubtedly found much to be said for a modified process of change and accommodation.

Finally, there was the international situation, or, to be more precise, the "Cold War." For Stalin, the deterioration in East-West relations which occurred after 1947 served to justify the imposition of rigid controls both at home and throughout the bloc. His successors, however, were primarily concerned with consolidating their power as well as with introducing political and economic reforms. It is little wonder, therefore, that in the years immediately after Stalin's death the Soviet Union sought to effect a gradual reduction in the level of international tensions. It is even less surprising that, having once decided to modify its position of implacable hostility towards the West, the leadership of the Soviet Union would, in time, also find it necessary to modify the process of change and accommodation which had controlled the evolution of the bloc during its formative years.

TOWARDS A NEW ORDER

Although the impact of these factors was immediately apparent in terms of Soviet behavior toward the rest of the bloc, their impact upon the process of change and accommodation was neither as direct nor as obvious. Thus, for example, in the three years following the death of Stalin, we find the Soviet Union moving to correct many of the problems associated with the previous era. Among the steps taken in this connection were: an end of one-man rule in Hungary, which resulted in a loss of power for the pro-Stalinist elements headed by Rakosi; sale of the joint stock companies to the governments of Eastern Europe; dissolution of the Cominform; an attempted reconciliation with Tito; the promise of further economic credits for China coupled with an agreement to abolish the Sino-Soviet joint stock companies and to return both Port Arthur and Darien to Chinese control; institution of the Warsaw Treaty Organization; and, in February 1956, the denigration of Stalin in a speech delivered by Khrushchev before the delegates assembled for the XXth Congress of the Communist Party of the Soviet Union (C.P.S.U.). In reviewing these and other developments of the period it is important to recognize that the initiative for change came, in each instance, from the Soviet Union. With the notable exceptions of Moscow's fleeting courtship with Tito and the concessions made to China, accommodation appears to have remained the exclusive obligation of the other members of the bloc.

More important than the specific measures taken during this period, however, was the move, again initiated by the Soviet Union, to develop an alternative basis for the conduct of intra-bloc relations. Initially, at least, the movement took the form of vague pronouncements concerning the creation of a "socialist commonwealth," and assurances to the governments and people of Eastern Europe that the new order did not constitute a return to Stalinism. Capping this effort was the publication in October 1956 of the "Principles of Development and Further Strengthening of Friendship and Cooperation Between the Soviet Union and Other Socialist States." Following as it did the intervention in Hungary, this document called for the building of relations among the members of the bloc "on a basis of full equality, respect for each other's territorial integrity, independence and sovereignty, and non-interference in each other's internal affairs." Taking note of past abuses, it went on to express regret over the necessity of having had to intervene in Hungary, and pledged a willingness on the part of the Soviet Union to "discuss with the other socialist countries measures to ensure the further development and strengthening of economic contacts between socialist countries with a view to eliminating any possibility whatever of violation of the principle of national sovereignty, mutual benefit and equality in economic relations." Finally, the Declaration offered to discuss with the other members of the bloc the status of Soviet advisors and Soviet military units stationed in Eastern Europe.

Needless to say, in the years which have elapsed since the publication of this Declaration the gulf separating promise and performance has remained substantial indeed. Yet the fact remains that after 1956 the process of change and accommodation did undergo a gradual modification. In part at least, the modification appears to have been intentional—that is to say, it reflected a conscious decision on the part of the Soviets to rely on institutional integration and ideological supremacy as the primary instruments for holding the bloc together. Whereas Stalin relied principally on the force of his personality and the force of the Red Army, and whereas he insisted on keeping the members of the bloc divided through a system of bilateral arrangements, Khrushchev and the men who succeeded him have consistently stressed the benefits of integration and, to that end, have encouraged greater participation in various multi-lateral arrangements within the overall structure of the Council of Economic Mutual Assistance. In so doing, of course, they have had to face the prospect of institutionalized opposition grounded, as it were, in the legitimate pursuit of "many roads to socialism."

To much greater extent, however, modification of the process of change and accommodation can be characterized as unintentional. To be sure, in the period after 1956, the Soviet Union demonstrated an increasing willingness to tolerate national diversity. Political as well as economic deviation from the Soviet model was, or at least seemed to be, viewed by Moscow as an essential prerequisite for the maintenance of the bloc as a functioning system. What Moscow did not seem to recognize, initially at least, was that change initiated from within has a way of getting out of hand; particularly where permissible limits of diversity are ill-defined and external constraints are susceptible to evasion by one or more of the members.

Prior to 1961, and the open break with China, the gradual nature of the changes taking place throughout Eastern Europe—and, for that matter, within the Soviet Union itself—seemed to have kept pace with a gradual reapportionment of the responsibility for accommodation. In other words, change initiated by individual members of the bloc did not pose a threat to the integrity of the system. As a result, the Soviet Union, for its part, appears to have been willing to bear a greater part of the obligation for accommodation.

CRISIS IN THE BLOC

After 1961, however, the precarious balance that had characterized previous efforts to modify the process of change and accommodation began to deteriorate. On the one side, there developed mounting pressures for internal reform. Although such pressures were neither universal nor uniform in their intensity, they nevertheless manifested themselves against a background of worsening relations between Moscow and Peking. On the other side, there developed added opportunities for initiating change—opportunities which appear to have been, at least in part, related to the effort of the Soviet Union to enlist support of the other members of the bloc in its ongoing struggle with the Chinese.

The convergence of necessity and opportunity seems to have placed the Soviet Union in a position where the initiation of change increasingly favored the other members of the bloc, while the obligation for accommodation became more and more a responsibility of the U.S.S.R. Confronted with this situation, Moscow nevertheless continued to temporize, except, of course, in the case of Albania where the challenge to Soviet authority—assuming as it did a pro-Chinese orientation—was so obvious that it could not be ignored.

In the case of Rumania, however, the U.S.S.R. clearly adopted a wait-and-see policy, apparently on the assumption that the Rumanian Communist Party not only had an interest in making sure that the internal reforms did not get out of hand, but more importantly, that the Party was strong enough to deal with any and all internal challenges to its authority.

Then, in January of 1968, the situation in Czechoslovakia began to change. The fall of Novotny, followed by the adoption of the Action Program by the Central Committee of the Czechoslovakian Communist Party (CCP) on April 5th, presented the Soviet Union with a situation that was both unique and—from the point of view of the bloc—potentially very dangerous. The uniqueness of the Czech situation lay in a number of factors. First, there were the contemplated reforms, the extent of which, as can be seen in the documents presented here, went far beyond anything previously attempted in the bloc. Secondly, and probably even more disquieting, was the anti-Soviet character of the popular response to the promise of reform. Thirdly, whereas the Rumanian Communist Party had consistently demonstrated an ability to regulate both the character and extensiveness of its reform program, the CCP and, more particularly Alexander Dubcek, projected a much less reassuring image. With its members divided between Czechs and Slovaks on the one hand, and pro- and anti-Novotny elements on the other, the Party appeared to be experiencing considerable internal dissension. Its image certainly was not helped either by Dubcek's apparent inability to eliminate all supporters of Novotny from positions of authority or by the continued expression of anti-Soviet sentiment in the face of official pleas for moderation. Fourthly, there was the fact that Czechoslovakia does share a common border with West Germany and, as such, has traditionally occupied a position of special importance in the eyes of the Soviet Union.

For the Soviet Union as well as for other members of the bloc, the situation as it developed in Czechoslovakia after January must have appeared doubly dangerous. At worst, there was the distinct possibility that the reforms would get out of hand and that, in time, this would lead to pressures for withdrawal from the bloc. Should that happen, disintegration of the system would be just a matter of time. At best, there was the equally distressing possibility that, given Czechoslovakia's economic potential, the reforms could be successfully carried out without jeopardizing the position of the Party. Should that happen, the Soviet Union would then be faced with the equally unpleasant choice of acknowledging the legitimacy of not only the economic but the political reforms as well. The implications of such a choice both for the bloc as a whole and for the internal political situation in each of the member countries—particularly the German Democratic Republic—are so obvious as to preclude further elaboration.

Considered in this context, the military intervention initiated on August 20th is not surprising. What is surprising is that it did not occur sooner.

Although no one can say with certainty why the Soviets waited eight months to intervene, the delay would seem at least in part to reflect the degree to which the process of change and accommodation has actually been modified in the years since Stalin's death.

In reconstructing the events which preceded the intervention, one finds, for example, that the ouster of Novotny did not evoke any significant reaction on the part of either the Soviet Union or the other members of the bloc. In fact, considering the conditions in Czechoslovakia at the time of his ouster, it is quite probable that his removal met with the full approval of the Soviet leadership. Whether Moscow actually gave prior consent is a matter of some speculation. Nevertheless, the change in leadership was carried out in the absence of any public opposition from the Soviet Union. However, in the months following the January plenum of the Central Committee of the CCP, the public reaction of the Soviet Union to developments in Czechoslovakia became increasingly hostile. At first the Soviets seem to have reconciled themselves to the necessity for, and the legitimacy of, the reforms set forth in the Action Program adopted by the CCP in April. Judging from the statements in *Pravda* and *Isvestia* during the period immediately preceding and following adoption of the Program, Moscow's principal concern seems to have been less with the reforms than with the ability of the CCP to maintain effective control over the situation. Thus we find, for example, the appearance of articles supporting the right of the CCP to initiate change which also contain warnings about the danger of counter-revolutionary activities and an insistence upon the primacy of the CCP as the vanguard of the working class within Czechoslovakia. Between April and mid-July, mounting Soviet concern over the course of events in Czechoslovakia appears to have been characterized by a continued willingness to tolerate reform and by an increasing uneasiness over the danger of a counter-revolution led by so-called "anti-socialist" elements. Throughout this period, however, the Soviet press continued to make a clear distinction between the CCP and forces in the country who were hostile to socialism. Accordingly, in reporting publication of the statement "2000 Words to Workers, Peasants, Employees, Scientists, People in the Arts, to All Citizens" in the Czech press, *Pravda,* on July 11, noted that the statement "does not conceal its sympathies for the capitalist system." This same article went on to comment, however, that "healthy forces in the party and in the country view this document as an overt attack on the socialist system, on the CCP's guiding role and on Czechoslovakia's friendship with the Soviet Union and other socialist countries."

The practice of distinguishing between the "anti-socialist" elements in Czech society and the CCP was, however, gradually abandoned by the Soviets in the weeks that followed. In a series of attacks directed first against "some Czech leaders" and then against the Central Committee of the CCP, Moscow went to great pains to point out that the U.S.S.R. felt conditions in Czechoslovakia were getting out of hand and that, unless corrected, they would constitute a threat not only to the CCP but to the rest of the bloc as well.

From the middle of July until the intervention on August 20th, articles in the Soviet press alternately emphasized the need for corrective action and the danger of "imperialist intervention." Although the attacks abated somewhat following the conferences at Cierna and Bratislava, they resumed with an even greater intensity shortly thereafter.

What emerges from this brief review is the fact that it was apparently not the initiation of change by the CCP which prompted the military intervention on August 20th, but rather the inability of the CCP to convince the Soviet Union that the changes being initiated did not constitute either a threat to the survival of Communism in Czechoslovakia, or a danger to the rest of the bloc. In retrospect, Moscow appears to have been willing to accommodate itself both to the fall of Novotny and to the prospect of internal reform. What it could not accommodate, however, was the initiation of change by elements within Czechoslovakia whose aims included the termination of Communist rule in that country. Initially, at least, the Soviet Union apparently thought that the CCP could handle the situation. Thus, it sought to emphasize the danger without indicting the CCP. When it became apparent that Dubcek and his supporters were either unable or unwilling to move decisively against these elements, Moscow decided to drop this polite distinction and launched instead a series of direct attacks against the CCP. Even so, care was taken to accuse the Czechs of nothing more than a failure to understand the gravity of the developing situation. In return for its moderation the Soviet Union received assurances from Prague that it did not consider the danger of counter-revolution to be very real. These assurances, coupled as they were by publication of the so-called "Statement of 2000 Words" and General V. Prchlik's subsequent comments concerning the ineffectiveness of the Warsaw Treaty Organization, probably convinced the Soviets of the need for more strenuous measures. Although the agreements reached at Cierna and Bratislava have never been fully revealed, it would seem safe to conclude from what is known that the purpose of these meetings was to impress upon the Czechs the importance of curbing what the Soviets and other members of the bloc undoubtedly viewed as a very dangerous situation. That they failed to accomplish this purpose is attested to by the subsequent intervention which began on August 20th.

CONCLUSION

The purpose of this analysis has been two-fold. On the one hand, I have sought here to provide a perspective for viewing recent developments in Czechoslovakia. To that end I have tried to emphasize the ongoing process of change and accommodation which has characterized the evolution of the Soviet Bloc. Caught up, as it were, in the press of recent events, it is easy to lose sight of the fact that the bloc has come a long way since the Stalinist era. No longer does the initiative for change reside solely with the Soviet Union and no longer can the obligation for accommodation be said to lie entirely with the other members of the bloc. The years that have elapsed since Stalin's death have witnessed a gradual sharing of the power which once resided almost exclusively in the Center. As a consequence, responsibility for initiating change, particularly after 1961, has become increasingly more of a shared responsibility. In the process, so has the obligation for accommodation.

This is not to suggest that the bloc is today a system composed of members who are equal in all respects. The Soviet Union, if only by virtue of its size and power remains pre-eminent. Nor is it to suggest that there are no limits to the modification of the process of change and accommodation. The intervention in Czechoslovakia, like the earlier intervention in Budapest, indicates that limits do exist, even if vaguely defined, and that these limits are transcended at the point where the initiation of change is likely to require that the Soviet Union accommodate itself to the dissolution of the bloc.

Herein, or so it seems, also lies the real significance of the Czech experience. The intervention, coming as it did after eight months of attempts by the Soviet Union and other members of the bloc to pressure the CCP into action, was probably occasioned less by fear of reform than by a genuine concern that in the absence of a strong Communist Party, responsibility for initiating change within Czechoslovakia would gradually fall to those identified as "anti-socialist" elements, and that, as a consequence, the CCP would eventually find itself in the position of having to accommodate itself to its own extinction. For the Soviet Union and other members of the bloc, the intervening months between January and August witnessed in Czechoslovakia the evolution of a process of change and accommodation not unlike that which had been operative throughout the entire bloc in the period since Stalin's death. When viewed in this context the intervention thus appears to have had a dual function. Not only did it serve to re-establish the permissable limits of diversity for the bloc as a whole, but within Czechoslovakia itself it sought to insure that in the future change would be initiated by the

CCP. Whereas the obligation for accommodation would continue to reside with the rest of Czech society.

The second, and related, purpose of this analysis has been to set the documents that follow in perspective. Read against the background of the developing crisis within the bloc and within Czechoslovakia itself, the documents serve to illuminate the full extent of the modifications wrought in the process of change and accommodation throughout the bloc. More importantly, they attest to an initial modification of this same process within Czechoslovakia. In the case of the former, military intervention in Hungary merely halted for a time the modification. Whether the same will be true within Czechoslovakia is something which the reader must decide for himself. These documents will provide a basis for his decision.

1

This document, like those that follow is probably best understood as an exercise in simultaneous communication with several different audiences. There is, in the first instance, the internal audience; an audience composed of the "masses" (Czechs, Slovaks, workers, peasants, intellectuals, etc.), the Czechoslovak Communist Party (CCP), and the Czech Government. In addition, there is the external audience. Here it is useful to distinguish between the Soviet Union, members of the bloc and other "fraternal parties," on the one hand, and the non-Communist world on the other.

Reading and, more importantly, interpreting a document of this type presents a number of problems, which for the most part, are inherent in any effort to communicate: they involve the meaning of words, the constraints of the media, the intentions of the speaker and the values of the audience. To try and resolve these problems in the limited space available here would amount to an exercise in futility. Nevertheless, in order to better understand what follows, they should be identified.

Let us recognize at the outset that words are value-laden symbols. As such, they may have one meaning for a Marxist, let us say, and a completely different meaning for one who is wedded to liberal democracy. Traditionally, the Communists have exploited this feature in instances where communication among the "initiated" has been involved. Not only does the use of what we would regard as jargon facilitate communication but it offers the added advantage of privacy—a necessary factor when sensitive issues are aired in a public forum. For men like Dubcek it is difficult and, in this case at least, probably unnecessary to abandon the practices of a lifetime. He is communicating with those who understand only too well the numerous references to "some comrades" or to "anti-socialist elements."

In a related vein, let us also acknowledge the fact that here, as anywhere else, "something is lost in the translation." Although reproduced in its entirety, the speech was obviously not delivered in English. The "cost" of translation is probably not very high, however, if only because of the fact that this speech, like the other documents, originated with the Czechs themselves. Presumably, it reflects careful scrutiny by the powers that be.

A more serious problem is that which attaches to the limitations or constraints of the media; in this case, an official speech intended for public consumption. As a formal statement of intent, the speech was undoubtedly made with the understanding that it would receive careful scrutiny by all concerned, including, it might be added, the Soviet Union. That knowledge, together with the realization that once made, a public statement is difficult to repudiate, almost certainly accounts for the moderate tone of the speech and the conciliatory nature of references made to the past. To expect otherwise would be asking for the impossible.

Then, of course, there are the problems associated with the audience or, to the extent that more than one audience is involved, with the necessity for simultaneous communication with divergent groups whose interests, attitudes, and expectations do not always converge. For the speaker, the problem is essentially one of balancing the need to communicate with the need to conciliate. Thus, we find criticisms of the past coupled with praise for the accomplishments of the present; the promise of democracy coupled with the insistence that it be "socialist democracy"; the awareness of alienation coupled with commitments to humanism; assertions of independence and sovereignty coupled with the pledge of greater support for the cause of "socialist unity." Whether Dubcek succeeds in carrying off his "balancing act" is a matter of opinion. For the reader, however, the attempt makes it difficult to establish with certainty when he is speaking to the internal audience and when he is not.

Finally, there is the problem of objectivity: the speaker's, the reader's, and my own. For myself, the notion of total objectivity, like that of total rationality, is nonsense. We all have our value preferences and I certainly am no exception. The most I can do is make explicit that which is implicit in this and succeeding commentaries. To that end let me say that I carry no brief either for the "captive nations" school or for the "convergence" theorists. To assume, as in the case of the former, that Communist political systems are founded on "error," presided over by cynical opportunists who, in a somewhat detached fashion manipulate entire populations for their own selfish ends and therefore cannot endure, is to ignore the history of the last fifty years. For those who wish to read this speech as the death knell of Communist rule in Czechoslovakia, I would recommend they reflect upon the source and the nature of the proposed reforms. I would offer the same advice to those who might interpret the speech as another installment in an inevitable process of convergence. In particular, I would urge that they give thoughtful consideration to the references made to ideology, the role of the Party, and the nature of the political system.

For myself, I prefer to see this speech and the documents that follow as a sign of maturity on the part of a developing political system; a system which up to now at least has demonstrated not only a significant capacity for making mistakes but, and more to the point, an equally significant capacity for being able to live with its mistakes. This is not to suggest that the system lacks either the ability to correct its mistakes or the capacity to initiate change. It is to suggest—and here I part company with the "convergence" theorists—that the initiation of change, in Czechoslovakia as in other Communist political systems, has been prompted not by pressures from below, although, such pressures have, and still do operate, but *primarily* by a desire on the part of those who, as the principal beneficiaries of the system believe in and work for its survival. To argue differently is, or so I would contend, to confuse liberalization with liberalism, reform with renunciation and superficial similarities born of parallel development with a merger of identities. It is, in addition, to misread the principal message of this speech. That message, simply stated, is that elements within the CCP had decided the time had come to initiate change; that having made this decision they and nobody else would preside over its implementation; and, that as a result they and the system would emerge stronger, not weaker.

THE INTERNAL AUDIENCE

In presenting this message to the internal audience, Dubcek manages what amounts to a skillful orchestration of variations on a common theme; namely, unity, socialism and humanity. First there is the past or, more specifically, the period prior to the January plenum of the Central Committee of the CCP. In dealing with this period, he fully admits that errors were committed; errors which, among other things, served to divide the Party from within, the Party from the "masses", Czechs from Slovaks, the Party from the Government and the Government from the people. As might be expected, his criticism is both selective and, judging from what is known of the conditions which obtained throughout Czechoslovakia at the time of Novotny's ouster, relatively mild. Thus, the audience is pointedly reminded that while mistakes were made, they were accompanied by many accomplishments. It is also reminded of the fact that the mistakes of the past occurred as a result of individuals in the Party and the Government who, for one reason or another, failed to apply socialist principles in their dealings with the "masses." In this way he establishes two points: first, that responsibility for the economic stagnation, political oppression and growing alienation which had developed in Czechoslovakia prior to the January plenum lies with individuals—particularly Novotny, although he is not singled out by name—and not with the Party; second, that the belief system or ideology which, it should be noted, serves to legitimize the primacy of the CCP, is still relevant to the organization of life in Czechoslovakia. The implication in each instance is quite clear. On the one hand, he has by his acknowledgement of error committed in the past, established the need for reform. On the other hand, by linking these errors to individuals who failed to follow the principles of socialism, he has also established the right of the CCP to continue to preside over the initiation of change.

This, of course, is the same message that is conveyed by his assessment of the present, i.e., the period of time between the convening of the January plenum and the delivery of the speech. In dealing with this period he again emphasizes the theme of unity, socialism and humanity. The variation is, however, slightly more optimistic. Thus, he stresses not the widening gulf between the Party and the "masses," but a convergence born of reforms carried out in the best socialist tradition. Despite the gains made, he is careful to point out that progress has been slow. In part, this is attributed to the complexity of the problems; problems which he suggests have been carefully analyzed by the CCP as a prelude to the proposal of the Action Program. In part, the limited progress made during this period is seen as the fault of "some comrades" who are reluctant to accept the onset of a new era.

In analyzing events since the January plenum, Dubcek once more emphasizes the need for reform. The gains recorded during that period are presented as proof of the willingness and ability of the CCP to guide the future development of Czechoslovakia. Failure to resolve all of the problems confronting the country is not the fault of the CCP. Again it is the individual who is to blame; the individual who as a Party member cannot or will not conduct himself in accordance with the principles of socialism. Yet the Party will not be deterred from pushing ahead. For those who might doubt either its sincerity or ability in this regard there is the Action Program; the end-product of careful scrutiny by the CCP of the problems confronting Czechoslovakia. There are, moreover, assurances to recalcitrant members who will not conform that the Party understands and speaks for the "masses," and therefore it is acting in the highest traditions of socialism. The implication is, of course, that those who wish a return to the old ways are acting against the "masses" and are therefore in "error."

Once again the message is driven home. Reform is essential. Moreover, the Party recognizes the need for change and is prepared, despite the opposition of a few die-hards, to carry on with its efforts to lead the Czechoslovakian people to a better future under socialism.

Dubcek concludes his message to the internal audience by outlining in general terms the provisions of the Action Program. The reforms contained in the Program itself will be dealt with in a subsequent commentary. For now, it is sufficient to note that the speech, in dealing with the future, continues to emphasize the theme of unity, socialism and humanity. The variation of that theme when projected against the future is, if anything, even more optimistic. Thus the audience is offered the promise of reforms which, if implemented, will help to bring the Party and the people even closer together. Reforms, moreover, that will help to heal old wounds between Czechs and Slovaks in the crucible of federalism; open government to the people; free the economy from the mistakes of the past;. and, in the context of a socialist democracy, create opportunities for personal fulfillment that will eliminate alienation once and for all.

To be sure, the road ahead will not be easy. The problems to be faced are complex and the solutions are difficult. Moreover, there is the danger that elements in the society will seek a return to the old ways or, what is even worse, reject the promise of a future under socialism for the decadence of bourgeois democracy.

Yet, or so the audience is told, the road can be traversed. The CCP, as the Action Program amply demonstrates, is fully aware of the problems, and has already begun devising solutions. Together with the "masses" it will in the future, as in the past, continue to deal "scientifically" with the difficulties facing the nation. This will require that changes be made. It is, however, important that these changes be carefully considered. To move too quickly would be to give the anti-socialist elements in the society an opportunity to sabotage the work of the Party and the "masses." It might also give those who are disturbed about developments since the January plenum an opportunity to turn the tide in their favor. Again, the CCP is aware of the danger and, with the help of the "masses," will see that neither danger ever materializes.

The message for the future, as for the past and the present, is one of change; change initiated and presided over by the CCP. It is a message not of repudiation but regeneration. It is a message which offers liberalization, not liberal democracy. Finally, it is a message of strength and belief, not of weakness and denial.

THE EXTERNAL AUDIENCE

The projection of this message to the external audience is keyed to a somewhat different theme. That theme, in the case of the Soviet Union, other members of the bloc and "fraternal parties," invokes a plea, a promise and a warning. The plea is for understanding and is most prominently reflected in those portions of the speech that purport to deal with the need for change. It is there that he describes the shortcomings of his predecessor. It is there too that he speaks of the accomplishments of the past and the wishes of the "masses." Leaving aside the internal implications of these comments, it would appear that his aim here is to convey to the "socialist camp" the necessity for initiating change. By emphasizing the gravity of the situation he seems to be suggesting that the CCP and, by implication, he himself, acted out of necessity as much as choice. Whether this was indeed the case is another matter. The point is that if the CCP could accommodate itself to the will of the "masses," why then should not the rest of the bloc accommodate itself to the CCP.

The promise is an assurance that the changes contemplated in the speech will in no way jeopardize either the primacy of the CCP as the "vanguard of the masses" or the integrity of the Soviet Bloc. Viewed in this context, the explanation of the term "socialist democracy" as well as the comments concerning the unwillingness of the CCP to tolerate "anti-socialist" elements, the retention of the People's Militia and the National Front, the need for moderation, etc., were probably intended as much for external as for internal consumption. The same can surely be said for his references to proletarian internationalism, his remarks concerning the Warsaw Treaty Organization and his statements dealing with the Vietnam conflict, and the German question.

The warning is more implicit than explicit. It is a warning against interference in the internal affairs of the CCP. Thus, for example, we find references to the principles of equality, sovereignty, and non-interference are accompanied by the assertion that "the socialist elaboration of our future road is inviolable." Similarly, in commenting on the outcome of an earlier meeting in Dresden with other leaders of the bloc Dubcek takes care to point out that the "exchange of opinions must be understood in the sense that the principle of non-interference in the internal affairs of other parties will continue to be valid."

This message, when projected to the non-Communist world, assumes the character of an illusion. It is the illusion of "freedom." For the western reader, it is easy to be misled by this speech. The reforms proposed here seem, on the face of it, to mark the creation of a democratic political order. Yet, as I have tried to show, the message of the speech is not one of rejection but of renovation. Dubcek is not a liberal-democrat, he is a Communist. As such, he undoubtedly believes in the capacity of his system to provide a better future for the people of Czechoslovakia. The content of the speech when carefully analyzed certainly gives us no reason to assume otherwise.

CONCLUSION

In sum, the message of this speech is the same for both the internal and external audience: that elements within the CCP, for whatever reason, had decided the time had come to initiate change; that having arrived at this decision they, and they alone, had decided to preside over the process of implementation; and, that as a result they, and the people of Czechoslovakia, would be better off for the effort. Internally, the message is presented as a call by the CCP to a better future under socialism. To the Soviet Union, members of the bloc, and other "fraternal parties" it is a plea for understanding, a promise of internal stability and continued loyalty to the "socialist camp," and a warning against interfering in the internal affairs of the CCP. To the non-Communist world it is the illusion of "freedom" projected against the substance of an abiding belief in the ability of the prevailing system, once modified, to provide a better future for the people of Czechoslovakia.

This is my interpretation; the reader, here as throughout, is invited to provide his own.

THE SPEECH DELIVERED BY COMRADE ALEXANDER D U B Č E K AT THE PLENARY SESSION OF THE CENTRAL COMMITTEE OF THE COMMUNIST PARTY OF CZECHOSLOVAKIA

on April 1st 1968

A p r i l 1968

THE SPEECH BY COMRADE

ALEXANDER D U B Č E K

Dear Comrades,

We were asked by the January plenary session of the Central Committee of the Communist Party of Czechoslovakia to work out an action programme that would ensure the attainment of objectives set by that session. Our draft programme should also prepare the ground for the elaboration of a longer-term programme of the Party. We wish to submit our draft action programme to you today together with other materials.

Let me give you, by way of introduction, a short explanation of the materials, an appraisal of their importance and ideas, and also submit a brief report as to how the Central Committee presidium of the Communist Party regards the development which our society and our Party have been going through since the January plenary session.

Naturally this evaluation of the development can only be of a preliminary character in view of the dynamism, scope, and depth of the movement after the January plenary session. You, members of the Central Committee gathered here, will surely make your own addition and improvements to it.

However, one thing is obvious and indisputable: the movement since the January session is undoubtedly socialist and democratic, called to life by our Communist Party, and is also characterized by an unwonted activity of our citizens.

It is clear that, from the point of view of our long-term prospects, the period we have been going through since January is extremely important. It has not only been a very serious test of values, but even a telling proof of the ability of our Party to imbue the social development with a new spirit. The situation deserves and undoubtedly will call for a profound analysis and explanation. Today, however, it requires a great concentration of efforts, sacrifice, will and singleness of purpose, patience and perseverance of the avant-garde party of the socialist society.

The process of new tasks and methods of fulfilling our mission, encountering old attitudes and habits, full of contradictions in intself, surges through the whole Party. That is right. We could not start on new roads otherwise.

On the one hand we can witness new hopes of the really broad masses, an unexpected activity of social organizations and of the Party in the first place, an activity admired even abroad, but was surprising even for us at home, which greatly enhanced the attractivity of our country and of our policy. However, many are wondering and so surprised as to express fears whether the Party has not been recoiling under the pressure, whether it is not being driven by the development and whether it will be able to oppose wrong actions, harmful demands that always crop up during such a process.

We must seek answers to all these questions, we must go into their causes and judge them correctly, The Central Committee presidium has reviewed the situation, at least for operational purposes, several times lately and published its attitude.

We must, however, try to grasp more profoundly the meaning of the development of the past months. I think we are most likely to come near to this if we understand the most essential characteristic of the dispute which has been growing in the society and in the Party during the last few years.

The essence of the dispute lay in the appraisal of the social and economic situation as it developed in Czechoslovakia after the political and economic defeat of the bourgeoisie, and after laying the political and economic foundations of socialism. The putting into effect of a new phase of the socialist revolution at the stage of non-antagonistic relations necessitated, at the same time, the development, further shaping, and establishment of a political system to meet this new situation. The problem is one of intensifying the role of the Party and generally its attitude to the present tasks of social development. We have to apply to a fuller extent, the basic principles of the theory of Marxism-Leninism, the principles of socialist construction in which we have already achieved outstanding successes, the principles of the leading role of the Party. It was and it is a matter of marching forward, of unfolding these principles. We are beginning a new stage of our proletarian socialist revolution, we have to set up such a political structure, to adopt such political methods of work that will correspond to the new conditions which **we have so far been lagging** behind. We have to set purposefully to elaborate and realize such a role of the Party in society which will establish - and it has done so already in this short time - the Party as the vanguard of society and its progress, as a political leading force of this society, to restore the confidence of people in it.

We were right in stressing the political aspect of the present problems. Otherwise we could hardly proceed successfully in fulfilling the policy of the 13th Congress, and this is our main concern, that we want to put into

a 5

practice, that we shall continue to elaborate. The Party is thus taking an ever more marked and convincing stand in the forefront of the movement and is not only defending the stage achieved. This, I think, is a sufficient retort to those who feared lest the new attitude should weaken the policy of the 13th Congress. We are bound to say publicly and clearly that the Central Committee of the Communist Party of Czechoslovakia stands and will continue to stand for the concentrated fulfilment of this Party policy. It was just this conviction and resolve that urgently called for an intensification of socialist democratism, for an explanation of the new conditions and tasks of our socialist society. It is with regard to the binding conclusions of the 13th Congress and experience from their being put into effect that we have to formulate even such tasks that have already been overcome and thus add new touches to emphasize the basic line in the period between congresses and prepare a new formulation answering the experience and the new conditions.

It should be said - and you will certainly have a vivid memory of the origin of the events at the last three plenary sessions - that the Central Committee of the Party could not channel the actual course, vigour, and complexity of the events of the past three months into a definite pattern either at the January plenary meeting, or before the district Party conferences. You, members of the Central Committee, know very well what it was like when we were parting in January, that the Party leadership which opened the door to this process and put itself at its head did not and could not have any time schedule for the development of the events.

The peculiarity of this process is actually that it was mostly, especially in the speed of its flow, called forth by a creative and, at the same time, spontaneous activity of the broad masses led by communists, which thus acted in the sense and in accordance with the conclusions of the

6 a

plenary meeting of the Central Committee without any instigation and ordering about from above. This, too, bears out the correctness of the January decision. It was therefore necessary, even desirable, to know better the opinion of the Party rank and file and of the broad masses of inhabitants, which made itself heard so conspicuously at the annual meetings and conferences in basic organizations, and especially at district conferences. To do anything before the Party conferences would have meant interfering with the process without having more profound knowledge of Party opinion.

We are more and more confirming that social movement cannot be simply decreed, that reason cannot be imposed upon it from outside, but that under our conditions this reason lies first of all in the knowledge, interests, and movements of the broad masses, and that it is the task of the Party to discover this reason, to give it final shape, to improve it, to emphasize progressive thinking and deeds, to oppose incorrect views, and to return the knowledge thus enriched to the social movement of the broad masses, to point it out to them, and so raise them to a higher social level. This difficult task must be borne by the whole Party.

There is therefore nothing more and nothing less at stake than a full application of the fundamental Marxist concept of the role of the broad masses and the role of the Party and of politics. The Party can play its role only if it fully leans on the interests and experience of the really broadest masses and on a scientific understanding of their application. Also in our latest political movement it was and is practice that helps from below to put finishing touches to the programme of a new political system. This movement seized the existing political and social forms and, where these forms proved to be capable of absorbing the new contents, it made use of them. If, however, the existing forms were insufficient, this democratic movement of the broad masses started to break them.

Let us not fear this wave, but let us take it as a lesson. Let us adopt and apply, in every more important social issue, the principle of tackling weighty problems in time and with the assistance of people. Only they will help us to get near to the truth and to truthful conclusions, only with them, and if it is their cause, can we achieve something, can we make changes and attain some goals. The Party can only carry out this essence of political activity well if it makes it, that is conceives it and puts it into practice, as a whole, together with communists in the appropriate fields - in production, culture, government - if it makes it jointly with the communists in the particular fields of work or walks of life. It may be more difficult, more complicated, but it is the only correct political procedure.

Such an attitude is welcomed by an overwhelming majority of communists and the population at large. This is borne out by the results of public opinion polls, thousands of resolutions, letters, conclusions of annual meetings and district conferences. What is important is not figures, but the tendency: confidence in the Party is growing, and so is self-confidence inside the Party.

Activity is evident in all social categories, among workers, the intelligentsia, agricultural workers, though still characterized with a certain irregularity and sometimes spontaneity. It is our duty, the duty of the whole Party and of all communists, to imbue this activity with a really creative character. A revival can be witnessed also in the inner life of large social organizations - in the trade unions and among the young people.

Economic results of the first two months of this year show that the hectic period of discussions, polemics, appraisals, and resolutions did not leave any unfavourable signs on the working morale. On the contrary, we are being increasingly convinced that the development of democracy is the only way of strengthening a conscious discipline. We also have full confidence in our working people to be able to understand that the newly started tendency of development can be effectively supported by deeds, by purposeful work in factories, in the fields and workshops as well as in scientific thinking and in the arts.

We can, therefore, say quite unambiguously that the decisions and conclusions of the January plenary session proved to be correct, and also absolutely necessary, because the state as it existed - accumulation of many ripe and untackled problems - threatened an acute political crisis. The vehemence of the whole society's response supplies a proof. At the same time, of course, it is a commitment for the whole Party and for us in the Central Committee to apply all our efforts to a resolute realization of socialist democracy, to analyze this decisive positive development and to carry it on. On the other hand not to ignore the extremes which harm the movement, and thus to be at the head of a further development of this socialist democracy. Everybody in this Republic, all the more so a Party member, must be aware that we do not have in mind just any sort of democracy, but socialist democracy. That this cannot mean a weakening of the leading role of the Party, but only a new adaptation in the spirit of Leninism, effective, purposeful, meeting the new conditions. That there is no question of an impairing of the influence on and tasks towards the socialist state, but of the best expression of the principle of democratism and the necessary centralism, so that the democratic element of the development of our society, inherent in the socialist state, might find an ever better expression.

We see the essence of socialist democracy in that it directly affects all social strata, in that it is democracy not only in respect of institutions, but that it governs also all other provinces of the social life of people.

Freedom of speech is a very important precondition for expressing opinions and interests. These, however, will necessarily clash with each other and with the social reality. Institutional safeguards of their objective appraisal and solution is a further necessity which must be thoroughly elaborated and put into legal form. All of this would have no sense, of course, if the submitted and recognized problems were not tackled, if they were not grappled with in the social sphere at all, and in economy in particular, if the social activity were not transformed into economic activity. The wealth of thoughts must be reflected in a growth of cultural and material wealth. It will always be, again and again, the honest, purposeful and good work that pushes us forward. Nothing else can be promised.

We consider socialist democracy to be a system in which the working man has his own standing and value, his security, his right, and his future. It is based upon human participation, coherence, and cooperation. We wish to meet people's longing for a society in which they can feel to be human among humans. This active, humane, integrating part of socialism, a society without antagonism, that is what we want to realize systematically and gradually, serving the people. It is a very gratifying task to serve humanity, one which has been waged by Marxist revolutionaries for more than a hundred years. We are carrying on their work and want to link up imaginatively with everything that is progressive and positive in the history of our nations.

If we want to make socialist democracy a living thing - and let there be no doubt about that - we must and we shall be guided in our work, by the living theory of Marxism-Leninism and shall actively defend its ideology against various attacks. We shall fight for its purgation, for its realization in the full sense of the term, and thus we shall best enhance the attractiveness and convincingness of socialist ideas in our class-split antagonistic world.

The main bearer of ideas of a further and full realization of the socialist revolution is the working class which was and still remains the pillar of social progress. It is most, socially and politically, interested in an all-round development of our society, it is part and parcel of social progress which can bring it and hence the whole society a further general liberation. The speed of changing the whole society depends on its revolutionary self-surpassing.

It is as true, now as in the past, that the working class will have to find its way - again and again, in every new situation - to understanding its role in society, and it is the duty of the Party to be its friend in this respect to help the working class better understand its tasks at the new stage of development. We have to keep in mind, of course, that just as the whole society, even the working class is differentiated by the varying attitude of its members to the spirit of political progress of social development.

In view of the Party being armed with scientific theory, in view of the whole historical achievement of our Party and in view of the fact that the revitalization process and the opening of a new stage in our country was initiated by our Party, we think we have the right to declare: the Communist Party of Czechoslovakia continues to be, and is now even more rightly, the decisive, organized, and progressive force of our society. The main method in the activities of the Party must be such a political practice in which the Party will continuously seek public control and make full use of the results of science and erudition and of the inspiring existence of the arts. This too will be a permanent well of fresh water upon which the Party may draw for a constant progressive development and against stagnation.

The tasks facing us, the socialist, non-antagonistic

character of our society, and the longing to satisfy, to the highest possible extent, all the needs of our society, preparation of the scientific and technical revolution, all this makes it possible, but also demands, a strengthening and development of the unity of our society. One of the main tasks of the Party at present and in the future, all the more so is that we understand this unity dialectically. We have to respect the increasing differentiation, and achieve unity by meeting specific requirements. In addition, we have to overcome whatever is bad in the heritage of the past as regards relations among individual classes and social categories, between the nations.

When going over to a new chapter of the socialist revolution, I think we have to thank all those who for tens of years took part in its preparation by carrying on a revolutionary fight for a remoulding of society. It was an immense task, hard, full of searching, often accompanied by misunderstanding, self-denial, sacrifice, personal courage. Not only we, but history will surely appreciate that period of the birth, preparation, and putting into practice of socialist ideals in our country as a period literally bursting with historical events, a period of an immense activity of communists-revolutionaries.

I also wish to thank all of those who, in the past twenty years, honestly and boldly carried out their tasks, who make up an overwhelming majority of our society, and whom we have chiefly in mind in our strivings. Without the honest and meticulous work of millions it was not possible in the past, and it will not be possible in the future, to bring the present intentions of the Party to fruition - to meet the longings and realize the ideas of our nations.

In the interest of the future we shall try to get rid of everything that has become obsolete or that has proved to be incorrect. The Central Committee gave impulse to this,

12 a

at its January plenary meeting, by the self-criticism then applied, and it accelerated the process. The idea is to further develop and strengthen everything positive that has been accomplished. It is really unfounded if this process is used by individuals for a sweeping rejection and debasement of everything done before. We cannot reject and debase a bold and honest work because of faults and of achievements that have become anachronistic. We shall consider and rectify the wrongs and faults of the past, but that does not mean to disparage and slander the past which is bound up with officials and members of the Party, economic workers, anti-nazi fighters, workers, peasants, citizens of our Republic. Our thanks are due to them and to their efforts for everything positive in our past.

Now, together with these unambiguous conclusions and standpoints we must at least try to judge how in these past three months the Party as a whole has carried on, the practical part of political management, how we have managed to understand the ideas and moods of the working people in the various social categories, how we project them into our policy, put the finishing touches to them and realize them, where we see the problems of that period.

A really new situation has emerged. Instead of one apparently homogenous social interest in the country which coincided with the ideas of some leading comrades, we are now faced with many differentiated, overlapping and mutually clashing interests and attitudes expressing various short- and long-term partial interests of the most varied social categories.

It is my opinion that the Central Committee of the Communist Party of Czechoslovakia can at this very stage commence the task of fulfilling the real mission of the Party as the leading force in our society. It can start with an analysis of the people's real interests, with evaluating their common and their differing aspects, their

a 13

expressions of progressiveness and conservatism, to make clear what of these real interests are part of the interests amd requirements of the whole society, to arrive at conclusions in the strategy and tactics of its advance with regard to individual social categories. In carrying through the logical development of society as a whole the Party may consciously place itself at the service of the real needs and interest of the people, solicit their confidence in materializing them.

Naturally, in the short time we have so far had at our disposal, these ideas can hardly be more than an outline of a programme. People therefore ask for guarantees that this process will not stop. Although we are still only at the beginning of our revitalizing process, some personnel and institutional guarantees of its further development have already been created.

What, in our opinion, is the main problem now, at this moment? I should say the main problem of the moment is to trim our revitalization process, to make it more concrete, to consolidate it. So far all the attention is centred around personal changes, but a more substantial stage is already in the making. A mere change of persons is no way to reach the fundamental goals, but at the same time the fundamental change cannot be forced along hastily, in an improvised way and at the speed characterizing the past few weeks which neither we nor the public can bear indefinitely.

A period is just beginning when a system of safeguards and stimuli of an organized progress is to be set up, when a mechanism must be developed to achieve our aims not in a haphazard and catastrophic way, but calmly, smoothly, and democratically. Our plenary session is sure to play a great role in this respect, insofar that it will be the first step towards fulfilling the action programme. Here,in preparing the action programme - we have, I think, fulfilled the objectives of the January meeting within a short and busy period. We thought them to be decisive at this stage. A Central Committee plenary meeting without planning further activities, for which an action programme would provide preconditions, would only complicate and hamper the materialization of the conclusions of the last three meetings, all the more so because the level of today's knowledge, based upon district conferences, provides scope for developing the spirit of the conclusions of the past meetings and enables dissociation from some expressions of demagogy, anarchy, and various extremes which could only interfere with the process of democratization. Nobody and nothing can halt the creative development of our socialist society. It can, however, be slowed down and affected by impatience, subjectivism in reverse and other extremes alien to this socialist development.

Our political work, however, will not be easy either tomorrow or in the future. The criticizing ferment of the past few months indicated the way our political work has to take. Apart from undoubtedly positive features the democratization process brought up many old, and also some new weak spots and shortcomings. Evidently this process of criticism has not yet touched all the old features we have to overcome but, what is more important, it does not always touch the essentials of our social life, but very often only its superficialities. The criticism, it is true, reached and reaches almost all spheres of our social life, but it often concentrates only on the consequences without taking into account the causes. And so various faults and shortcomings are simply stated and more or less put in connection with certain persons. Meanwhile it is clear, that we have to lay stress on an improvement of methods. We are lacking a more profound historical and analytical survey on the origins of these faults and shortcomings. I think, especially in connection

a 15

with the preparations for the 14th Congress, that for a further positive course of democratization of our social life, it will be necessary to get down to a really thorough analysis of the entire economic and political development to date in our socialist society.

It is, of course, not only a matter of the past. The analytical method must be concerned especially with the present. Today, tomorrow, and in the future, the development will be controversial, the new will clash with the old. It is essential to recognize in time what is what and where to go in for greater, more general details. Such a deeper sounding is imperative for all those who have a say in social processes.

Hand in hand with this programming role of the Party, the Party activity proper and political work as such, political influencing, must return, at all levels and in all sectors, to a more consistent organizational work among the people, to a more lively contact with the people, to a direct investigation of their real views. This applies to Party officials, but it also applies to every Party member, as this is the essence of his Party membership - to get to know the Party policy, to take a part in its shaping, to participate in its being put into effect, in explaining it.

This activity in the Party has become very weak. In appraising the upswing of Party life these days we have to realize that a return to such a concept of the duties of the Party member will be complicated and strenuous. We are resolutely criticizing the haughty and administrative methods in Party work which paralysed the activity of members. We must at the same time realise that it has left deep marks, consequences in practice, habits and, with some people, even a tendency to seek alibis, to rely on instructions. This is true also of members in all spheres of social activities. Contact and understanding with people whose social-political

16 a

interests and problems are being tackled are indispensable. To order people about is not possible and right no matter what form may be used, administrative or theoretical postulates, or means aimed at affecting public opinion. This must be faced not only by members drawing the attention of various Party bodies up to the Central Committee to the wrong opinions but by opposing them ideologically themselves. They are expected to defend the Party policy, to explain it, to win people over for its realization.

I think that from our plenary meeting, we must address with full confidence and also with exacting requirements, the ranks of our membership who must get our full support, the basic organizations committees elected at annual meetings, the district Party committees elected at annual conferences. We must not chicane and scandalize, without reason, the work of thousands who, consciously, full of loyalty to the Party, courageously and mainly honestly fulfilled the tasks of our socialist construction. We are asking the active Party members, the overwhelming majority of our members to which the Central Committee looks for support - and we are convinced that this request will be met - to show their self-sacrifice again as it was always so typical for them and to develop activity among workers in factories, fields, building sites, and all other working places. This is the direction our socialist policy for the people must take with more vigour than ever before. It is their interests and worries that we must pay attention to in the first place, it is they whom we must understand, in good or bad situations. I think that every communist, every democratically thinking person understands that he can realize his ideals only in unity with the life of our working people. Every type of sectarianism is harmful.

Important in this respect is the role of district committees which, after the district conferences and backed by the realistic content of our policy, will do a good deal of work among the citizens, especially in securing the fulfilment of economic tasks which should get much more attention in pre-election political activities, no matter whether the elections take place in June or in the autumn. This important task would be jeopardized if the conclusions of some district conferences were to be questioned. If it is found that some replacements of officials are necessary here or there, no new conference is required, especially if the call of some individuals is not in harmony with the opinion of an overwhelming majority of Party members. Democracy does not mean never-ending conferences. The discussion and consultations must be followed by a conclusion binding for all members, and then by the deed. Conferences were and are the highest Party organs in the districts, and in the periods between the conferences it is the district committees elected by the conferences. The principle of democratic centralism, which must be fully respected in the intra-party life, without which the Party would lose its capacity of action, requires the minority to submit to the conclusions, to the decisions of the majority, and to apply its opinion by adhering to intra-party rules.

Just a little note. There are rumours, a sort of doubting, as to whether the people´s militia should continue to exist. Of cours it should. The people´s militia is firmly incorporated in a uniform system of the country´s defence, it has its own share of duties which it will certainly carry out. Doubts about its role are quite unfounded.

I think,comrades,that generally speaking,in pushing through democratic relations their scope and depth must be observed to a greater extent.This especially refers to personnel and cadre problems. We must establish an atmosphere that would make it possible for Party officials to be criticized,to make this a natural feature,to prevent criticism breaking out only when things have gone to the extreme,and then using force.At the same time,however,we must reach a state when the criticized persons can take a stand, when they can explain untruthful or incorrect reproaches. A mass obsession in this respect or even its inciting can only bring tragic consequences, as we were able to see for ourselves in the past. Wrongs cannot be undone by causing new wrongs. In the struggle of the new with the old we must do all possible to rally the Party of the platform and around the goals submitted by the Party Central Committee. Here, in this political scope, let differentiation and unification take their course.

We do not want and cannot proceed so that the rectification of shortcomings would be contrary to our basic principles of ethics, we do not want to have to rectify the rectifications. We declare this idea binding on the communists in all sectors and in all Party bodies. We know our people well, and even if some individuals might succumb to their passions, organizers of an incorrect course which would not comply with the ethics of our Party work would never find understanding with our public.

A further problem, lesson, and requirement to be met - and this will be among the first for us to strive for at a further stage of our socialist democracy, is really to develop an ever richer content - that is the knowledge that the criticism bore the stigma of one-sidedness practically right through. For a long time it was a monologue as it hardly found any opponents either from the ranks of the conservative wing, or even from the progressive wing. It found its expression, among other things, also in the fact that, even though there are both objective and subjective reasons for it, little was heard from the technical and economic intelligentsia. It is necessary to take into fuller account the desirability of a larger share of the public expression of the attitude of workers and peasants for the future course of this democratization process. The reasons are of course various. A role was played in this respect by information available, its speed of supply and its level, immediate availability of public involvement and so on. It resulted in a certain perturbation and fears with some of the comrades in factories and agriculture because their interests were left unheeded. We have to keep this in mind at all levels of Party activities, in the economic life, in trade unions, in the youth movement, and to redress the situation. Our journalists, radio and television workers must realize this in order to improve their very useful and beneficial work and, by giving more attention to the thoughts and opinions of workers and peasants, to improve to an even greater extent our capacity of rallying for action.

People working in this field and communists did much in accomplishing our aims through the mass media of information. They correctly used the conclusions of our January plenary meeting in preventing people getting informed by a whispering propaganda or from abroad. This is enhanced by supplying information on discussions going on in the Central Committee presidium and the secretariat. They may feel rewarded by an immense interest shown in their work. However, this interest binds them, at the same time, to a very high political or even a statesmanslike responsibility as every wrong or unobjective news or transmission has a mass repercussion, calls for a standpoint, an explanation. If we want to refine, and we shall do so, democratism with a clear socialist tendency, then responsibility for its good functioning and for preventing anybody from meddling with it rests indeed on all component parts, all levels of management.

It is necessary to appreciate the self-evident truth that the speed in submitting problems may be easily increased, but their solution, their realization - unless we indulge in subjectivism in reverse has its own objective limits and requires a good classification of tasks. Unrealistic, irritated demands with an addition of demagogy may bring im-

20 a

mediate popularity, but if they are not met they cannot establish the trust without which we cannot understand each other. And we do need mutual trust if we are to factually assess and bring together the multitude of interests.

We would be short-sighted were we not to see a further feature of the post-January development - a revival of certain non-socialist moods, even of some angry cries demanding revenge. We drew attention to these in the presidiums published statement of February 21. Our standpoint is, that the Party will not be caught unprepared, not even by possible attempts at a legalization of these moods under the disguise of democracy or rehabilitation, and that it will refute any attempts at a weakening and atomization of progressive socialist tendencies. I am reiterating that the democracy we have in mind is and must be, even in future, of a definitely socialist character, and that no anti-socialist tendencies will have a chance to take advantage of this. The decisive feature is that the general character of the revitalizing process in our society is by far not determined by certain extreme tendencies and excesses which try to express these moods. But wherever they may crop up, we must oppose them on basic ideological grounds so as not to be retarded on our way. The main and decisive factor of our development is the unfolding of socialist democracy, the road to which was opened by the October, December, and January plenary meetings of the Central Committee of the Communist Party of Czechoslovakia.

This must remain the basis of our policy even in the future. On this basis, and that has been confirmed by the past three months, an immense energy of our Party and of our nations was put into motion. This is the basis on which the efforts of workers, agricultural workers, and intelligentsia are consolidating. We have, therefore, to go on looking ahead, to develop all that is new and all the positive features of our socialist construction.

Comrades,

allow me to say a few words about our work as members of the Central Committee and the Presidium. I think that we must regularly and self-critically ponder over it, especially in such a fermenting political period as this, in order to improve our work in practice too, in the way we resolved at the January Plenary Session, in order to strengthen leading Party work and rid it of outdated, unsuccessful and incorrect methods.

A state has originated in the Party following the January Plenary Session of the CC of the Czechoslovak Communist Party in which discussion about the problem dealt with by the Central Committee has continued for quite a long time. As you all know well, this was an extremely serious discussion on the position of the Party in the society. The complexity of the discussion, the contradiction of the process of unification marked the conclusions of the Central Committee's January Plenary Session with incomplete and diverse, and particularly non-analytical information - including that provided by members of the Central Committee about the reasons, which led to the decisions at the January Plenary session. This contributed considerably to the fact that many Party organisations did not grasp well enough or sufficiently appraise the resolutions and especially the importance of the content of the Plenary Session's debate. A different situation arose where correct understanding and verbal report of the conclusions and content of the Plenary Session's debate, helped it to

22

a

be grasped fully. This led to an unbalanced state, which really made the situation difficult for functionaries. We take this for a fact resulting from the state of our Party before the January Plenary Session and it is impossible to arrive at any conclusion but that in future we should pay greater respect to the importance of a more unified approach to the basic questions by members of the Central Committee before the Party public. This is not a matter of uniformity. That would harm the cause. The point at issue is that the Party - if it is to be a Party of action of revolutionary practice - must adhere to the principles of democratic centralism so that in its activity, in action it can proceed as united as possible.

We assumed that we should first manage to present to the Party the draft Action Programme, which might function as an outstanding unifying factor, a factor of unity on the basic problems of progress and development of our socialist society. However, the succession of events was more rapid. This was promoted by increasingly comprehensive information about the essence of the conclusions to the active Party group and the course of the latest Plenary Sessions imparted from a different angle, I should say, "the Šejna case" disturbing the public, as well as other circumstances.

We were aware that the decision of the January Plenary Session would influence the growth of the political activity of citizens, that it would bring about a new political atmosphere, speed up the raising of demands - including social demands - which are frequently justified and which will have to be solved gradually and systematically, though not all at once. The government will have to seek ways of solving them setting a course and give reasons for it so that the solution is realistic. Under the pressure of time we were faced with other new problems, for the solution of which the Central Committee had not been sufficiently pre-

a 23

pared in advance. This relates to certain problems of the work of the Czechoslovak Union of Youth, the tasks and position of the National front and the political parties, the activities of cultural and art unions and many other problems.

Many questions and problems have accumulated for solution over the past period. The January Plenary Session brought them to the surface. It is possible to say today, even more then in January, that the Central Committee has assumed its task, but that it was already high time.

At the beginning, the Presidium of the Central Committee of the Czechoslovak C.P. was meeting once a fortnight. We believed that, contrary to the past, it should not deal with details, but with really fundamental political problems of the society. But they are many today. Therefore we had to meet much more frequently lately. However, it is difficult in this respect to make up what was neglected in the period after the 13th Congress. In this period of just over two months it was beyond our strength to adopt an attitude without proper analysis towards the large quantity of problems posed by this development.

It proved to be correct that the Presidium of the Central Committee took a stand on many important principal problems, for instance, at the Congress of agricultural cooperatives, at the February session of the Presidium of the Central Committee of the Czechoslovak C.P. at the enterprise conference at Kladno, where the present position and tasks of the working class were discussed, and at the district conference in Brno.

But we must also ponder over how to achieve that the attitudes being published from the session of the CC Presidium of the Communist Party of Czechoslovakia should reflect the situation more profoundly, more emphatically point out the reasons of the given phenomena to the entire Party, serve more as instruction for activity and thus stimulate even greater activity of communists, and their zest and will to solve serious social problems.

In this respect, we shall have to rely more effectively on, while channelling the work of the Party apparatus, which we cannot do without. The apparatus itself, its workers, particularly through the active Party group, must help more efficiently towards better, really analytical work of Party bodies. The work of the apparatus must be increasingly orientated, improved and made more efficient in this direction. It must have the position which is really its due - no more, no less. It is impossible not to see its important position in the system of our Party work. Therefore it is also out of place to negate indiscriminately the work of the Party apparatus. Its overwhelming majority is made up of brave and honest communists whose aim is to serve devotedly the Party and our people.

There were proposals during the first conferences that we should call a Plenary Session of the Central Committee of the CP of Czechoslovakia. The Presidium of the CC of the Communist Party of Czechoslovakia adhered to the set course in preparations for the first Plenary Session after January. This was mainly because it was too much to work out a course for the future work of the Central Committee, which would proceed from the principles of the Action Programme in this short time. The Presidium thought it decisive for the future course of work to concentrate on the content of Party work in the next period and carry out personnel changes only on this basis, and not vice versa. Without knowing the conclusions of the response to the January Plenary Session and the intensity of Party activity, which became evident at the district conferences, the CC Plenary Session would be unable to advance. The district Party conferences attested to the Party´s maturity and to the ability of communists to make a correct estimation of the situation.

Although we do not want to, and must not, fall into giving directives for particular processes, we could give positive replies to certain questions only in the spirit of the prepared Action Programme. I have in mind for example the problem of youth organisation. In the coming period the youth organisation should respect the differentiation of the interests of young people, while preserving the unity of the Czechoslovak Union of Youth in what unites all the different groups of young people, so that the strength and importance of youth are not split in this fundamental issue. I believe that young people will not only state their demands, but also what they want to do. What is common to, and what unites young people will become evident on the basis of these interests. I think that the unity of a differentiated youth organisation should be as natural as the unity of other important social organisations. In this we must not ignore the fact that the struggle for the unity of youth organisations has been fought for decades so that youth as a whole could apply their political influence more efficiently. This is also why the youth movement should not give up its unity.

I spoke here about certain problems in achieving a more coherent functioning of the Party in society. I should also like to say that by no means can we, nor do we want to, return to some sort of authoritative relationship towards society, towards individual social groups. We should demonstrate this also by subjecting the decisions and conclusions of the Central Committee from the past period to a really profound analysis that would be as objective as possible. We should annul and practically outpace those which proved to be erroneous. I want to inform the Central Committee in this connection that we have also thought of including a political assessment of the Party attitudes towards the 4th Congress of the Union of Czechoslovak Writers of last September on the agenda of this session. As a result of the pressure of time and the insufficient ideological analysis of various aspects of this Congress we have arrived at the conclusion that it is correct to concentrate first on solving the basic political problems of this time and tackling others without haste afterwards.

At the same time we think it inevitable in the interests of normalizing relations between the Party Central Committee and the writers' organisation to cancel immediately the validity of those conclucions of the Central Committee which administratively interfered from a position of power in the ideological conflict which needed to be settled by ideological means. Therefore we recommend that the September 1967 decision of the Central Committee on the transfer of Literární noviny into the sphere of the Ministry of Culture and Information be rescinded and that the proposal of the Central Control and Auditing Commission of the Communist Party of Czechoslovakia revoke the resolution on the expulsion of comrades Klíma, Liehm and Vaculík from the Party, on the punishment by reprimand with caution of comrade Kohout and on the introduction of Party disciplinary measures against comrade Milan Kundera.

Dear comrades,

Allow me now to pass to a brief explanation of the materials submitted to you. In them we stress the political aspect of work, above all the deepening of the content and methods of Party work.

We must purposefully create preconditions already today to be ahead of schedule in our future work. This means to work out with the help of solidly based scientific analyses the key problems of the new policy which is now being formed and which will continue being formed with the advance of preparations for the 14th Party Congress, and to accumulate prerequisites for the formation of a prospective programme. In this respect, we must activate and coordinate the

a 27

work in all spheres of scientific research, not give way to rashness, and reject the insincerity of cheap slogans and promises. On the other hand though, we must not be afraid to set ourselves the boldest aims the feasibility of which can be scientifically anticipated.

The importance of the choice and leadership of communists, who work in State and non-State institutions and organisations, and especially the importance of Party branches in which they are grouped must be stressed in connection with the new concept of the relationship of the Party to these organisations. Communists in non-Party organisations must be able to work out their policy independently and create scope for its implementation by winning the confidence and support of non-communists through the correct statement of their interests. The growing importance of the mission of communists should become and will be more clearly evident also in the fact that new members will be joining the Party mostly from the ranks of those who have best proved their worth and have grown into respected public officials.

It will be necessary to build up an objective Party system based on the system of democratic relations between all the components of the Party structure on an entirely new foundation. Consistent struggle against undesirable and undemocratic tendencies, lively and permanent confrontation of practical measures with the Party's Action Programme and with the democratic process of policy-making, of protection of rights and interests of communists, will be the main purpose of this system.

It will be necessary now to concentrate the best forces of the Party for practical action and at the same time for working out the general line of the next Party Congress, which would fully correspond to the new stage of the development of our society. In view of the situation and demands of

28 a

many district conferences we believe that it is necessary not to take a decision on the convocation of the 14th Congress, but to analyse the possibility of speeding up and intensifying its preparation while starting to work out a long-term programme of the CP of Czechoslovakia.

The reasons stimulating the speeding up of preparation for the Congress will certainly be intelligible to our comrades. For if we really want to take the lead in the current, and especially future, social changes we cannot do so predominantly through propaganda nor by personnel changes only. We can lead and inspire mainly by a realistic and clear policy. Its basis for the next period is the Action Programme. However, we should not forget that development is very dynamic. What is good today will be no longer sufficient tomorrow. Our nations rightly expect that, at the future Party Congress, we shall be able to state a clear programmatic standpoint, in its entirety. This means inclusive of the problems of the growth of the standard of living, basic objectives of the fifth five-year plan, prognoses of long-term economic development, etc. Otherwise, the proceedings of the Congress will bring nothing and would only result in wasting the initiative and activity to which we have stimulated the Party and masses.

The Party Congress presupposes the completion of the Action Programme, its extension into the guideline of the 14th Congress, though in unity with the economic programme. Otherwise, the workers will not understand us. The Congress will certainly take up everything that was viable and really progressive in our past policy and in the history of the Party, that stood the test of historical proof of values. And this guide-line will also clearly disengage from everything that was unrealistic and wrong.

There will certainly be an opportunity in the process of the implementation of the Action Programme and preparation

a

for the next Congress - i.e. on the basis of an active and matter-of-fact attitude, in everyday work - for the Party public to decide responsibly who should be given the mandate of member of the Central Committee of the CP of Czechoslovakia at the Congress.

In order to succeed fully in what we shall energetically strive for we must create the necessary preconditions in Central Committee bodies and in the central apparatus of the Party already at this Plenary Session. To reorganise the Presidium and the Secretariat of the Central Committee is the first task. We must logically proceed in this from the results of the past Plenary Sessions. The new Presidium and the new Secretariat must then prepare proposals for a complete adaptation of the structure of the central apparatus. Suggestions - although they cannot be regarded as complete - have been submitted to you. We are submitting them to you for study and for comment as working material, which has not yet been approved by the Presidium of the Central Committee of the CP of Czechoslovakia. We shall take a decision on them after they are completed and debated by the presidium of the Central Committee of the CPC, probably at our next Plenary Session.

All-round rationalization of the state administration in accordance with the spirit of the proceedings and conclusions of the December and January plenary sessions of the Central Committee is part of the policy of strengthening our socialist system. We have taken the first step in this direction by the election of the new president. We are fully confident that the election of comrade Ludvík Svoboda will contribute to the unification of progressive forces, to the

30 a

consolidation of political conditions in the state, and that all our efforts will benefit from it.

A very important task is to intensify the work of the government. The government must work, from the beginning, at a level in keeping with its constitutional function and the requirements of the new era. It must be not only a team of ministers, but also a collective body actually governing the republic and ensuring the needs of the society, expressed in the policy of the Communist Party and the National Front. In its work it must fully respect the will of the supreme body of state power, the National Assembly, cooperate with it in an active way, and systematically account to it for its work. Gradually, the government must get rid of excessive, for the government disproportionate, operative management of the economy and culture by directives, and be, above all, a body of conceptual and perspective management and effective state administration, sufficiently firm and exact to ensure that desirable order and democratic discipline prevail in our country.

In forming a new government, it will be right to count with the most urgent changes in the structure of the ministries, as proposed by the presidium of the Communist Party Central Committee and the government. In the foreseable future the new government should propose other necessary structural changes and adopt fundamental measures aimed at improving its work.

Mainly, however, we must proceed from the necessity of substantially changing the composition of the government, in keeping with the new conditions of its work and function. The public expects that those people will be appointed to government posts who will represent guarantees that the spheres assigned to them will be administered well. We must respect and apply the democratic principle that fundamental changes and turning points in politics are connected with the changes of political personalities asked to carry out the changes.

One of the first tasks of our Central Committee, the government and the National Assembly will be to accelerate the consolidation of the situation in the security forces and in the army.

Many critical words have been directed lately against the Ministry of Interior, and security bodies. The public was disquietened by a large number of facts which had come out in connection with the work of some security agencies in the 1950s, and by certain recent events. The measures, including the cadre measures, which are being taken at present will support everything that is sound at the Interior Ministry. Party conferences and meetings of the ministry personnel confirm that the sound forces within the security services represent the overwhelming majority. These forces guarantee that the confidence of the public in security services will be restored.

I am sure you will agree with me that the social need for security services is beyond any doubt. Only recently, Prague was perturbed by the report that another young member of the Public Security had lost his life in a struggle with a criminal. We must show full, sincere understanding for the difficult, responsible work of the security service, and we must extend a helping hand to the comrades in the service.

The Party regards reliable protection of the secure life of the country's peoples as an important political task. The defence of the republic is the concern of all the people, all Party, state, social and economic bodies and organizations. The resolutions and letters addressed to the Central Committee confirm that the communists in the armed forces, and other servicemen, fully and unequivocally support the results of the October, December and January plenary sessions of the Central Committee. They support the progressive trends in the Party and in the society, especially the process of democratization and rectification of errors in the methods

32 a

and work of the Party and state bodies. The communists in the army, security forces and units of the People's Militia have our full confidence, and will be given full support of the Central Committee for their highly responsible, demanding service and work.

The communists in the army realize that the revitalization process in our society and Party applies, to the full extent, to the army. Also we see in that, and in the necessary cadre changes in the army command, the guarantee that not even a shadow of doubt will ever fall on the absolute loyalty of the army to the people and to the progressive development of our society.

We must continue building our army, and improving it on socialist principles, on the basis of full centralism and indivisible authority of command, as a defence bulwark against the external enemy, against the imperialist agressors. The army must be built as a firm link in the alliance of the Warsaw Treaty armies.

The building and operations of the Czechoslovak armed forces, army and security, must proceed under the democratic control of responsible state bodies. It will be right to create appropriate guarantees in this respect. At the same time, to a much greater degree, the problems concerning the army and security must become the subject of interest and democratic supervision of the whole public.

As regards the National Assembly, we must fully ensure the application of the constitutional rights of this supreme state institution, already in its present form and under the conditions of the valid constitution and other laws, with possible necessary partial amendments. It is necessary to recommend inevitable cadre changes in the presidium of the National Assembly. Finally, it will be necessary to draw up new principles for the activities of the communists in the National Assembly. In this connection, the necessity to

a 33

set up without delay an armed forces and security committee of the National Assembly is urgent.

The communists in the National Assembly should come forward with the initiative for the inception, without delay, of qualified work on the preparations of a new constitution which will give legal expression to the social transitions in our society, and which will become a firm legal base of the democratic structure of our life, as a permanent principle of advancing, modern socialist society. The principles of the draft constitution should become the subject of broad, democratic discussion of the public and of experts.

Fundamental changes must also be carried out in the constitutional expression and protection of the principle of equal rights of the Czechs and Slovaks. Experience from development hitherto, and especially following the constitution of 1960, prove convincingly how various aberrations have affected this sphere of state law, supremely important for the unity of the two nations, practically annulling the elementary rights of Slovakia, of the Slovak national bodies. The existing organization of the Slovak national organs is the target of justified criticism. It is our task to develop the relations between the Czech and Slovak nations on sound foundations, to strengthen the common Czechoslovak statehood.

It is, therefore, necessary, to prepare a new constitutional law in the foreseeable future, even before the elections to the National Assembly and to the Slovak National Council. This constitutional reform, which should be a continuation of the positive concepts and proposals which have been born in the periods of the anti-fascist resistence and of the beginnings of the national and democratic revolutions, will fundamentally change the status and authority of Slovak national bodies. The amendment should be based on the wishes and needs of our nations and nationalities, should fully ensure their national development, and thus contribute to the even greater activity of communists, and their zest and will to solve serious social problems.

In this respect, we shall have to rely more effectively on, while channelling the work of the Party apparatus, which we cannot do without. The apparatus itself, its workers, particularly through the active Party group, must help more efficiently towards better, really analytical work of Party bodies. The work of the apparatus must be increasingly orientated, improved and made more efficient in this direction. It must have the position which is really its due - no more, no less. It is impossible not to see its important position in the system of our Party work. Therefore it is also out of place to negate indiscriminately the work of the Party apparatus. Its overwhelming majority is made up of brave and honest communists whose aim is to serve devotedly the Party and our people.

There were proposals during the first conferences that we should call a Plenary Session of the Central Committee of the CP of Czechoslovakia. The Presidium of the CC of the Communist Party of Czechoslovakia adhered to the set course in preparations for the first Plenary Session after January. This was mainly because it was too much to work out a course for the future work of the Central Committee, which would proceed from the principles of the Action Programme in this short time. The Presidium thought it decisive for the future course of work to concentrate on the content of Party work in the next period and carry out personnel changes only on this basis, and not vice versa. Without knowing the conclusions of the response to the January Plenary Session and the intensity of Party activity, which became evident at the district conferences, the CC Plenary Session would be unable to advance. The district Party conferences attested to the Party's maturity and to the ability of communists to make a correct estimation of the situation.

in our opinion, centre without delay their main attention on care for the daily needs of the population.

In the past few months, we have already practically started on the road towards solving a number of questions of socialist democracy. Freedom of speech and criticism, freedom of press - these are no longer demands, but realities. We have begun solving definitely all problems of the rehabilitation of all unjustly persecuted people - communists and non-communists. There is also full-blooded development of initiative in our social organizations, especially in trade unions. The National Assembly and the Slovak National Council are beginning to understand their new role. Changes in certain important state, party and social functions also belong to the realities of the past weeks.

However, these are all only first steps. What will be necessary now? Above all, we must give a legal form to all positive features of the current revitalization process, we must pass laws which will guarantee that the freedoms of speech and criticism, freedom of the press and freedom of assembly will be, in connection with socialism and the inviolability of our statehood and socialist achievements, permanently protected by laws, by the fundamental parts of our political system, by the fundamental rules of our public life.

No democracy - and thus not even our socialist democracy - can live for long only on the fact that opinions can be freely expressed, that criticism is permitted. That in itself is only decisive,if free and sound criticism removes old obstacles from the road of social progress. In order to live and to rule democratically in our society even then, when the obstacles have been eliminated everywhere and for good, we must have a well-thought out and well functioning system of institutions, bodies and organizations, which will work in a new and effective way, where new policy will be pursued, and these bodies will be permanently under democratic supervision of citizens. Therefore, we are faced with the very urgent task of consolidating political conditions, developing the whole existing system of political management in our society so as to make it into a system fully combining socialism and democracy, a system capable of factually and in a qualified way solving all problems arising from the needs of the life of our society, a system in which the relationships of responsibility and control will be determined, in which it will be clearly stated who is responsible for what and to whom, in which independent authority and independent responsibility of everyone for his tasks will be exactly fixed.

This will require systematic work on the part of government bodies and elected state bodies, social organizations and of the Party in the next few months.

All these problems will be dealt with in an atmosphere of genuine socialist democracy. This means the beginning of a situation - which will now be of a permanent character - when we, the communists, will have to defend and argue in public, our views and standpoints in discussion with all the others. The communists will stand in the vanguard of the development, and will have the status of leadership to the extent to which they will be able to win and keep it by ideological and political means, under democratic conditions. Authority is not given once and for all - neither to the individual, nor to a party organization, nor to a party. Authority must be unceasingly renewed, on the basis of the results of work. The Party and its members must be at the head of the progressive development,must lead and sweep the other masses of the working people into the vortex of the tasks.

The relationship of the communists and non-communists, the relationship of the Party and the rest of the society is thus becoming the key question of today. Quite naturally, this is being discussed both within and outside the Party. In doing so, we must proceed from the reality of contemporary processes. The process of revitalization has put into

a 37

motion the whole mechanism of social life. The purpose and aim of the democratization process is clear: to create an improved type of socialist democracy, in keeping with Czechoslovak conditions. It is in the interest of the Party and to the benefit of the whole society that the process should be completed in a relatively quiet way, without any major oscillations. Any other transition might seriously endanger the aims we are following, might thwart the historical opportunity which is offered to us today for our socialist development.

The present process, taking place on a socialist basis, must give a truly democratic scope to the interest of all social groups, must guarantee the permanence of our international ties. These vital demands cannot be met without the leading role of the Communist Party. No other organized force exists in our society which could guarantee the socialist character of the current social process and its even democratic development.

In solving the problems of relations of the Party to state and social institutions, we proceed from this realistic position. The past situation in this sphere, especially as regards the National Front, was not entirely satisfactory. It has been negatively affecting the authority and activity of these bodies, as well as the authority of the Party. We welcome and appreciate that the social organizations are beginning to assert themselves as independent, autonomous parts of the political system. We especially welcome and wish to develop the revitalization process in the trade unions, because it enhances their status in the National Front.

The whole National Front, the political parties which form it, and the social organizations, participate in the formulation of state policy. The political parties of the National Front are partners, their political activities proceed from the common political programme of the National

38 a

Front, proceed fully from the socialist character of social relations in our republic. The Communist Party regards the National Front as a political platform which does not divide the political parties into government and opposition parties in the sense that opposition would be formed against the line of state policy as the policy of the whole National Front, and that a political fight for power in the state would be waged.

The formation of political forces striving to deny this concept of the National Front, to exclude the National Front from political power, was on the whole overcome already in 1945 after the tragic experience of both our nations with the prewar political development of ČSR.

In the National Front and in the whole political system, we shall apply the Marxist-Leninist concept as a concept of leading policy so that we shall use all means of political work - in all parts of our system and directly among the masses of the workers and all working people - to win for it such support which will ensure its leading position by democratic political means.

All this contributes, and will contribute even more, to the realization that the responsibility for the development of our society and our state will be a common one, fully and really shared by all, communists and non-communists alike.

For many communists, who have become used to the old methods, it will not be easy. The Party as a whole is, however, bound to succeed. We are firmly convinced of it, because there are many creative forces within the Party, and to fear the new process would be to underestimate deeply these creative forces.

Our political system will certainly not revert to the state in which its foundation would be only the relations of the political parties. In the system of socialist democracy, we are concerned with more than a copy of the parliamentarism typical for formal democracies. The aim is to increase the real independence of social and group-interest organizations, to make the representative bodies of the state - up to the National Assembly - into bodies where political decisions of the state are actually made. During the process of further development of our political system, it will be desirable to give consideration especially to the question of how even the whole scale of interests of the people in certain spheres of the social division of labour - in the economy, in the industries and agriculture, in social services, education, science and culture - will directly assert itself in the system of socialist democracy to a more marked degree. Socialist democracy must differ from formal democracy, inter alia, also insofar that it will be the working people who will have the decisive word in the management of the society.

Naturally today, we cannot yet define the future model of a functioning socialist democracy. The democratic forces and phenomena are at the beginning, and not at the end. We must follow their movement, and strengthen and elaborate it further. The first steps we are taking today are sufficient only for what is most urgent in the given situation, and would be insufficient, even one-sided, for further perspectives. In connection with the preparations of the 14th Party Congress, we should consider how to develop the whole political system so that we could use all knowledge and international experience to make of it a much more intensive union of democracy with socialism under specific Czechoslovak conditions.

Another important task of the future period is the consolidation and development of our national economy. In the current discussions, it is increasingly demanded that the present stage of our national economy be quite frankly and critically evaluated, that it be stated clearly and with full responsibility what our situation really is and that it be said quite clearly and responsibly how and by which methods we want to consolidate our economy. I think that an analysis of the present state of our national economy should be given by the new Government when it submits its program. This analysis should precede the report on the ways and methods by which we want to and must ensure a balanced, smooth and effective development of our economv.

We want to consistently introduce the new system of economic management. We must stop talking only about improving the system of management and say clearly that it is to be a profound economic reform designed to create a new system for the functioning of the socialist economy. We know that it will be a system based on a synthesis of the plan and the market, a synthesis which must be first of all elaborated. In this synthesis, the criterion of economic activities will be not only formal indicators of a directively-conceived plan, but economic instruments ensuring the aims of the whole society, objective criteria of the market and of social-political priorities, resulting from objective economic interrelations and which are fully binding on every state which wants to make its economy permanently prosperous. It should be a system which will fully appreciate high-quality and effective work and which will assure that people are remunerated not only according to the physical and mental energy they expended but, above all, according to the real results by which they contributed to the satisfaction of all the needs of the society. A system which will set free the creative initiative of the working people, will enable the growth of capable people and will create a wide scope for natural

a

selection in making appointments to leading positions.

The main condition for the consistent and rapid implementation of the new system of management is today the institutional adjustment of relationships in the economic sphere and the creation of a new organisational structure in the whole sphere of production. In this connection, I want to emphasize - and this also answers many questions and comments from district conferences - that we are putting through, and shall continue to put through, further measures designed to democratize economic management. As regards enterprises, we expect them to gain such a measure of independence as will enable them to fully develop business activity. Within enterprises, democratic managing bodies will operate to which directors and other leading economic executives will be accountable. In addition to this, the trade organisation will also assert itself in putting through the interests of employees and in exercising control over management.

Profound changes in the system of management will be supplemented by extensive changes in the structure of production which, at present, is not in keeping with Czechoslovak conditions and, moreover, has departed from the objective tendencies of the progressive development of the productive forces which are becoming increasingly predominant in all industrially advanced countries. It will be a difficult transformation which will affect many partial interests. But we have no other choice. At the same time, we must take care that those who are not responsible for the present unsatisfactory production structure should not be the worse for the changes.

The government will have to submit to the National Assembly a set of immediate measures by which these important tasks will be consistently ensured. It will be necessary to carry out changes in the structure of investments, i.e. to allocate means especially to agriculture and to the consumer and food industry, as well as to the non-productive sphere, particularly to housing construction and the whole field of services. Since our resources are limited, each measure which will make their use more effective can help to reduce the economic imbalance and achieve a faster growth of the national income. The most important reserves of greater effectiveness are, in our view, the viving activity of the people and the application of that which has always been typical of Czechoslovak workers and technicians and which has been rendered inactive by the old system of management, i.e. an independent approach to tasks, the application of know-how, abilities and skill, as well as of initiative, resulting from the restored feeling that the people's work is their own creative personal contribution to the successful effort of the whole society. This will be stimulated not only by the application of the principles of the new system of management but also by the current process of revitalization in our public and political life.

These measures are closely interrelated with the program concerning the standard of living. Prosperity can be achieved only on the basis of a modern and highly efficient economy which is able to assert its qualities in tough competition on the world market. All other roads towards prosperity are provisional, temporary and full of risk.

At present, we can solve only the most urgent social problems, those we formulated in the document adopted at the plenary meeting in December. In this conection, I want to emphasize that we must seek possibilities of making cuts also in the field of central management and public expenditure; these cuts will be used for improving the social conditions of the population. However, the achievement of a more substantial improvement will depend to a decisive extent on how we shall be able to run our economy in future. The changed system of management should contribute not only towards rationalizing the state and economic apparatus but

a 43

also towards making it cheaper and at the same time towards eliminating many abnormalities and bureaucratic anomalies.

In addition to these measures which we shall implement in the next few months, we must intensify the elaboration of the long-range conception of the development of the Czechoslovak national economy which will not only comprise changes in the structure of production and in its more consistent integration in the world division of labour, but also in which we shall proceed from the new structure of the needs of our population.

Today, attention concentrates mainly on the material and social needs of the people. However, we want to, and must, achieve even more. Socialism, and especially socialism based on broad democratic principles, must create a new humanism of the modern era, one which other systems are unable to give to mankind in spite of all their technical progress, it must create better conditions for the development of man than have been so far created by any other society. This means that when we strive for normalizing the economy, we do not regard this task as an end in itself but as an instrument designed to promote the full development of man, of human personality. It must therefore aim at creating, for every individual person, conditions in which everyone will be able to assert himself in all spheres of work and life. An immense role will, in this sense, be played by science and art. We therefore strive not only for a fast development of the individual branches of science, which are interrelated with the growth of the productive forces, and with the scientific and technical revolution, but also for the development of the humanistic scientific branches and all spheres of art which will help people to find a new way of life corresponding with the era of the scientific and technical revolution and with the socialist principles of our society.

In solving present-day economic difficulties, i.e.

the economic imbalance, we must take into account the factor on which we could not count before the January plenum of the Central Committee, the factor which could not be counted upon by economists but which must be today seen by politicians, i.e. the activity which is setting in motion the creative mind and energy. Economic effectiveness and economic difficulties can, in no case, be solved at the expense of the living standard of the people. Resources and reserves for solving this vitally important task must be found in production. In solving the present tasks, it is therefore necessary to take fully into account the moral factor emerging with new revitalizing and renascent power after the January plenum. People must be infused with faith in themselves, with faith in knowledge, skill and intellect. This faith in the working people is today a moral force but will tomorrow certainly be a material force on which we shall be able to count fully in our drive for the further development of our national economy, for further growth in the living standard.

The period since the January meeting of the Central Committee of the CP CZ has been characterized up to this day by lively foreign political activities of our Party in spite of the fact that the stormy internal political developments have apparently relegated international policy to second place. However, it has again been confirmed that we are implementing and shall implement all the complicated and exacting internal tasks in a certain concrete international situation.

In this relatively short period of time, several multilateral meetings have taken place which are important for strengthening the cooperation of the socialist countries and for further efforts to achieve unity of the internal Communist movement. In terms of time, first place among them is held by the Budapest consultative meeting of Communist and workers' parties. I do not intend to give a more detailed evaluation of its results but, in this connection, we want to emphasize two aspects of this meeting. It is important that the delegations which participated in the Budapest meeting, under complicated conditions reached unity on a number of points which are of decisive importance for convening and preparing a world conference of the Communist parties. This is an encouraging success. Secondly: the Budapest meeting was a step forward in seeking new forms of unity while preserving the independence of the fraternal parties and their mutual international collaboration.

The delegation of the Communist Party of Czechoslovakia undoubtedly made a positive contribution to the talks. It tried to assert a sober and realistic view of the contradictory problems of the present world as well as of complicated questions of the cooperation of the Communist parties. Our delegation strongly supported demands for a substantial extension of ties with all the anti-imperialist forces. It adopted a clear attitude to past incorrect evaluations of the League of Communists of Yugoslavia and it raised its voice in support of sensible efforts to develop relations with those fraternal parties which hold different views on a number of questions.

The recent meeting of the Political Consultative Committee of the Warsaw Treaty in Sofia and the meeting of the highest representatives of certain socialist states in Dresden were also important. The first meant much for political cooperation, the second, I believe, will become an impulse for a more thorough and open discussion on the problems of economic cooperation, both within the framework of the Council of Mutual Economic Assistance and on a bilateral basis.

It is natural that we have taken advantage of all these meetings to supply information on developments in our country and to explain correctly the positive sense of the process of democratization. As you know, I myself met earlier Comrade Brezhnev, Comrade Kádár and Comrade Gomulka. Such meetings will take place in future with representatives of other fraternal parties also. Comrades Koucký and Kriegel held talks in this sense with delegations of many fraternal parties in Budapest as well as on other occasions. A broad exchange of views took also place during the visit of the delegations of fraternal parties and states at the time of the celebrations of the 20.th anniversary of the February events.

Our last discussion to date took place at the recent meeting in Dresden. It must be stated that the representatives of the socialist countries and the central committees of their parties at this meeting showed understanding for the present views of the Central Committee of the Communist Party of Czechoslovakia on developments in our Republic and on questions of mutual cooperation. The discussion and the exchange of opinions must be understood in the sense that the principle of non-interference in the internal affairs of other parties will continue to be valid.

I am sure that I express the identical view of the entire Central Committee if I once more emphasize that in the same way as the socialist character of our future road is inviolable, so are equally inviolable the basic values of the Czechoslovak foreign political orientation: firm alliance and all-round cooperation with the Soviet Union and the socialist states, based on the principles of equality, mutual benefit, non-interference and international solidarity. This basic orientation of our policy is in harmony with the most vital needs of the security of our nations and with the development of our national economy. No one will ever succeed in casting any doubt on the unserving Czechoslovak-Soviet friendship. This friendship is not only a matter of historical experience of the people of our country but, above all, the outcome of a realistic appraisal of the present situation of the Republic in the surrounding world. If our country is now, at the present time, not exposed to any acute threat from outside, which sometimes

a 47

gives rise to not exactly profound conclusions as regards the existence or non-existence of danger, it must be seen that this is precisely the consequence of our alliance with the Soviet Union, the consequence of the safeguard we have in the Soviet Union.

The idea that in today's antagonistically divided world we could stand somewhere in the background appearing and behaving neutralistically and speculating that if things should go badly for our nations we should invite others to bleed for us, is impossible not only from the political but also from the ethical point of view.

Proletarian internationalism, its practical application in relations to other socialist countries as well as towards the whole international Communist movement, respect for our essential common interests, our assistance to everything representing social progress in the world, constitutes today, and also for the future, the basis of the foreign policy of our socialist country.

This is also the aspect in which we view our intention to activate generally the foreign political activity of our state. We must require this activity to have an elaborated conception and to assert with greater initiative our standpoints on important international problem, our active contribution to the common, scientifically substantiated, international political activity of the socialist states. This will, in particular, mean pursuance of a more effective European, and primarily Central European, policy contributing to the consolidation of peaceful relations in Europe and to the expansion of cooperation among countries with different social systems.

Our interest concentrates especially on a peaceful solution of the German problem which is of cardinal importance for European security and in which an important role is played by the existence and the policy of the German Democratic Republic. Positive efforts for the creation of a peaceful atmosphere and good relations among the nations of Europe and in the world in general represent the chief line of our international policy.

At the same time, however, the activities of world imperialism and particularly the activization of revenge-seeking forces in the German Federal Republic forces us to continue strengthening and maintaining our armed forces, our Czechoslovak People's Army on a high level. The American aggression against the Vietnamese people is too strong a warning for us to be able to underestimate it. This is also why- and certainly in harmony with the evaluation by members of the Party Central Committee - we are for taking the necessary measures for extending the mechanism of the Warsaw Treaty so that it corresponds to present-day conditions. Concretely, this means to improve the activities of the joint command, which was recently discussed at the Sofia and Dresden meetings. As was shown at the Dresden conference, especially in Comrade Kosygin's speech on the economic sphere, we have still many untapped reserves in this respect. The State Planning Commission has been therefore charged with preparing an initiative proposal for intensifying cooperation with the Soviet Union where we are bound by the raw material basis, but also with other socialist states, especially with our neighbours - with Poland, Hungary and the German Democratic Republic.

The action program could outline only very briefly certain foreign political tasks. It will depend on initiative efforts especially of the Ministry of Foreign Affairs and naturally also of the whole Government the National Assembly, the Central Committee and its Presidium smaller to no extent that these principles are concretized as soon and as well as possible in order that Czechoslovak foreign policy may ensure all the indispensable external conditions for the successful internal socialist development of our country.

Comrades,

The action program which has been submitted has a double purpose: first of all, to create unity in action for the implementation of the main tasks of our development, to give sufficient impetus for the development of the socialist initiative of the people, to show the road by which it is possible to eliminate the obstacles which have until now been standing in the way of further development corresponding to present-day conditions, obstacles consisting first of all in excessive centralism, in administrative-directive methods rooted in the field of political management.

The second and deeper sense of the program lies in the fact that it opens up scope for basic structural changes in our society and for the creation of a new dynamic of socialism which would be in harmony with the changed social, economic and cultural conditions as well as with specific national conditions. The implementation of this program can, and must, open up the road towards the sollution of other more complicated and more important questions concerning the organisation and the dynamic development of our socialist society in directions which could now be only indicated. Greater activity of socialist development can be created only by setting into motion new powerful forces of social life, and - relying on creative Marxist thinking - carrying out bold, but at the same time well-considered, experiments. In the course of this process, it is necessary to deepen and perfect the new general line of the Party.

This is why the program has been drafted as a fundamental political view of the present stage and its needs. It cannot be understood as a directive enumeration of concrete tasks but as a political platform which must be creatively developed. It is an open document which will be further perfected in the course of its implementation. The program does not want to, and cannot in advance, determine the detailed course to be adopted by individual organisations and institutions but it opens up sufficiently wide scope to enable them to determine and concretize these tasks themselves in the spirit of the basic lines. Any other approach would be at variance with the spirit of the program. If people are to indentify themselves with the aims of the program, they must participate in their formulation.

I should like to say a few words about work with the action program, especially about its role in the current general process of democratization. We must be aware of the character of this process, its rate and its rapid acceleration. Things which, a fortnight ago, appeared as something basically different from the general view are today becoming generally accepted and may already tomorrow be out-of-date. In connection with the action program we may also hear that people already know its content. It is an actual fact that certain ideas of this program have already been published, some of them have even been discussed. However, knowledge, acceptance or non-acceptance of its ideas are one thing.This can be achieved in a short time. But the main thing - implementation, elaboration and concretization - is something different. This activity is more difficult, frequently also little effective, ordinary and routine work, it requires perseverance but is indispensable if the program is to serve any purpose.

The current of democratization, the social mechanism which began to operate, will indubitably develop even further. Only if the Party submits in its program demands which, from the present point of view, are sufficiently bold, if it regards the program as the basis and a starting-point, shall we be able to be constantly at the head of the creative process and enforce its socialist character. We must endeavour to master the social interests operating in society. It is therefore desirable to orientate ourselves to progressive demands - even if perhaps they appear to us at this moment to be too radical - in order that we may be able to keep up with this process, in order that the Party may stand at its head, so that there might not be a great difference between the potential interests of the people and the program of the Party.

As regards organisational procedure, we recommend that immediately after its adoption by the Central Committee the program be submitted to the National Front and that, after it has been discussed and amended, it be submitted - this time already as the program of the National Front - to Parliament. This will be in harmony with democratic principles and with the demands requiring the assertion of the leading role of the Party.

Simultaneously with this, it will be correct to submit the program to gatherings of working people at various places, particularly in enterprises, so that they may familiarize themselves with it. Immediately after the plenum of the Central Committee, it will be useful to organise also meetings and gatherings in the decisive cities and at larger places of work too. This method should be one of the main sources of information immediately after the meeting of the Central Committee. We now have an excellent and extraordinary opportunity to approach our people and to show them how purposefully and energetically our Party intends to pave the way to progress and socialism.

In conclusion, I want only to emphasize that the action program is to become an important political platform on which to unify the revitalizing efforts of the Party,and all the people in the interests of the successful development of our socialist society.

On the basis of the action program, attention must be already focussed ahead. It is necessary to pass on to practical deeds at every place of work, to pass over from words to deeds, to act and organize work so as to make everyone feel that he is needed, that he is counted with.

2

The document which follows is undoubtedly the most significant of the collection. Its significance attaches to the fact that here, in the Action Program of the Communist Party of Czechoslovakia, the reader will find spelled out in considerable detail the foundations for a new political, social and economic order. This is not an order based either on the principles of liberal democracy or the free private enterprise system, but rather on the principles of Marxism and an economy oriented toward socialism.

In reading the Action Program it is important to recognize that the proposals made here originated with the Czechoslovak Communist Party (CCP). Accordingly, they represent the thinking of men who, although profoundly disturbed by conditions around them, are nevertheless undoubtedly convinced of the capacity of their system to meet the challenge of renewal. It would be a mistake, therefore, to read this Program either as a confession of weakness or an admission of failure, although, as the reader will discover, it contains elements of both. It would also be a mistake to interpret this Program as a total repudiation of the past. The measures outlined here appear to attest to an awareness of the fact that conditions within Czechoslovakia have changed and that if the system is to survive it too must change. Moreover, they appear to attest to a belief in the ability of the CCP to oversee the innovation.

If this is so, then the message of this Program is that when confronted with the spectre of irrelevance, Communist political systems must respond, and must respond creatively; they must, moreover, do so without destroying themselves in the process; finally, and by implication, unless they can demonstrate this capacity they are, like any other political system, doomed to extinction.

THE INTERNAL AUDIENCE

The message is conveyed to the internal audience on three different levels. Speaking, as it were, to the Party, the Program underscores both the urgency of the challenge confronting the CCP and the necessity for meeting this challenge in a way that will jeopardize neither its own survival nor the survival of the system. In this connection, the Program gives considerable space to the errors of the past as well as to the problems of the present. The theme throughout appears to be less one of recrimination than of reconciliation. As articulated in the Program, this theme finds expression in the emphasis on the need to recognize past errors so as to insure that these mistakes will never be repeated. The call to introspection is thus presented in a way that will inspire confidence rather then demoralize. For those who, because of their close association with the policies of the past, might find this exposition of previous abuses a rather painful exercise, the Program offers the promise of "salvation" through "repentance." For those who might be inspired to carry this process of self-criticism too far, the Program stands as a pointed reminder that it was the CCP which recognized the need for reform, and it is the CCP which will lead the way to the future. Finally, for those who opposed the policies of the past, the Action Program represents both a vindication and a victory.

Although this review of the distortions of the past may serve to intimidate the few, it can hardly be expected to inspire the many. To accomplish the latter, the Program combines an enumeration of the problems that lie ahead with a projection of what life will be like once these problems are resolved. Such an approach can be considered doubly useful. First, it inspires by holding out the promise of rewards to members of the Party who demonstrate a willingness to accept the challenge of renovation. Secondly, for those in the Party who might be somewhat reluctant to accept this challenge, it offers inspiration of a negative nature—namely, the dire consequences that await a Party which is no longer relevant.

The Program seeks to motivate in yet another way. In offering a plan of attack which reflects the initiative of the CCP, it implies that the steps to be taken will not lead to the destruction either of the system or of the Party. Thus the prospect of change is made more palatable, while the prospect of resisting change is made unattractive. Since the future of the Party is secure, and since these measures will serve to strengthen rather than weaken that position, there is little to be gained by obstructing implementation of the Program. But there is much to be gained by wholehearted acceptance of the measures set forth therein.

The same theme is employed in conveying the message to the "masses." Again, the need for change is keyed to both a frank acknowledgement of past errors and an equally frank acknowledgement of the willingness of the CCP to adapt to the changing conditions within Czechoslovakia. In each instance, however, the acknowledgement is a qualified one. The past is viewed as a period of both significant shortcomings and significant accomplishments. The crisis during these years centered around the reconstruction of a war-ravaged nation and the building of socialism. In the period immediately after World War II, there was a threat to the very existence of the Party. This, however, was successfully overcome and the work of reconstruction was begun. The years that followed are treated as a period of sacrifice, hardship and rapid change; they are also treated as a period in which an inexperienced Party confronted with new and demanding tasks was required to adopt policies which—while suitable for this particular stage of the country's development—were nevertheless retained long after they were needed.

The treatment of the past here, as elsewhere in the documents, is marked by an emphasis on individual and institutional shortcomings rather than Party error. The "masses" are told that while the CCP recognized the need to change with the times, "leading *bodies* and *institutes* of the Party and the State" found it difficult to accept the necessity of adjusting their behavior in accordance with the requirements of each succeeding stage of development (Italics mine). Abuses such as "sectarianism, suppression of the democratic rights and freedoms of the people, violation of laws, signs of licentiousness and misuse of power" are ascribed to the shortcomings of individuals and institutional deviation from the Party line.

Again, as in the case of Party members, although a confession of errors may serve to placate the "masses," it hardly constitutes a suitable foundation from which to proceed to the building of a better future. In apparent recognition of that fact, the Action Program—in addition to rescuing the reputation of the CCP—attempts to salvage as much as possible of the legacy of the past. The "masses" are told that many gains were made during these early years—gains which provide a solid basis for tackling the problems that lie ahead.

By the way of providing further inspiration, the Program takes the position that while much remains to be done the worst is, in effect, over. In line with this position, there is the assertion that *"at the end of the fifties our society entered another stage of development."* This assertion, preceded as it is by an exposition of past errors and followed by references to the need for a major renovation of the entire system, in effect constitutes a pledge by the CCP that there will be no turning back. The development theme is thus employed to demonstrate that neither the Party nor existing conditions will permit a return to the economic stagnation, political repression and popular alienation which characterized the earlier period.

The theme has an even more important function, however. In tying past, present and future together, it conveys to the "masses" the idea of progress or forward movement within the context of the existing system. The Action Program, when viewed in this context assumes the character of simply another installment in an ongoing process of continuity and change—a process which, it should be noted, envisions an enduring future under socialism.

The major source of inspiration is, of course, the Program itself, and more particularly the specific reforms outlined therein. For the most part these reforms speak for themselves. Considered at one level, they constitute a pledge on the part of the CCP to not only eliminate the accumulated shortcomings of past years but to work for the development of a society that is united, socialist, and humane—a society in which the CCP is truly responsive to the needs of the people—needs which are expressed freely and without fear of reprisal—a society wherein the Government becomes more than a hollow instrument of repression; a society, moreover, in which the active participation of the "masses" in the process of renovation is supported by the establishment of legal safeguards against an arbitrary and capricious government; in which youth is allowed to partake of a rich cultural heritage in a system of education that encourages individual thought and personal development, and the nationality question is resolved so that Czechs and Slovaks live together in equality and harmony. Finally, a society in which the economy, once freed from the stifling control of a bureaucracy that is top-heavy and unimaginative, develops the capacity to provide the material basis for a full and happy life.

Considered at another level, however, these reforms represent an admission on the part of the CCP that a system which is dedicated primarily to the maintenance of internal security is not a system which is likely to foster internal development. As such, the system, if it is to survive, must change. That change cannot be piecemeal or superficial. It must be fundamental in character and far-reaching in its impact. It must, moreover, be presided over by a Party that is both competent and flexible; a Party that rewards imagination, expertise, and competence rather than unquestioning obedience to higher authority; a Party which tolerates legitimate dissent as the price for remaining relevant to the needs of society; a Party that is capable of demonstrating its right to control the destinies of the people by providing leadership which is conducive to the fulfillment of popular aspirations.

This is not a Party, it should be added, which presides over its own annihilation. Nor is it a Party that permits its will to be thwarted by those "right-wing anti-socialist elements" within Czechoslovakia who would reject the promise of socialism for the corruption of bourgeois democracy. It is instead a Party of strength—strength which is derived not from the forceable repression of opposition, but from opposition to forceable repression. A Party which is capable of distinguishing between legitimate dissent and subversion.

This, then, is the message delivered at the third level. It is a message of resolution and strength, calculated to serve as a reminder to those who would interpret this Program as a repudiation of the system, that the CCP recognizes the need for renovation and is willing to accept the uncertainties which accompany change. It is not, however, willing to accept an end to its primacy as the leading force in the construction of a socialist society. Development there will be. Liberalization there will be. Revolution there will not be. As this Program indicates, the CCP is prepared to deal with the challenge of development. It is, as the Program makes absolutely clear, also prepared to deal with the challenge of denial.

THE EXTERNAL AUDIENCE

To the external audience the message is presented with equal clarity. To the Soviet Union, members of the bloc, and other "fraternal parties" it is less a gesture of defiance than a statement of intent. The Program follows the established pattern of first providing a requirement for change and then outlining the methods to be employed in meeting that requirement. In the case of the former, there are references scattered throughout the text covering not only the need for change but the role of the CCP as the initiator of change in Czechoslovakia. The impression conveyed is not one of a Party being dragged along by irresistible forces of change but of a Party which has acted, albeit belatedly, to curb a growing threat to its own survival. The Action Program is in this way depicted as a product of necessity as well as choice. It is also, and more importantly from the standpoint of the bloc, depicted as a Czech response to a Czech problem and thus is not presented as a model to be followed by anyone else.

The process of outlining methods to be employed in meeting the needs of the present as well as of the future combines an attempt to establish the fact that the changes will be beneficial with an attempt to establish the equally important fact that the primary beneficiary of the Action Program will be the CCP itself. To that end, references to specific changes are generally coupled with statements concerning either the source of the change, i.e., the CCP, or comments dealing with the abuses of the past which, in one way or another, have made the changes necessary. Here too, understandable care is taken to avoid giving the impression that the Action Program is intended for external consumption. By linking the reforms to internal conditions, the CCP is able to minimize its references to ideology. In a system where, theoretically at least, there is a shared legitimacy of experience, this is understandably an important consideration.

The references to foreign relations which appear at the end of the Program serve to underscore in a literal sense the message to the "socialist camp." Utilizing a theme of continuity and change, these comments alternately stress a desire to assume a more active international role and assurances that such a desire in no way constitutes a danger to the Soviet Bloc. In the Program as in the other documents, special reference is made to the question of Czechoslovakia's relations with the German Democratic Republic and the German Federal Republic. The references reflect both the sensitive nature of the question and the fact that the CCP fully understands the political-military implications of its strategic position within the bloc.

The message as presented to the "socialist camp" is thus stated in such a way as to minimize possible objections either to the specific reforms or to the adoption of the entire Program by the CCP. The clarity with which the message is stated, the moderate tone of the arguments advocated, the reliance on internal necessity as the justification for the changes to be initiated, and the numerous indications of the primacy of the CCP, its awareness of the internal dangers and its commitment to strengthening the instruments of State security, add up to a Program which should have been palatable to the Soviet Union, if not to the other members of the bloc. Whatever the reasons behind the intervention, it would not appear that the Action Program was a primary or even decisive factor. On the contrary, it would not be surprising at all if, in the months that follow, this Program is implemented as stated.

To the non-Communist world the message of the Action Program is stated in a somewhat obscure fashion. On the surface the Program would appear to be a break with the past, a break occasioned by disillusionment with the old order and a desire to create a better way of life for the people of Czechoslovakia. Upon closer scrutiny, however, the Program appears to constitute not a break with, but an extension of, the past—an extension prompted both by disillusionment with the old order and by confidence in the ability of that order to withstand the ordeal of change.

It is for this reason that the Program deserves careful study—study conducted in an atmosphere which is free of polemics and maudlin sentimentality. For if the reforms proposed here say anything at all, it is that Communist political systems—or at least this Communist political system—have a capacity for self-regeneration which is considerable indeed. This is not to suggest that this, or for that matter any other, political system is indestructible. Nor is it to imply that the system has an unlimited capacity to absorb change. It is instead to suggest that the same system which produced the pressures for change also produced this Program. That in itself would seem to be a significant accomplishment.

The accomplishment becomes even more significant, however, when one realizes that the Action Program seeks not to destroy but to modify the system in the light of changing conditions within Czechoslovakia. It may be argued, of course, that in time such modification would have brought about the end of Communist rule in that country. The point is that the individuals who formulated this program appear to have been willing to take that chance. In the final analysis, this may well be the most significant aspect of the Action Program—significant not only for the non-Communist world but for the Communist world as well.

CONCLUSION

The Action Program reflects both an awareness of the need for change and a commitment to meet that need within the framework of the existing system. The reforms contemplated by the Program suggest not a rejection of the system but its renovation. That renovation, involving as it does a series of far-reaching reforms, further suggests a belief in the capacity of the system to absorb change. Finally, that belief, coupled as it were with the desire to provide a better future under socialism for the people of Czechoslovakia, would seem to indicate, at least in this case, that Communist Party State systems are capable of meeting the challenge of political development.

THE ACTION PROGRAMME OF THE COMMUNIST PARTY OF CZECHOSLOVAKIA

adopted at the plenary session of the Central Committee of the Communist Party of Czechoslovakia on April 5th 1968

Prague, April 1968

THE CZECHOSLOVAK ROAD TO SOCIALISM

The social movement in the Czech lands and in Slovakia during the 20th century was carried along by two great currents - the national liberation movement and socialism.

The national liberation struggle of both nations culminated in the emergence of an independent state in which, for the first time in history, the political unity of the Czechs and Slovaks in a single state was realized. The founding of the Czechoslovak Republic marked important progress in the national and social development of both nations. The democratic order eliminated the old monarchist remnants and created favourable conditions for fast progress in all spheres of national life.

The pre-war bourgeois order, however, did not solve the onerous class antagonisms and was not able to lay reliable foundations for the lasting prosperity of the new economic entity and to guarantee the workers and employees full employment and a secure existence. Its nationalist regime, though liberal towards the minorities, ignored the individuality of the Slovak nation and did not succeed in eliminating the influence of extreme nationalism and in introducing the harmony desirable among all nationalities of the Republic. Under the conditions prevailing at that time in capitalist

a 3

Europe, not even the independence of the Czechoslovak Republic could be permanently safeguarded.

The progressive forces tried to give an answer to these shortcomings. Their most energetic component was the Communist Party of Czechoslovakia which was striving for a socialist conception of the Czechoslovak society.

In the broad wave of the anti-fascist movement which was born in connexion with the breaking up of Czechoslovakia as it existed between the wars, and especially in the course of the national liberation struggle, the integration of socialism with the national and democratic movement began to take shape.

During the national and democratic revolution of 1944-45 the national and democratic values of socialism were united for the first time. The democratic and national movement began to be socialized and socialism became a really national and democratic affair. The road to socialism taken by Czechoslovakia, at the beginning of which, in 1944-45, stood the Slovak National Uprising and the Prague Uprising is the source of the most progressive traditions of modern Czech and Slovak history.

The Republic, whose liberation was the result of the heroic fighting of the Soviet Army and the national liberation struggle of the Czechoslovak people, was restored on new foundations. These facilitated the solving of the most acute national problems in the country; the existence of the Republic as a State was ensured by close alliance with the Soviet Union; by nationalization the Republic gained an economic system providing conditions not only for rapid restoration but also for further development of the economy towards socialism. The considerable expansion of informal political freedoms was the true culmination of the whole democratic tradition of Czechoslovakia's development. Socialism became the embodiment of the modern national programme of the Czechs and Slovaks.

Czechoslovakia was the first industrial country to realize socialist reconstruction. The policy of Czechoslovakia's road to socialism, as pursued from 1945 to 1948, was an expression of the endeavours to respect the complexity of the specific internal and international conditions of Czechoslovakia. It contained many elements the understanding of which could contribute towards achieving our present aim of democratizing the socialist order.

We identify ourselves with traditions of the liberation struggle in which patriots participated at home and in various parts of Europe and the world, 375,000 of whom gave their lives for these ideals. We will support a scientific examination of the history of both nations, the conclusions of which cannot be decreed by anyone, but can only be the result of the study of history itself. The February victory of the working people was an important milestone in the socialist development of post-war Czechoslovakia, which created preconditions for accelerating the advance to socialism. After February 1948 the Party took a new road of socialist construction with a fund of great confidence and support of the broadest strata of the population.

This was a difficult road. In a divided world in the grips of cold war, our nations had to increase their efforts to safeguard their hardly won national existence and had to concentrate on reinforcing their own defence and that of all the other socialist states. The building up of the new Republic, which was far from having the internal resources essential for developing the economy, was closely connected with the progress and problems of the whole socialist camp. The inclusion of the Republic in the system of socialist states brought substantial changes in the direction of development of the national economy and also in its internal structure, in the character of the state and the social order. This was a matter of respecting the joint tasks of these ıntries in which the combating of economic and cultural retardation interwoven with the creation of new forms of ownership, played a leading role.

These connexions and tasks influenced the speed, form and content of the profound economic, social and political reconstruction which the Republic was going through during the building of socialism. They impelled an exceptional exertion of energy of the working class and the whole people, great sacrifice of communists and the dedicated work of tens of thousands of functionaries.

With the size, exceptionality and challenge of the changes, however, correspond the contradictions of development, the grave shortcomings, unsolved problems and deformations of socialist principles which are known as the personality cult.

The construction of the new social system was marked by insufficient experience, lack of knowledge, by dogmatism and subjectivism. Many signs of the times, conditioned by the sharpened international situation and compulsory acceleration in building up industry, were understood as the generally valid forms of the life and development of a socialist society. The stage of development of the socialist states at the beginning of the fifties and the arrest of the creative development of knowledge concomitant with the personality cult, conditioned also a mechanical acceptance and spreading of ideas, customs and political conceptions which were at variance with Czechoslovak conditions and traditions. The leading bodies and institutes of the Party and the State of that time are fully responsible for that acceptance. The centralist and directive-administrative methods used during the fight against the remnants of the bourgeoisie and during the consolidation of power under conditions of heightening international tension after February 1948 were, in this situation, unjustifiably carried over into the next stage of development and gradually grew into a bureaucratic system. Sectarianism,

6 a

suppression of the democratic rights and freedom of the people, violation of laws, signs of licentiousness and misuse of power appeared in the internal life of the Republic, which led to undermining the initiative of the people and, what is more, gravely and unjustly afflicted many citizens - communists and non-communists. The irreparable losses suffered by our movement at that time will remain for ever a warning against similar methods.

The extraordinary exertion of the energy of our people brought great historic successes. Basic socialist social changes have been accomplished and the socialist order has sunk its roots deeply and firmly into our land. Our society, in which the means of production are mainly in the hands of the socialist state or of workers' cooperatives, has got rid of capitalist exploitation and the social wrongs connected with it. Every citizen of the Czechoslovak Socialist Republic has the right to work and enjoys basic social security. Our society has gone through a period of industrialization and now disposes of an extensive industrial base. We have achieved noteworthy successes in the advancement of science and culture; the possibilities of the broadest strata of the people gaining appropriate education have increased to an unheard of extent. The international status of the Republic among the socialist countries is firmly secured.

At the end of the fifties our society entered another stage of development. On this fact was gradually formed the political line which we want to apply in a creative way and to develop. Characteristic of the present stage are:

- antagonistic classes no longer exist and the main feature of internal development is becoming the process of bringing all socialist groupings in the society closer together.
- methods of direction and organization hitherto used in the national economy are outdated and urgently demand changes, i.e. an economic system of management able to enforce

a turn towards intensive growth;

- it will be necessary to prepare the country for joining in the scientific-technical revolution in the world, which calls for especially intensive cooperation of workers and agricultural workers with the technical and specialized intelligentsia, and which will place high demands upon the knowledge and qualifications of people, on the application of science.

- a broad scope for social initiative, frank exchange of views and democratization of the whole social and political system - becomes virtually the condition for the dynamics of socialist society - the condition for us being able to hold our own in competition with the world, and to honourably fulfil our obligations towards the international workers movement.

Surmounting the causes of profound social crisis

Already at the time when this Party line was being formed and starting to be applied, it ran up against lack of understanding for the new tasks, with recidivism of redundant methods of work which arose at the time of sharp class struggle in Czechoslovakia, with the opposition of those who in one way or another found the deformations of the socialist reality convenient.

We want to disclose frankly what these mistakes and deformations were and what were their causes so as to be able to remedy them as soon as possible and to concentrate all forces on the fundamental structural changes in our lives which we are facing at the present time.

Already after the 20th Congress of the Communist Party of the USSR, which was an impulse for revival of the development of socialist democracy, the Party adopted several mea-

8 a

sures which were intended to overcome bureaucratic-centralist sectarian methods of management or its remnants, to prevent the means of class struggle being reversed against the working people. Many communists and whole working collectives tried to open the way to progressive development of the economy, the living standard, science and culture. The more definitely was the class antagonism overcome and the foundations for socialism laid, the more urgent was the stress placed upon promotion of cooperation of all working people, of all social strata, groups and nationalities in Czechoslovakia and on fundamental changes in methods employed during the time of sharp class struggle. At the same time, there was rightly seen in the development of socialist democracy the main social conditions for realization of the humanistic aims which are characteristic of socialism. However, they met with lack of understanding, inhibitions and, in some cases, even with direct suppression. The survival of methods from the time of the class struggle evoked an artificial tension among the social groups, nations and nationalities, different generations, communists and non-party people in this society. Dogmatic approaches impeded a full and timely re-evaluation of conceptions of the character of socialist construction.

The measures adopted did not therefore bring the anticipated results. On the contrary, over the years, difficulties piled up until they closed in a vicious circle. Subjective conceptions were not overridden in time, as if construction of the new society were dependent only upon accelerated extensive development of production. This led to a precipitated expansion of heavy industry, to a disproportionate demand on labour power, raw materials and to costly investments. Such an economic policy, enforced through directive administrative methods, no longer corresponded to the economic requirements and possibilities of the country and led to exhaustion of its material and human resources.

Unrealistic tasks were placed upon the economy, illusory promises were made to the workers. This orientation served to intensify the unfavourable structure of production which did not correspond with the national conditions in which local skilled labour could be not sufficiently applied, caused considerable technical retardation in Czechoslovak production, put a brake on development of public services, upset the equilibrium of the market, worsened the international status of the Czechoslovak economy, especially of the exchange of Czechoslovak products of labour abroad and finally, had to end in stagnation and, in certain cases, even in the reduction of the living standard of the people.

These shortcomings were directly caused by the maintainence and constant restoration primarily of the old directive system of management: Economic means, forms of supply and demand, and marketing ties were replaced by directives from the centre. Socialist enterprise did not expand. In economic life, independence, diligence, expertize and the initiative of the people were not appreciated, but, rather the contrary, subservience, obedience and even kowtowing to higher ups were.

A more profound reason for keeping up the outlived methods of economic management were the deformations in the political system. Socialist democracy was not expanded in time, methods of revolutionary dictatorship deteriorated into bureaucracy and became an impediment to progress in all spheres of life in Czechoslovakia. And so, political mistakes were added to economic difficulties and mechanism was created which resulted in helplessness, conflict between theory and practice. Much endeavour, activity and energy of workers of the Party, the State, the economy, science and culture was squandered away. When to this was added the adverse external circumstances of the early sixties, serious economic crisis followed. It is from there that the difficulties with which the workers are still confronted daily, emanate: the slow increase in wages of many-years standing, stagnation of the living standard and especially the constantly increasing retardation of the infrastructure in comparison with advanced industrial countries, the catastrophic state of housing and insufficient building of houses and apartments, the precarious state of the transport system, poor quality goods and public services, lack of cultural standard in living environment and conditions in general which tangibly affect just the human factor, possibilities of developing human energy and the activity of man, all of which are decisive for a socialist society. Embitterness grew among the people and a feeling that despite all successes which had been achieved and despite all efforts exerted, the socialist society was making headway with great difficulty, with fateful delay and with moral political defects in human relations. Quite naturally, apprehensions arose about socialism, about its human mission, about its human features. Some people became demoralized others lost perspective.

The main link in this circle was that of remnants or reappearance of the bureaucratic, sectarian approach in the Party itself. The insufficient development of socialist democracy within the Party, the unfavourable atmosphere for the promotion of activity, the silencing or even suppression of criticism - all of this thwarted a fast, timely and thorough rectification. Party bodies took over tasks of State and economic bodies and social organizations. This led to an incorrect merging of the Party and State management, to a monopolized power-position of some sections, unqualified interference as well as the undermining of initiative at all levels, indifference, the cult of mediocrity and to unhealthy anonymity. A consequence of this was the spreading of irresponsibility and lack of discipline. Many correct resolutions were never fulfilled. This adversely affected theoretic thinking, making it impossible to recognize in time the short-

a 11

comings and the danger connected with the outdated system of management. Amendments in the economy and politics were held up.

All of these questions became a focus for clashing of those forces which were insisting upon fundamental changes with the bearers of the old conception. At the same time, this led to a clarification of the position, and essential social progress was pushed ahead. At the December sessions of the Central Committee, thorough and factual criticism was made of the main causes of the aforementioned shortcomings, and their bearers, and corrective measures were instigated in the leading bodies of the Party themselves. One of the immediate causes was said to be that inside the Party there was too great a concentration of decision, that there arose an extraordinary status of individuals, in the first place of A. Novotný. This criticism allowed the whole Party and the society to start overcoming the old approach and sectarian bureaucratic practice on the basis of self-critical evaluation of the work to date, from top to bottom, so as to create real unity of the society on the same basis of social democratism, thoroughly to put into practice the principles of the new system of economic management, to modernize and rationalize life in Czechoslovakia, to open up long-term perspectives of gradually including Czechoslovakia in the process of the scientific-technological revolution - so that in all spheres of this society the power of socialism will be revived and will start out along a new road of socialist development.

A policy of unity and confidence

Decisive for the socialist development of this country was the creation of the broad reliance of progressive forces of the town and country headed by the working class and the unity of the Czech and Slovak nations.

The resolution of the 13th Congress of the Communist Party of Czechoslovakia set the task: "In the internal life of the country to continue strengthening the union of the working class which is the leading force in the society,with the agricultural cooperative workers and the socialist intelligentsia as the political base of the State, to help the mutual rapprochement of classes and strata of the nations and nationalities in Czechoslovakia and to consolidate their unity." The sense of the present policy is to stimulate continuously democratic relations of cooperation and confidence among the various social groups without differentiation, to harmonize their efforts, to unite their forces on the basis of the development of the whole society.

All social classes, strata, groups, both nations and all nationalities of the society agree with the fundamental interests and aims of socialism. One of the big advantages of socialist development to date is, that a decisive factor in assessing the standing and activity of the people in this society is their working merits and progressive social activity and not their membership of this class or that stratum. The Party resolutely condemns attempts to put the various classes, strata and groups of the socialist society in opposition to each other and will eliminate everything that creates tension among them.

On behalf of unity and the interests of the whole society, there can be no overlooking the various needs and interests of individual people and social groups according to their work, qualification, age, sex, nationality and so on. In the past we have often made such mistakes.

Socialism can only flourish if scope is given for the assertion of the various interests of the people and on this basis the unity of all workers will be brought about democratically, This is the main source of free social activity and development of the socialist system.

The Party is backed, and will continue to be backed, by the working class which has shown that it is able to carry the main weight of socialist endeavour. Under prevailing conditions, we rely especially upon those, who, with their awareness i.e. profound understanding of the real interests and tasks of the working class in the revolutionary reconstruction of the whole society, with their qualifications, and their cohesion with modern technology, the high effectivity of their work, their social activity, contribute markedly to the further progress of Czechoslovak production and to the whole society as such. The working class began the revolutionary struggle so as to abolish every sort of exploitation, to erase all class barriers, to facilitate the liberation of people and with them to transform the conditions of human life, the character of human labour, to make way for the full self-realization of man, and by all this to change even itself. These long-term interests of the working class have not yet been fully realized. The workers, however, now have in their hands new technical, social and cultural means, which allow them to continue changing their working and living conditions, to expand the elements of purposeful creative endeavour in their activity. We are determined to open up wide the road to the assertion of all creative and by far not fully utilized energy which the working class has for these tasks.

In the past, the workers did not always have the possibility of asserting their immediate and specific interests. Therefore the Party will strive to activize the social life of the workers, to provide scope for making use of all their political and social rights through political organizations, and trade unions and to strengthen the democratic influence of collective teams of workers in the management of production. It will strive for the alleviation

14 a

of exhausting labour, for the humanization of work and for improving the labour conditions of workers.

One of the most significant results of the transformation of the social structure was the creation of social groups, organically cohering with the workers - agricultural cooperative workers. This fact must be appreciated politically. The Party will strive for the absolute economic equalization of agriculture with industry and for appraising the social importance of agricultural work. In accordance with the conclusions of the 7th Congress of Agricultural Cooperatives we shall support the setting up of all-state agricultural cooperative organizations and raise their political authority; we want to abolish all administrative, bureaucratic obstructions which impede the independent initiative of agricultural enterprises, everything that endangers the security of cooperative venture and that emanates from lack of confidence in the ability of the agricultural cooperative workers to act independently and in a socialist way.

Likewise it will be necessary to understand that the character of our intelligentsia has gradually changed, it has become an intelligentsia of the people, a socialist intelligentsia. It represents a force, which takes part, in a creative way, in the development of the society and makes the wealth of science and culture available to all people. Today, the workers will find in the intelligentsia their integral component part and their own inner force. The constantly closer collaboration of the technical intelligentsia with the workers in productive collectives simultaneously records the process of surmounting former class barriers. The Party will support the growing unity between the intelligentsia and the other working people, it will combat underestimation of the role of the intelligentsia in this society, which was the case of late, it will combat everything that upsets relations between the intelligentsia and the workers.

a 15

It will strive for just remuneration of complex and creative mental labour.

Just as with the working class, so with the agricultural workers and the intelligentsia, the Party will rely mainly upon those who best understand and most actively assert social interests and who, by effective work, most markedly contribute to social progress. Cooperation of all groups of the socialist society will be effective and possible only providing everyone becomes aware of his responsibility to the other, and does not give preference to narrow professional interests.

The fundament of Czechoslovak statehood is the voluntary and equal co-existence of Czechs and Slovaks. By the forming of socialist relations, pre-conditions will be given for the strengthening of the fraternal co-existence of our nations. Our Republic can only be strong providing, there will be no sparks of tension, or signs of nervosity and suspicion in the relations of the Czech and the Slovak nations and all nationalities. We must therefore resolutely condemn all expressions which would undermine the principles of the equality and sovereignty of both socialist nations and which occured in the past. The unity of the Czechs and Slovaks can be strengthened only on the basis of an unhampered development of their national individuality in harmony with progress made in economy, with objective changes in the social structure of both nations and on the basis of absolute equality and voluntariness. Our Republic will be that much stronger, the more developed will be the two nations, the greater will be the use made of the enormous economic and cultural resources in Slovakia, in the interest of the progress of the whole Republic. Indifference to national interests or even endeavours to suppress them, is considered by the Party to be a gross distortion of its programme, of its political course. The Party will consistently defend the Leninist prin-

16 a

ciple that the overlooking of the interests of a smaller nation by the larger is incompatable with socialist relations between nations. It will oppose any kind of endeavour to place the continuous searching for the best methods of development in the constitutional relations of our nations, established on equal rights and voluntariness, in the light of weakening of the Republic. Communists of both nations and all nationalities in this country defend the principles of internationalism; the communists of every nation and nationality are themselves surmounting nationalistic relics in their own surroundings.

Under socialist conditions, each of the national minorities - Hungarian, Polish, Ukrainian, German and so on - have the right to their own national life and consistent fulfilling of all other constitutional rights.

The Party stresses it will oppose all expressions of antisemitism, racism and any anti-humanistic ideology,which would set the people against each other.

Various generations of our society have grown up under different conditions and naturally vary in their outlook on many questions of our life. The Party strongly rejects endeavours to put into contradiction the interests of these generations, it will devote special care to harmonizing and satisfying the needs of the different age groups.

It is true that our system, on the basis of the dedicated work of the older generation, as compared with the pre-Munich Republic has provided better conditions for the young people. Nevertheless, we have still remained greatly indebted to the youth. Shortcomings and mistakes in political, economic and cultural life, just as in human relations, affect the young person especially strongly, contradictions between words and deeds, lack of frankness, phrasemongering bureaucracy, attempts to settle everything from a position of power - these deformations of socialist life must pain-

a 17

fully affect students, young workers and agricultural workers, arousing in them the feeling that it is not they, their work, their efforts which are decisive for their own future life. An urgent task is that of restoring contact with young people everywhere and of making them responsible which pertains to them for their independent work under socialism.

This especially applies to improving working conditions, and possibilities of young people being active in social and cultural life and of consistently erasing everything that evokes non-confidence towards socialism in young people. We are all glad about the enthusiasm of the youth, their positive and critical initiative, which is a condition for them finding their cause and future in socialism and communism.

Neither should we overlook the material conditions, the social necessity, respect for and social assertion of the old people, which makes possible for them a dignified and well-merited retirement. This society should give great attention to ensuring the active participation of members of the resistance movement to whom the respect of everyone is due.

The deformations of the Party and State policy also include the fact that in the past the problem of women, especially those in employment was not considered a serious political matter. In State, economic and cultural policy, women should have access to such positions which comply with principles of socialist democracy and the significant role taken by women in creating material and spiritual values of the society.

In the further development of our society we must reckon with the activity of all strata of the population in public life and constructive endeavour. We can say quite openly that we are calculating with believers too, who, on the basis of their faith wish, as equals, as builders of a socialist society, to take their part in helping to fulfil all our exacting tasks.

To develop democracy and eliminate equalitarianism

The assertion of the manifold interests of the social groups and individuals, and their unification, calls for the elaboration and implementation of a new political system in our lives, a new model of socialist democracy. The Party will strive for such a development of the State and social order as will correspond to the actual lay-out of interests of the various strata and groups of this society, as will give them the possibility of expressing their interests in their organizations and of voicing their views in public life. We expect that in an atmosphere of mutual confidence between people and their institutions civic responsibility will grow at the same time and that norms of human relations will be respected.

Meanwhile, the Party will strive to link the democratic principles of the social system with expert and scientific management and decision. In order to be able to judge responsibly what is in the interest of the whole society, we must always have before us other alternatives for appraisal, expertly justified proposals for solving all disputable matters, and we must ensure that the people get much more information, more candidly.

Today, when class differences are being erased, the main criterion for evaluating the status of people in society is how the person contributes towards social progress. The Party has often criticized equalitarian views, but in practice levelling has spread to an unheard of extent and this became one of the impediments to an intensive development of the economy and to raising the living standard. The harmfulness of equalitarianism lies in the living standard. The harmfulness of equalitarianism lies in the fact that it puts careless workers, idlers and irresponsible people to advantage as compared with the dedicated and diligent workers, the unqualified compared with the qualified, the technically and expertly backward people as compared with the talented and those with initiative.

When attempting today to do away with equalitarianism, to apply the principle of actual achievements in the appraisal of employees we have no intention of forming a new privileged stratum. We want in all spheres of social life, the remuneration of people to depend upon the social importance and effectivity of their work, upon the development of workers initiative, upon the degree of responsibility and risk. This is in the interest of the development of the whole society. The principle of actual achievements raises the technical standard, profitability and productivity of labour, respect and authority of the managers responsible, the principle of material incentive, it stresses the growing importance of qualification of all workers.

One of the key conditions of the present and future scientific, technical and social development is to substantially increase the qualifications of managers and experts at all levels of economic and social life. If the leading posts are not be filled by capable, educated socialist expert cadres, socialism will be unable to hold its own in competition with capitalism.

This fact will require great changes in the existing cadre policy in which for years the aspects of education, qualification and ability have been underrated.

Application of the principle of remuneration according to the quantity, quality and social usefulness of work calls for a de-levelling of incomes. It does not however mean neglecting the interests of citizens in the lowest income group, the interests of families with many children, citizens with reduced working ability, pensioners and certain categories of women and youth. On the contrary, consistent application of the principle of differentiated remuneration according to actual work achievement, is the only effective means for such a development of resources which would enable a raising of the standard of living and, according to the spirit of socialist humanism, determine and ensure good living conditions for all strata of the society. We want to make it quite clear that honest work for the society and efforts to improve qualification are not only duly remunerated but they must also enjoy due respect. The socialist society respects those who achieve exceptional results, who are active and show initiative in advancing production, technical, cultural and social progress; it respects the talented people and creates favourable conditions for their assertion.

The leading role of the Party - a guarantee of socialist progress

At present it is most important that the Party practices a policy fully justifying its leading role in society. We believe that at present this is a condition for the socialist development of the country.

The Communist Party, as a party of the working class, won the struggle with capitalism and the struggle to carry out revolutionary class changes; with the victory of socialism it becomes the vanguard of the entire socialist society. Especially during the present time has the Party proved its ability to lead this society, when from its own initiative it launched the process of democratization and ensured its socialist character. In its political activity the Party intends to depend particularly on those who have understanding for the requirements of the society as a whole, who do not see their own personal and group interests against those of socialism, those who use and improve their abilities for the benefit of all, who have a sense for everything new and progressive and are willing to help advance it.

The Communist Party enjoys the voluntary support of the people; it does not practice its leading role by ruling the society but by most devotedly serving its free, progressive socialist development. The Party cannot enforce its authority but this must be won again and again by Party activity. It cannot force its line through directives but by the work of its members, by the veracity of its ideals.

In the past, the leading role of the Party was often conceived as a monopolistic concentration of power in the hands of Party bodies. This corresponded to the false thesis that the Party is the instrument of the dictatorship of the proletariat. This harmful conception weakened the initiative and responsibility of the State, economic and social institutions and damaged the Party's authority, and prevented it from carrying out its real functions. The Party's goal is not to become a universal "caretaker" of the society, to bind all organizations and every step taken in life by its directives. Its mission lies primarily in arousing socialist initiative, in showing the ways and actual possibilities of communist perspectives, and in winning over all workers for them through systematic persuasion, as well as by the personal examples of communists. This is determined by the conceptional character of Party activity; Party bodies do not deal with all problems but should encourage activity and suggest the solution to the most important ones. At the same time the Party cannot turn into an organization which would influence the society only by its ideas and programme. Through its members and bodies it must develop the practical organization functions of a political force in society. The political and organizational Party activity coordinates the practical ef-

22 a

forts of the people to turn the Party line and programme into reality in all respects - in the social, economic and cultural life of the society.

As a representative of the interests of the most progressive part of all the State - and thus also representative of the perspective aims of the society - the Party cannot represent the entire scale of social interests. The political expression of the many-sided interests of the society is the whole National Front, as an expression of the unity of the social strata, groups of interests and of the nations and nationalities of this society. The Party does not want to, and will not take the place of social organizations,but, on the contrary, it must take care that their initiative and political responsibility for the unity of the society is revived and flourishes. The role of the Party is to seek such a way of satisfying the various interests which would not jeopardize the perspective interests of the society as a whole, but which would promote them and create new progressive interests. The Party policy must not lead to non-communists getting the impression that their rights and freedom are limited by the role of the Party. On the contrary, they must see in the activity of the Party a guarantee of their rights, freedom and interests. We want, and shall achieve, a state of affairs when the Party right at basic organization level, will have informal, natural authority based upon its working and managing ability and the moral qualities of communist functionaries.

Within the framework of democratic rules of a socialist state, communists must over and again strive for the voluntary support of the majority of the people for the Party line. It is necessary to alter Party resolutions and directives if they fail to express correctly the needs and possibilities of the whole society. The Party must endeavour for its members - as the most active workers in their spheres of work - to have corresponding weight and influence in the whole society, to hold functions in State, economic and social bodies. This, however, must not lead to the practice of appointing party members to functions, without regard to the principle that leading representatives of institutions of the whole society are chosen by the society itself and by its various components and that functionaries of these components are responsible to all citizens or to all members of social organizations. It is necessary to abolish the discriminating practice and the creation of a "Cadre ceiling" for people not members of the party.

The basis for the Party s action ability is its ideological and organizational unity based upon broad intra-Party democracy. The most effective weapon against introducing methods of bureaucratic centralism in the Party is the strengthening of the influence of Party members, of forming the political line, reinforcing the role of really democratically elected bodies. Elected bodies of the Party must first of all guarantee the application of all rights of its members, the making of decisions collectively, and, that all power will not be concentrated in a single pair of hands.

Only down-to-earth discussion and exchange of views can be the pre-condition for responsible deciding of collective bodies. Confrontation of views is an essential expression of a multilateral responsible attempt to find the best solution, to advance the new against the obsolete. Each member of the Party and Party bodies has not only the right, but the duty to act according to his conscience, with initiative, criticism, with different views on the matter in question, to oppose any functionary. This practice must become deeply rooted if the Party is to avoid subjectivism in its activity. It is impermissible to restrict communists in these rights, to create an atmosphere of distrust and suspicion of those around who voice different opinions, to persecute the minority under any pretext - as has happened in the past. The

Party, however, cannot abandon the principle of requiring the fulfilling of resolutions once they are approved. Within the Party, all its members are equal regardless of whether they hold any function in Party bodies or in bodies of State and economic organizations. Nevertheless, he who occupies a higher position, also carries greater responsibility. The Party is aware of the fact that there will be no more profound democracy in this society if democratic principles will not be consistently applied in the internal life and work in the Party itself, among communists. Decisions on all important questions and on the filling of posts by cadres must be ensured by democratic rules of negotiation and by secret ballot. The democratization of Party life also means the strengthening of work contacts between the Party and science. In this line we shall make use of consultations, exchange of opposing and contrary views since the role of science does not end by preparing analyses and documents. It should continue on Party grounds, by observing the processes evolved by the various resolutions and by contributing to their materialization and to the control of the correctness of the resolutions in practice.

The Central Committee of the Communist Party of Czechoslovakia set out on this road at its December and January sessions and it will make sure that in the months to come the questions of content and democratic methods of Party life, of relations between elected bodies and the Party apparatus are clarified throughout the Party and that rules will be elaborated defining the authority and responsibility of the individual bodies and links of the Party mechanism, as well as the principles of the Party's cadre policy which, among other things, will ensure an effective, regular change of leading officials, guarantees of the standard of information of members and relations of Party bodies to Party members in general. In preparing the 14th Party Congress the Party will make sure that the Party statutes correspond with the present state of its development.

a 25

FOR THE DEVELOPMENT OF SOCIALIST DEMOCRACY, FOR A NEW SYSTEM OF THE POLITICAL MANAGEMENT OF SOCIETY

In the past decade, the Party has many times put forward the demand for a development of socialist democracy. Measures taken by the Party were aimed at enhancing the role of elected representative bodies in the state. They emphasized the importance of voluntary social organizations and of all forms of popular activities. The Party policy initiated a number of laws which increased the protection of rights of every citizen. It was clearly stated in the theses of the Central Committee of the Communist Party of Czechoslovakia prepared for the 13th Party Congress that "the state of working class dictatorship had fulfilled its main historical mission in our country" and the guide line for further development of our democracy was given no less clearly - "the system of socialist democracy - the state, social organizations, and the Party as the leading force - purposefully endeavours to bring out the differing interests and attitudes of working people to social problems in a democratic way and to settle them inside the socialist society organizations correctly and with regard to nationwide needs and goals. The development of democracy must proceed hand in hand with strengthening of a scientific and professional approach to social management."

Nevertheless, harmful characteristics of centralized directive decision-making and management have survived up to the present day. In relations among the Party, the state, and social organizations, in internal relations and methods within these individual partners, in the relations of state

26 a

and other institutions to individuals, in the interpretation of the importance of public opinion and of people being informed, in the practical effect of personnel policy - in all these fields there are too many things souring the life of the people, while obstructing a professionally competent and scientific decision-making, and encouraging highhandedness. The reason may be sought, first and foremost, in that these relations in our political system have been built up for years as the instrument for carrying out the orders of the centre, and hardly ever made it at all possible for the decision itself to be the outcome of a democratic procedure.

The different interests and needs of people not foreseen by the system of directive decision-making were taken as an undesirable obstacle and not as new needs of the life of people which have to be respected by politics. That was why the often well-meant words of "an increase in the people's participation in management" could not help as in time this "participation of the people" came to mean chiefly help in carrying out orders and not in settling the correctness of the decisions. Thus it was possible that views, measures and interventions were enforced that were highhanded and did not comply either with scientific cognition, or with the interests of the various strata of the people and of individuals. Centralized decision-making put into effect in this way could not then be effective either and, on the contrary, led to a number of resolutions not being fulfilled and weakening of the purposeful management of social development. This, in turn, has in many cases kept such people in functions that are not capable of any other way of "management", who consistently revive the old methods and habits, who surround themselves with people who humour them and not with people whose capacities and character would be a guarantee of the successful carrying out of the functions. In spite of consistently condemning the "personality cult" we are still not able, therefore, to eradicate some character-

a 27

istics of our society typical for that period. This undermines the people s confidence in the Party being, in fact, able to change this situation, and old tensions and political nervous strain are again raised and revived.

The Central Committee is firmly determined to overcome such a state of affairs. As said above, it is necessary to prepare, for the 14th Congress, the fundamental issues of the development of the political system into a concept meeting the demands of life, just as we have elaborated the fundamental concept of the new economic system.

The main thing is to reform the whole political system so that it will permit the dynamic development of socialist social relations, combine broad democracy with a scientific, highly qualified management, strengthen the social order, stabilize socialist relations and maintain social discipline. The basic structure of the political system must, at the same time, provide firm guarantees against a return to the old methods of subjectivism and highhandedness from a position of power. Party activity has, so far, not been turned systematically to that end, in fact, obstacles have frequently been put in the way of such efforts. All these changes necessarily call for commencement of work on a new Czechoslovak constitution so that the draft of the new constitution may be thoroughly discussed among professionals and in public in all important points and submitted to the National Assembly shortly after the Party Congress.

But we consider it indispensable to change the present state of things right now, even before the 14th Congress, so that the development of socialism and its inner dynamics are not hampered by the outdated factors in the political system. Our democracy must provide more room for the activity of every individual, every collective, every link in the management, both at lower and higher levels, and in the centre, too. People must have more opportunity to think for

28 a

themselves and express their opinions. We must radically change the practices that turn the people's initiative and critical comments and suggestions from below into words that meet with the proverbial deaf ear. We must see to it that the incompetent but adaptive /to anything/ people are really replaced by those who strive for socialism, who are concerned with its fate and progress, with the interests and needs of others, and not with their own power or advantages. This will affect people both "above" and "below". It is going to be a complicated process taking some time. It is necessary to make clear everywhere - at all levels of management, in the Party, in state and economic bodies and in social organizations - which body or which official or which worker is really responsible, for what, where to look for guarantees of improvement, where to change institutions, where the working methods, and where to replace individuals. The attitude of individual Party officials to new tasks and methods, their capability of carrying the new policy into practice, must be the basic political criterion.

No responsibility without right

Who, which body and which official is responsible for what, what are his rights and duties, must be perfectly clear in all our system of management for the future, and we consider this to be the basic prerequisite for correct development. To this end, each component part should have its own independent position. Substitution and interchanging of state bodies, agencies of economic and social organizations by Party bodies must be completely stopped. Party resolutions are binding for the communists working in these bodies, but the policy, directing activities, and responsibility of the state, economic, and social organizations are independent. The communists active in these bodies and organizations must take

a 29

the initiative and see that the state and economic bodies as well as social organizations /notably the Trade Unions, the Czechoslovak Union of Youth, etc./ take the problem of their activities and responsibilities into their own hands.

The whole National Front, the political parties which form it, and the social organizations, will take part in the creation of state policy. The political parties of the National Front are partners whose political work is based on the joint political programme of the National Front and is naturally bound by the Constitution of the Czechoslovak Socialist Republic, is fully based on the socialist character of social relations in our country. The Communist Party of Czechoslovakia considers the National Front to be a political platform which does not separate the political parties into the government and the opposition in the sense that opposition would be created to the state policy as the policy of the whole National Front and a struggle for political power in the state were to exist. Possible differences in the viewpoints of individual component parts of the National Front, or divergency of views as to the policy of the state, are all to be settled on the basis of the common socialist conception of the National Front policy by way of political agreement and unification of all component parts of the National Front. Formation of political forces striving to negate this concept of the National Front, to remove the National Front as a whole from political power, was ruled out as long ago as 1945 after the tragic experience of both our nations with the prewar political development of the then Czechoslovak Republic; it is naturally unacceptable for our present republic.

The Communist Party of Czechoslovakia considers the political management of the Marxist-Leninist concept of the development of socialism as a precondition for the right development of our socialist society. It will assert the Mar-

30 a

xist-Leninist concept as the leading political principle in the National Front and in all our political system by seeking, through the means of political work, such support in all the component parts of our system and directly among the masses of workers and all working people that will ensure its leading role in a democratic way.

Voluntary social organizations of the working people cannot replace political parties, but the contrary is also true: political parties in our country cannot exclude common-interest organizations of workers and other working people from directly influencing state policy, its creation and application. Socialist state power cannot be monopolized either by a single party, or by a coalition of parties. It must be open to all political organizations of the people. The Communist Party of Czechoslovakia will use every means to develop such forms of political life that will ensure the expression of the direct say and will of the working class and all working people in political decision-taking in our country.

The whole existing organization, forms of activities, and incorporation of the various organizations in the National Front must be revised in principle under the new conditions and built up so that the National Front may carry out the qualitatively new tasks. The National Front as a whole and all its component parts must be allowed independent rights and their own responsibility for the management of our country and society.

Voluntary social organizations must be based on really voluntary membership and activity. People join these organizations because they express their interests, therefore they have the right to choose their own officials and representatives who cannot be appointed from outside. These principles should be the foundation of our unified mass organizations the activities of which are still indispensable but which should meet, by their structure, their working methods, and their ties with their members, the new social conditions.

The implementation of constitutional freedoms of assembly and association must be ensured this year so that the possibility of setting up voluntary organizations, special-interest associations, societies, etc. is guaranteed by law to meet the actual interests and needs of various strata and categories of our citizens, without bureaucratic interference and without monopoly of any individual organization. Any restrictions in this respect can be imposed only by law and only the law can stipulate what is anti-social, forbidden, or punishable. Freedoms guaranteed by law are applicable in this sense, in compliance with the constitution, also to citizens of individual creeds and religious denominations.

The effective influence of views and opinions of the working people on all our policy, opposition to all tendencies to suppress the criticism and initiative of the people, cannot be guaranteed if we do not ensure constitution-based freedom of speech and all political and personal rights of all citizens, systematically and consistently, by all legal means available. Socialism cannot mean only liberation of the working people from the domination of exploiting class relations, but must make more provisions for a fuller life of the personality than any bourgeois democracy. The working people, who are no longer ordered about by any class of exploiters, can no longer be prescribed by any arbitrary interpretation from a position of power, what information they may or may not be given, which of their opinions can or cannot be expressed publicly, where public opinion may play a role and where not. Public opinion polls must be systematically used in preparing important decisions and the main results of the research are to be published. Any restriction may be imposed only on the basis of a law stipulating what is anti-social - which in our country is mainly the criminal law. The Central Committee of the Communist Party of Czechoslovakia considers it necessary to define more exactly than hitherto in the shortest possible time by a press law, when a state body can forbid the propagation of certain information /in the press, radio, television, etc./ and exclude the possibility of preliminary factual censorship. It is necessary to overcome the holding up, distortion, and incompleteness of information, to remove any unwarranted secrecy of political and economic facts, to publish the annual balance sheets of enterprises, to publish even alternatives to various suggestions and measures, to extend the import and sale of foreign press. Leading representatives of state, social and cultural organizations are obliged to organize regular press conference and give their views on topical issues on television, radio, and in the press. In the press, it is necessary to make a distinction between official standpoints of state, Party and journalist bodies; the Party press especially must express the Party's own life, development and criticisms of various opinions among the communists, etc., and cannot be made fully identical with the official viewpoints of the state.

The Party realizes that ideological antagonists of socialism may try to abuse the process of democratization. At the present stage of development and under the conditions of our country, we insist on the principle that bourgeois ideology can be challenged only in open ideological struggle before all of the people. It is possible to win over people for the ideas and policy of the Party only by struggle based on the practical activity of communists for the benefit of the people, on truthful and complete information, and on scientific analysis. We trust that in such a struggle, all sections of our society will contribute actively towards the victory of truth, which is on the side of socialism.

At present the activity and responsibility of publishing houses, chief editors, of all Party members and progressive staff of mass communication media, must grow to

a 33

push through socialist ideals and to put into effect the policy of the Party, of the National Front, and of the State.

Legal norms must guarantee more exactly the freedom of speech of minority interests and opinions also /again within the framework of socialist laws and in harmony with the principle that decisions are taken in accordance with the will of the majority/. The constitutional freedom of movement particularly the travelling of our citizens abroad, must be precisely guaranteed by law; in particular, this means that a citizen should have the legal right to long-term or permanent sojourn abroad and that people should not be groundlessly placed in the position of emigrants; at the same time it is necessary to protect by law the interests of the state, for example, as regards the drain of some categories of specialists, etc.

We must gradually solve in the whole legal code the task of how to protect in a better and more consistent way the personal rights and property of citizens, we must especially remove those stipulations that virtually put individual citizens at a disadvantage against the state and other institutions. We must in future prevent various institutions from disregarding personal rights and the interests of individual citizens as far as personal ownership of family houses, gardens, etc. is concerned. It will be necessary to adopt, in the shortest possible time, the long-prepared law on compensation for any damage caused to any individual or to an organization by an unlawful decision of a state organ.

It is a serious fact that hitherto the rehabilitation of people - both communists and non-communists - who were the victims of legal violations in the past years, has not been always carried out in all its political and civic consequences. On the initiative of the Communist Party Central Committee bodies, an investigation is under way as to why the respective Party resolutions have not been fully carried out, and measures are being taken to ensure that the wrongs of the past are made good wherever it has not been done yet. No one having the slightest personal reason from his own past activity for slowing down the rectification may be either in the political bodies, or prosecutor's and court offices that are to rectify the past unlawful deeds.

The Party realizes that people unlawfully condemned and persecuted cannot regain the lost years of their life; it will, however, do its best to remove any shadow of the mistrust and humiliation to which the families and relatives of those affected were often subjected, and will resolutely ensure that such persecuted people have every opportunity of showing their worth in work, in public life, and in political activities. It goes without saying that even in carrying out full rehabilitation of people, we cannot change the consequences of revolutionary measures made in the past years in accordance with the spirit of class law aimed against the bourgeoisie, its property, economic, and social supports. The whole problem of a rectification of past repressions must be approached with the full responsibility of the state bodies concerned, and based on legal regulations; the Central Committee of the Communist Party of Czechoslovakia supports the proposal that the procedure in these questions and the problems of legal consequences be incorporated in a special law.

A wide democratic concept of the political and personal rights of citizens, their legal and political safeguards, are considered by the Party to be a prerequisite for the necessary strengthening of social discipline and order, for a stabilization of socialist social relations. A selfish comprehension of civil rights, an attitude to social property according to the principle "it's not my concern", a preferring of particular interests over those of the whole society - all these are features which communists will oppose with all their might.

The real purpose of democracy must be the achievement of better results of practical work based on wider possibilities of purposeful activity, in order to carry out the interests and needs of the people. Democracy cannot be identified with general speechmaking, cannot be understood in opposition to discipline, professionalism, and effectiveness of management. But arbitrariness and obscure stipulation of rights and duties makes such a development impossible. It leads to irresponsibility, to a feeling of uncertainty, and hence also to indifference towards public interests and needs. On the other hand, it is a more profound democracy and its measure of civic freedom that will help socialism to prove its superiority over the limited bourgeois democracy and will make it an attractive example for progressive movements even in industrially advanced countries with democratic traditions.

Equality of the Czechs and Slovaks - the basis for the strength of the public

Our republic, as a joint state of two equal nations - Czechs and Slovaks - must consistently ensure that the constitutional arrangement of relations between our fraternal nations and the status of all other nationalities of Czechoslovakia develops as required to strengthen the unity of the state, the development of the nations and nationalities themselves, and in keeping with the needs of socialism. It cannot be denied than even in socialist Czechoslovakia, in spite of outstanding progress in solving the problem of nationalities, there are serious faults and fundamental deformations in the constitutional arrangement of relations between the Czechs and Slovaks.

Let it be stressed that the assymetrical arrangement alone was not suitable, by its very character, to express and ensure the relations between two independent nations, as the respective standings of the two nations were necessarily expressed in different ways. The difference was mainly in the fact that the Czech national bodies were identical with the central ones which, having jurisdiction over all the state, were superior to the Slovak national bodies; this prevented the Slovak nation, to all means and purposes, in taking an equal share in the creation and realization of a country-wide policy. The objective shortcomings of such a solution were underlined by the existing political atmosphere and practice, adversely affecting the standing and activity of Slovak national bodies.

Under such conditions, the activities of Slovak national bodies were weakened, both in the fifties and in the fundamental ideas of the 1960 Constitution of the Czechoslovak Socialist Republic. Thus the Slovak national bodies got into a position from which their influence on the state machinery could be only of peripheral importance. These shortcomings, especially in view of the unsound elements of the political atmosphere of recent past could not be overcome even by the joint document of the Central Committee of the Communist Party of Czechoslovakia and the Central Committee of the Communist Party of Slovakia of 1964 on a strengthening of the role of the Slovak National Council.

This development necessarily caused misunderstanding to arise between our two nations. In the Czech lands the non-existence of their own national bodies gave an impression of superfluity of Slovak national bodies. In Slovakia the people were convinced that it is not the Slovaks who govern their own house but that everything is decided in Prague.

In the interest of the development of our socialist society it is therefore absolutely necessary to strengthen the unity of the Czechoslovak people and their confidence in the policy of the Communist Party of Czechoslovakia, to effect a crucial turn in the constitutional arrangement of

37

the relations between the Czechs and Slovaks and to carry out the necessary constitutional changes. It is now essential to respect the advantage of the socialist federal arrangement as a recognized and tried state form of the coexistence of two equal nations in a common socialist state.

For reasons of organization, the final federative arrangement must be preceded by the removal of the most pressing shortcomings in the existing unsatisfactory state of things in the legal relations between the Czech and Slovak nations as its integral part and development stage. It is therefore necessary to draw up and pass a constitutional law which will embody the principle of a symetrical arrangement as the goal to which our development after the 14th Congress will aim in the new constitution and which in a new way, on the basis of full equality, will solve the status of Slovak national bodies in our constitutional system in the nearest future - before the elections to the National Assembly and the Slovak National Council. It will have to

- constitute the Slovak National Council as a legislative body and the Slovak Council of Ministers as a collective executive body, and ministries as individual executive organs of the Slovak National Council, extending the real powers of all these organs so that the division of legislative and executive powers between the state and the Slovak bodies may basically comply with the principles of the Košice government programme;

- entrust the directing of national committees in Slovakia to Slovak national bodies and, in connection with an efficient arrangement between the state centre and the Slovak national bodies, set up a Slovak ministerial office for internal affairs and public security covering the full extent of responsibilities;

- adjust the competence of Slovak national bodies so that they may draw up and approve the economic plan and budget for Slovakia in all its items including the relevant economic tools. Set up a suitable structure of ministerial economic and executive bodies of the Slovak National Council and adapt the organizational pattern of the material and manufacturing basis in Slovakia accordingly;

- renew state secretaryship in central ministries, especially in the ministries of foreign affairs, foreign trade and national defence, the secretaries being members of the government;

- exclude, politically and constitutionally, the possibility of outvoting the Slovak nation as far as the state relations between the Czechs and Slovaks and the constitutional status of Slovakia are concerned;

- in addition, outside the scope of the constitutional law, to effect in real political practice the principle of equal rights of both nations in appointments to central bodies, diplomatic service, etc.

In preparing the 14th Congress of the Party and the new constitution it is necessary to submit, on the basis of all-round professional and political preparation, a proposal for a constitutional arrangement of relations between our two nations that will fully express and guarantee their equality and right of self-determination. The same principles shall be applied to the pattern of the Party and social organizations.

In the interests of strengthening the unity, coherence and national individuality of all nationalities in Czechoslovakia - of Hungarians, Poles, Ukrainians, and Germans - it is indispensable to work out a statute stipulating the status and rights of the various nationalities, guaranteeing the possibilities of their national life and the development of their national individuality. The Central Committee of the Communist Party of Czechoslovakia realizes that, in spite of indisputable achievements in solving the problems of nationalities, serious shortcomings exist. We deem it necessary to stress that the principles of our programme in respect of our two nations extend also to other nationalities. To that end, it is necessary to stipulate constitutional and legal guarantees of a complete and real political, economic, and cultural equality. The interests of the nationalities will have to be safeguarded also from the point of view of the pattern of state, regional, district, municipal, and local state power and administration. It is necessary to see that the nationalities are represented, in proportion to their numbers, in our political, economic, cultural, and public life, in elected and executive bodies. It is necessary to ensure an active participation of the nationalities in public life in the spirit of equality of rights and according to the principle that the nationalities have the right to independence and self-administration in provinces that concern them.

The power of elected bodies emanates from the will of the voters

The coming elections are to be the onset of implementation of the principles of this Action Programme in the work of the elected bodies of the state.

Although efforts were made in the past few months to improve the preparation of elections, it proved that it is not possible to effect the elections in the originally proposed term while meeting the requirements of the principles of advanced socialist democracy. It is therefore necessary to work out such an electoral system that will be in harmony with the changes in our political life. By means of the electoral law it is necessary to lay down exactly and clearly the democratic principles for the preparation of the elections, the proposal of candidates and the method of their election. The changes in the electoral system must be based, in particular, on the new political status of the National Front and the elected bodies themselves.

It is the national committees that make the backbone of the whole network of representative bodies in our country as democratic organs of state power. It must be in the national committees that state policy is formed, especially in districts and regions. In their work the principle of socialist democracy is to be fully applied: to bring out various interests and requirements of the people and to mould them into the general, public interest of communities, townships, districts, and regions.

The Party regards the national committees as bodies that have to carry on the progressive traditions of local government and people's self-administration. They must not be taken for local bureaucratic offices supervising local enterprises. The essential political mission of national committees is to protect the rights and needs of the people, to simplify the process of settling all matters with which the people turn to the national committee, to pursue public interest and oppose efforts of some institutions to dupe the people and ignore their requirements.

The Party regards the National Assembly as a socialist parliament with all the scope of activities the parliament of a democratic republic must have. The communists-deputies must see to it that the National Assembly works out a number of concrete measures before the new electoral period that will put into actual practice the constitutional status of the National Assembly as the supreme organ of state power in the Czechoslovak Socialist Republic. It is necessary to overcome formalism in dealings, the unconvincing unanimity concealing factual differences in opinions and attitudes of the deputies. From this point of view it is necessary to solve, in the nearest future, the relations between the National Assembly and Party bodies, and also a number of problems of internal activities of the National Assembly, particularly those concerning organization and competence. The result must be a National Assembly which actually decides on laws and important political issues,and not only approves proposals submitted. The Party supports a strengthening of the controlling function of the National Assembly in our entire public life and, more concretely, in respect of the government; from that point of view, it is necessary to subject the controlling machinery fully to the National Assembly, to establish it as its own body. Together with closer bonds between the National Assembly and our public opinion , all of this may, in a short time, increase the role and the prestige of the National Assembly in our society.

Division and supervision of power - guarantees against highhandedness

The communists in the government, too, must ensure as soon as possible that the principle of responsibility of the government towards the National Assembly covering all its activities is worked out in detail. Even under the existing practice of political management, the opportunity afforded for independent activity of the government and of individual ministers was not sufficiently made use of, there was a tendency to shift responsibility on to the Party bodies and to evade independence in decision-taking. The government is not only an organ of economic policy. As the supreme executive organ of the state it must, as a whole, deal systematically with the whole scope of political and administrative problems of the state. It is also up to the government to take care of the rational development of the whole state machinery. The state administration machinery was often underrated in the past; this machinery must consist of highly qualified people, professionally competent and rationally organized, it must be subject to a systematic supervision in a democratic way

42 a

it must be effective.Simplified ideas as if such goals could be attained by underrating and decrying the administrative machinery in general, were rather detrimental in the past.

In the whole state and political system it is necessary to create, purposefully, such relations and rules that would, on the one hand, provide the necessary safeguards to professional officials in their functions and, on the other hand, enable the necessary replacement of officials who can no longer cope with their work by professionally and politically more competent people. This means to establish legal conditions for the recall of responsible officials and to provide legal guarantees of decent conditions for those who are leaving their posts through the normal way of replacement, so that their departure should not amount to a "drop" in their material and moral-political standing.

The Party policy is based on the principle that no undue concentration of power must occur, throughout the state machinery, in one sector, one body, or in a single individual. It is necessary to provide for such a division of power and such a system of mutual supervision that any faults or encroachments of any of its links are rectified in time, by the activities of another link.This principle must be applied not only to relations between the elected and executive bodies, but also to the inner relations of the state administration machinery and to the standing and activities of courts of law..

This principle is infringed mainly by undue concentration of duties in the existing ministry of the interior. The Party thinks it necessary to make of it a ministry for internal state administration including the administration of public security. The schedule that in our state was traditionally within the jurisdiction of other bodies and with the passage of time has being incorporated into the ministry of the interior, must be withdrawn from it. It is necessary to elaborate proposals as soon as possible passing on the main responsibility for investigation to the courts of law, separating prison administration from the security force, and handing over of press law administration, of archives, etc. to other state bodies.

The Party considers the problem of a correct incorporation of the security force in the state as politically very important. The security of our lives will only benefit, if everything is eliminated that helps to maintain a public view of the security force marred by the past period of law violations and by the privileged position of the security force in the political system. That past period impaired the progressive traditions of our security force as a force advancing side by side with our people. These traditions must be renewed. The Central Committee of the Communist Party of Czechoslovakia deems it necessary to change the organization of the security force and to split the joint organization into two mutually independent parts - State Security and Public Security. The State Security service must have such a status, organizational structure, numerical state, equipment, methods of work, and qualifications which are in keeping with its work of defending the state from the activities of enemy centres abroad. Every citizen who has not been culpable in this respect must know with certainty that his political convictions and opinions, his personal beliefs and activities, cannot be the object of attention of the bodies of the State Security service. The Party declares clearly that this apparatus should not be directed and used to solve internal political questions and controversies in socialist society.

The Public Security service will fulfil tasks in combatting crime and in the protection of public order; for this its organization, numerical state, and methods of work must be adapted. The Public Security force must be better equipped and strengthened; its functions in the defence of public order must be exactly laid down by law and, in their fulfilment, the service will be directed by the national committees. Legal norms must create clearer relations of control over the security force by the government as a whole and by the National Assembly.

It is necessary to devote the appropriate care to carrying out the defence policy in our state. In this connection it is necessary to work for our active share in the conception of the military doctrine of the Warsaw Treaty countries, the strengthening of the defence potential of our country in harmony with its needs and possibilities, a uniform complex understanding of the questions of defence with all problems of the building of socialism in the whole of our policy, including defence training.

The legal policy of the Party is based on the principle that in a dispute over right /including administrative decisions of state bodies/ the basic guarantee of legality is proceedings in court which are independent of political factors and are bound only by law. The application of this principle requires a strengthening of the whole social and political role and importance of courts of law in our society. The Central Committee of the Communist Party of Czechoslovakia will see to it that work on the complex of the required proposals and measures proceeds so as to find the answer to all the necessary problems before the next election of judges. In harmony with and parallel to that, it is also necessary to solve the status and duties of the public prosecutor's office so that it may not be put above the courts of law, and to guarantee full independence of barristers and solicitors from state bodies.

Youth and its organization

We regard young people as those who are to continue in the socialist transformation of the society. The present political activity and the part young people take in the social process of revitalization proves the reproaches often addressed against them to be without any foundation. The decisive part of the working and student youth is, by its energy, critical approach, matter-of-factness, and initiation a natural ally and important factor in the creation and implementation of the programmed aims of the Party. For this reason, it is indispensable to open wide and confidently the doors of our Party to young people.

At the same time it is necessary to give young people of all social categories, in proportion to their age and abilities, full possibility of co-deciding on all their own and public matters in elected bodies; their organizations should be recognized as partners of Party and social organizations, economic bodies, national committees, and administration of schools in solving social, working, study, and other urgent problems of youth and children. Young people must be given the opportunity of timely application of their knowledge, qualifications, and talents in appropriate places including leading positions. Cultural, sporting and recreattion facilities must be built with their cooperation for them to spend their leisure in a healthy and effective way. The work of voluntary and professional trainers, coaches, instructors, and other workers who sacrifice their time and devote their abilities to children and youth as socially highly beneficial and praiseworthy must be appreciated.

In this connection, let us say a few words of self-criticism on the relations of the Party and the Czechoslovak Union of Youth. Until recently, we expected the latter or its representatives to pass on to the young people more or less ready-made instructions, often the result of subjective opinions, which tactlessly interfered with the internal affairs of the youth organization. We did not sufficiently influence young communists to take part in the creation of Party policies by making them consistently defend, develop,

46 a

and express the interests, needs, requirements, and viewpoints of the youth as a whole and of its individual categories. Thus the initiative of the youth and the role of its organization was impaired in public and political life. This tendency was strengthened by the incorrect principle of direct Party control of the Czechoslovak Union of Youth.

However, the independence of the youth and children's movement does not eliminate, but in fact presupposes ideological guiding, a systematic interest of the whole Party in the problems of youth and of children's education, the practical help of communists to children's and youth collectives and tactful attention to young people in everyday life.

The multiformity of needs, interests and frequently changing inclinations of young people, which itself is internally differentiated as regards age, social strata, qualifications, etc., requires also a diversified and differentiated organization of children and young people. Apart from partial interests and inclinations of the moment of individual categories of young people, there are the pressing immediate and prospective needs and interests affecting the whole younger generation, which can be expressed and pushed through only by joint action of all the important youth categories; this calls for a suitable form of organization and social representation of young people. We are of the opinion, without, of course, wanting to prescribe any pattern of youth organization, that a form of federation would be most fitting for the present needs and situation of youth and children's movements.

It will depend, to a great extent, on the present officials of the Czechoslovak Union of Youth and of other social organizations to assist this process, to prevent both a suppressing and an unnecessary diversification of the sound initiative of young people, to make use, purposefully, of all experience and opportunities in the search for the best formed development of our socialist youth and children's movement.

THE NATIONAL ECONOMY AND THE STANDARD OF LIVING

The 13th Congress approved conclusions stating that the improvement of our economy and the transition to intensive economic development cannot be achieved by traditional approaches or partial improvements of the directive system of management and planning, but by a basic change of the mechanism of socialist economy. The idea which prevailed was the idea of an economic reform based on a new economic system, the revival of the positive functions of the socialist market, necessary structural changes of the economy and a profound change in the role of the economic plan which would cease to be an instrument for issuing orders and would become an instrument enabling society to find the most suitable long-range trends of its development by scientific methods; a change from an instrument designed to enforce subjectively determined material proportions into a programme of economic policy, ensuring an effective development of economy and the growth of the standard of living. The implementation of the first important steps of the economic reform has met with the active support of the working people, experts and the broad public.

Certain features of the economic development over the past two years, better utilization of production factors, the drop of the share of material costs in the social product, the growing demands placed by consumers on the technical level and the quality of products etc., fully confirm the correctness of the conclusions adopted by the 13th Congress. These positive features of the economic development have not so far resulted in a better satisfaction of the needs of society and have not led to reducing the tension on the internal market. This is objectively caused by the fact that the former tendencies are still strongly apparent, that the old structure of production and foreign trade still survives and that production is being only slowly adapted to the changes and the growing demand of the market. This is connected with many inconsistencies and gaps in implementing the programme of economic reform.

Instead of a consistent effort to establish more objective market criteria which would expose the economic backwardness and old deformations of the economic structure and gradually eliminate their existence, there are still considerable efforts to deform these criteria, to adapt them to the given conditions and thus create an easy situation in which the backwardness and the deformations would remain concealed, could survive and thrive at the expense of us all.

The system of protectionism applied will regard to economic backwardness, connected with the policy of prices, subsidies and grants and mainly with the system of surcharges in foreign trade continues to prevail in the economic policy. The confused system of protectionism is creating conditions under which ineffective backward enterprises, managed in an unqualified way, may exist and are often given preferences. It is not possible to blunt for ever the economic policy by taking from those who work well and giving those who work badly. It is therefore necessary to objectivize value relations that the differences in the income situation between enterprises should really reflect actual differences in the level of their economic activities. Nor is it politically correct for the consumer to pay indefinitely for inefficiency by means of prices, taxes and indirectly by different forms of siphoning off means of effective enterprises.

Enterprises facing a demanding market must be given a free hand in making decisions on all questions concerning directly the management of the enterprise and its economy and must be allowed to react in a creative way to the needs of the market. A demanding market, together with the economic policy, will thus put pressure on production to become more effective and to introduce healthy structural changes. Economic competition,especially with advanced foreign firms, must be the basic stimulus for improving production and reducing costs. This competition cannot be replaced by subjective adjustments of economic conditions and by directive orders of superior bodies.

Socialism cannot do without enterprising

The programme of democratization in economy links the economic reform more closely with the processes facing us in the sphere of politics and the general management of society, and stimulates the determination and application of new elements which would develop the economic reform even further. The programme of democratization of the economy includes particularly the provision of ensuring the independence of enterprises and enterprise groupings and their relative independence from state bodies, a full and real implementation of the right of the consumer to determine his consumption and his style of life, the right of a free choice of working activity, the right and real possibility of different groups of the working people and different social groups to formulate and defend their economic interests in shaping the economic policy.

In developing democratic relations in the economy we at present consider as the most important task the final formulation of the economic position of enterprises, their authority and responsibility.

The economic reform will increasingly push whole working teams of socialist enterprises into positions in which they will feel directly the consequences of both the good and bad management of enterprises. The Party therefore deems it necessary that the whole working team which bears the consequences should also be able to influence the management of the enterprise. There arises the need of democratic bodies in enterprises with determined rights towards the management of the enterprise. Managers and head executives of the enterprises, which would also appoint them to their functions would be accountable to these bodies for the overall results of their work. These bodies must become a direct part of the managing mechanism of enterprises, and not a social organization /they cannot therefore be identified with trade unions/. These bodies would be formed by elected representatives of the working team and by representatives of certain components outside the enterprise ensuring the influence of the interests of the entire society and an expert and qualified level of decision-making; the representation of these components must also be subordinated to democratic forms of control. At the same time it is necessary to define the degree of responsibility of these bodies for the results of the management of socialist property. In the spirit of these principles it is important to solve many concrete questions; at the same time it will be necessary to propose a statute of these bodies and to use certain traditions of our works councils from the years 1945-48 and experiences in modern enterprising.

This naturally in no way reduces the indivisible authority and responsibility of the leading executives in managing the enterprise which, together with their qualifications and managing abilities, is the basic pre-condition of successful enterprising.

In this connection it is also necessary to reassess the present role of trade unions. In the centralized system, their function of supporting directive management blended with defending the interests of the working people. Moreover, they performed also certain state functions /labour legislation etc./. The resulting situation was that on the one side they took inadequate care of the interests of the working people and on the other they were accused of "protectionism". Even socialist economy places working people into a position in which it is necessary to defend human, social and other interests in an organized way. The central function of trade unions should be to defend with increasing emphasis employment and working interests of the workers and the working people, to appear from this aspect as an important partner in solving all questions of economic management; on this platform, the trade unions would develop more effectively also their function of organizing workers and employees for a positive solution of the problems of socialist construction and their educational function connected therewith. Communists in trade unions will proceed from these principles and ensure in an initiative way that the trade unions themselves analyze their position, the functions and activities of the central and union bodies on the basis of the whole Action Programme of the Party, that they evaluate the internal life of trade unions as an independent democratic organization and work out their own political line in solving these questions.

The enterprise must have the right of choosing its organizational integration. Supra-enterprise bodies /of the type of the present general and branch managements/ cannot be imbued with State administrative power. The individual branches must, with due regard to their conditions, be in future enabled to transform into voluntary associations, on the basis of the economic interest and requirements of enterprises. Enterprises must have the right to decide about the content of the activity of these associations, the right to leave them and become independent and to join such associations which will ensure in a better way the functions following from the concentration and specialization of production and from integration processes.

The withdrawal of enterprises from the existing supra-enterprise agglomerations and their free association cannot begin before the rules for this process are outlined by the government; during the transition period it will be necessary to ensure that even after becoming independent the enterprises should fulfill the precisely termed financial and cooperation obligations set to them before, and resulting from their previous membership in the supra-enterprise body.

It is necessary to put an end to the previous simplified, schematic approach to formulating the organizational structure of production and trade. The structure of enterprises must be varied, just as are the demands of our market. It is therefore necessary to count also with the development of small and medium-sized socialist enterprises, whose importance lies in the first place in the completization of production, in a fast supply of new items to the market and in a flexible reaction to the different demands of customers. In the development of the organizational structure of production and trade it is necessary to open up scope for economic competition among enterprises of all sorts and forms of enterprising, in the first place in the sphere of production and supply of consumer goods and foodstuffs.

Agricultural production contributes to a great extent towards the consolidation of our national economy.The latest period and particularly the future needs of the economy clearly emphasize this positive role of consolidation of agriculture whose composition should develop in a way which would gradually ensure a rational structure of nutrition to the population. This is why the Party considers it necessary to raise and concentrate the aid of the State and of all branches, especially the chemical and engineering industry, in ensuring the growth of crop and animal production. This is and continues to be the foremost taks of our economic policy.

Cooperative enterprising in agricultural production is of exceptional importance for the development of our economy. The Party supports the conclusions of the Seventh Congress of the Unified Agricultural Cooperatives, particularly the creation of a national organization of cooperative farmers, the right of the unified agricultural cooperatives to do business also in other branches and the possibility of selling part of farm products directly to the population and to retailers. The State bodies will help to ensure all-year employment for the farming population.

The Party considers the development of agricultural production in cooperatives and in State farms to be the decisive line of large-scale production in agriculture. It would be expedient for Communists to prepare proposals which will develop new forms of closer contacts of agricultural producers with supply and sales organizations of agricultural products so that these new forms may ensure direct contact of agricultural production with suppliers and the market and would be to a certain extent similar to the former farm cooperatives.

We shall support the development of different forms of credit in farming and recommend to examine the whole credit system in agricultural economy. At the same time, the Central Committee recommends that agricultural and other State managing bodies should seek and support also other forms of business in utilizing land in mountainous, hilly and border regions. In the border regions it is necessary to strive for the creation of further suitable conditions designed to intensify economic activities, i.e. to make better use of existing small workshops, to extend recreation possibilities and engage in further capital construction. This should help stabilize the settlement of the border regions and normalize their life. Even though the production

54 a

of individual farmers constitutes a relatively small part of overall production, it is important to facilitate their work, to improve their conditions of economy and to enable their cooperation with cooperative and State enterprises.

In keeping with the proposals made at the 13th Congress of the Communist Party of Czechoslovakia, it is also necessary to create possibilities for cooperative enterprising wherever cooperatives earn the money for their activity. It will be expedient to make individual cooperatives independent economic and social organizations with full rights, to abolish inexpedient administrative centralization of cooperatives and to create only such bodies superior to cooperative enterprises whose economic activity is advantageous for them. In connection with the development of cooperative enterprizing, it appears to be expedient to elaborate more thoroughly the co-ownership relations of cooperative farmers towards cooperative property.

A serious shortcoming existing in economic life over a long period of time is the low standard and shortage of services of all sorts which reduces the standard of living and arouses justified discontent among the population. The improvement of communal services /water, gas, sewerage, municipal transport, road cleaning etc./ will require considerable investments and can be achieved only gradually while ensuring their profitability. The unsatisfactory state existing in other services is caused by the way of their organization and their exacting administration, by low interest of the workers in their economic results, by the fact that certain services are unprofitable, by bad supply of material and low and wrong investments.

Neither the standard of productive forces, nor the character of work in services, repairs and artisan production correspond to the present high centralization in their management and organization which involves quite unnecessary

a 55

administration and burdens the services with inexpedient costs. This is why it is necessary to take immediate measures for improving and extending all existing forms of services /cooperatives, communal enterprises/, to simplify their management and organization in the spirit of the principles of the new system. In the sphere of services it is particularly justified to make individual shops independent and to remove unnecessary administrative links of management. Small-scale individual enterprising is also justified in the sphere of services. In this respect it is necessary to work out legal provisions concerning small-scale enterprising, which would help fill the existing gap in our market.

The role of the State in economy

The expansion of social wealth is the concern of our entire society. The actual tasks and responsibility fall both on enterprises and on managing bodies, particularly on the Government. It is therefore their common interest and task to make use of the growing political activity of the working people, which has been taking place since the December and January plenums of the Central Committee, and to win them over for the road which means the consolidation of the national economy.

To achieve this it is necessary to adjust the whole organism of the implementation of the economic policy of the State. The appropriate organizational questions must be solved by State and economic bodies. At the same time the Party considers it desirable that the final set up should correspond to the following principles:

Decision-making about the plan and the economic policy of the State must be both a process of mutual confrontation and harmonization of different interests - i.e. the interests of enterprising, consumers, employees, different

56 a

social groups of the population, nations etc. - and a process of a suitable combination of view of the long-term development of the economy and its immediate prosperity. Effective measures protecting the consumer against the abuse of the monopoly position and economic power of production and trading enterprises must be considered as a necessary part of the economic activity of the State.

The drafting of the national economic plan and the national economy policy must be subject to democratic control of the National Assembly and specialized control of scientific institutions. The supreme body implementing the economic policy of the State is the Government. This presupposes such an institutional set-up of central management which would make it possible in the process of decision-making to express and unify special interests and views and to harmonize, in the implementation of the economic policy, the operation of individual economic instruments and measures of the State. At the same time, the institutional set-up of the bodies of economic management must not offer opportunities for the assertion of departmental and monopoly interests and must ensure a marked superiority of the interests of citizens as consumers and sovereign bearers of the economic movement. In all central economic bodies it is indispensable to ensure a high level of specialization, rationalization and modernization of managing work, to which the necessary changes in cadres must be also subordinated. All this must be the concern of a group of government bodies which analyze the national economy, work on alternative solutions of this development and the national economic plan, compare the planned development with the real development in the market, and proceeding from these findings, take effective economic measures etc., and thus consistently and purposefully influence the real movement in the economic sphere (i.e. the activity of enterprise and their associations)in the direction outlined by the economic policy of the State.State bodies approach enterprises and their associations and integrated groups

57

in the same way as they approach other independent legal subjects. The means which are at the disposal of the State, are the result of the work of all the people and must be used for satisfying the needs of the entire society in a way which society recognizes to be reasonable and useful. An important part of economic management must be a well conceived technical policy based on the analysis of technical progress in the whole world and on own conceptions of economic development. The purpose of this policy will be to regulate the technical level of the production base and to create economic conditions which would arouse strong interest in seeking and using the most up-to-date technology.

In this connection it would be useful for the State bodies concerned to examine all kinds of public expenditure and for the Government to work out a programme of State and public measures designed to reduce expenditure. The State budget must become an instrument for restoring the equilibrium and not for its weakening. The Central Committee considers it necessary and possible to reveal and reasonably utilize extraordinary internal and external resources for achieving a speedy restoration of the economic equilibrium.

At the same time, the Central Committee appeals to all enterprises, their associations, plants and workshops to work out and implement, in connection with their enhanced economic authority, a programme of rationalization of all managing, productive and business activity, in order to achieve a concerted harmonization of work and to reduce production costs. The programme of rationalization is the precondition for an economic evaluation of existing capacities and for technical modernization of production.

We are putting great hope into reviving the positive functions of the market as a necessary mechanism of the functioning of socialist economy and for checking whether the work in enterprises has been expended in a socially use-full way. However, we have in mind not the capitalist, but the socialist market, and not its uncontrolled but its regulated utilization. The plan and the national economic policy must appear as a positive force contributing to the normalization of the market and directed against tendencies of economic imbalance and against monopolistic control of the market. The society must do the planning with due insight and perspective, it must scientifically discover the possibilities of its future development and choose its most reasonable orientation. This, however, cannot be achieved by suppressing the independence of other subjects of the market /enterprises and the population/, since this would on the one hand undermine the interest ensuring economic rationality, on the other hand it would deform information and decision-making processes which are indispensably necessary for the functioning of the economy.

The economic structure of Czechoslovakia, its technical standard, concentration and specialization must be developed in a way enabling it to react quickly to economic changes at home and in the world.

The level of the adaptibility and flexibility of the national economy is also the result of the skill and the technical and cultural standard of the working people, their ability to adapt themselves quickly to the changing technical and economic conditions of production. From the point of view of the resources of economic growth in Czechoslovakia, manpower, their abilities and quality, technical and cultural standard as well as their adaptibility and mobility are of quite exceptional importance. Even from the point of view of future economic growth, the Czechoslovak economy does not possess more promising resources than are its great human resources. Czech and Slovak workers and farmers have always been known for their know-how, their skill and creative approach to work. As a result of the directive method of management, the new generation has only partly taken over these qualities from the older generation. Instead of the feeling of satisfaction from well done work, there frequently developed indifference, mechanical fulfilment of tasks, and resignation to situations caused by incompetent and uninitiative management. The Party believes that the prime condition for eliminating these losses is to put to leading positions people who are really capable and who are able to secure natural authority in working teams by their professional and human level.

Effective inclusion in international division of labour

Experience resulting from the many years' isolation of economic units from the competitive pressure of the world market, has clearly shown that this creates exceptional conditions for the activity of economic units, conditions resulting especially in relative lagging behind the rate of technical progress and of structural economic changes this progress conditions, in the loss of competitiveness of our products on the world markets and in the creation of undue tension in external trade and payment relations. The limited raw material base of our economy and the limited size of the home market make it impossible to implement the changes in the material base of production carried along by the scientific and technical revolution without widely integrating our economy into the developing international division of labour.

The development of international economic relations will continue to be based on economic cooperation with the Soviet Union and the other socialist countries, particularly those aligned in the Council of Mutual Economic Assistance. At the same time, however, it should be seen that the success of this cooperation will increasingly depend on the competitiveness of our products. The position of our country in

60 a

the development of international division of labour will strengthen with the more general convertibility of our products. In our relations with the CMEA countries we shall strive for the fuller application of criteria of economic calculations and mutual advantage of exchange.

We shall also actively support the development of economic relations with all other countries in the world, which show interest in them on the basis of equality,mutual advantages and without discrimination. We support the development of progressive forms of international collaboration, especially cooperation in production and in the pre-production stage, the exchange of scientific and technical know-how, business in licences and suitable forms of credit and capital cooperation with interested countries.

The opening up of our economy to the pressure of the world market makes it necessary to consistently rid the foreign trade monopoly of the administrative conception and methods and to eliminate directive management in foreign trade transactions. In this sphere, the Central Committee considers it necessary to carry out an effective State commercial and currency policy, based particularly on economic rules and instruments of indirect management.

The Central Committee considers it indispensable to raise the authority and responsibility of enterprises for the concrete implementation of international economic relations. Production and trading enterprises must have the right to choose their export and import organizations. At the same time it is necessary to formulate conditions under which, if they are fulfilled, enterprises would be entitled to act independently on foreign markets.

The many years' isolation of our economy from the world markets has divorced home trade price relations from price relations in the world market. Under this situation, we consider it necessary to enforce the line of bringing the home and world market prices gradually closer together. This practically means a more energetic elimination of vario surcharges and subsidies to prices of the foreign market. Enterprises must be aware that this is only a temporary protection, they are receiving from the State and on which they cannot count indefinitely, and must therefore work out a programme of such changes in production which will enable them already in the next few years to do without subsidies and surcharges. Another side of this policy of eliminating price surcharges and subsidies must be a more broad-minded approach to those branches and enterprises in the national economy, which are from the point of view of the national economy capable of selling effectively their products in foreign markets. The Party considers it expedient to speed up the necessary changes in the present system of price relations and put them gradually in order both by the pressure of the market forces and by creating a proper rational price system through purposive economic policy of the State. This policy must be accompanied by energetic measures designed to ensure internal stability of the currency. This presupposes the development of the production of effective and good-quality funds of products marketable on foreign markets, the achievement of equilibrium in the internal market of commodities, money and labour, an effective restrictive investment policy, the achievement of equilibrium in the balance of payment and the creation of necessary currency reserves.

The phased opening up of our economy to the world market, whose final aim is to create conditions for the convertibility of our currency must be carried out in an extent that would not pile up too many social problems and would not endanger the growth of the standard of living. However , it must be realized that we are living in conditions of sharp competition and that every concession today will worsen the prerequisites of effective economic development and of the growth of the standard of living in the future.

62 a

Problems of the standard of living - an urgent task of the economic policy

The basic aim of the Party in developing the economic policy is the steady growth of the standard of living. However, the development of the economy was in the past one-sidedly focussed on the growth of heavy industry with long-term returnability of investments. This was done to a considerable extent at the expense of the development of agriculture and the consumer goods industry, the development of the production of building materials, trade, services and non-productive basic assets, particularly in housing construction. This one-sided character of the former economic development cannot be changed overnight. If, however, we take advantage of the great reserve existing in the organization of production and work, as well as in the technical and economic standard of production and products, if we consider the possibilities offered by a skillful utilization of the new system of management, we can substantially speed up the creation of resources and on this basis to raise the growth of nominal wages and the general standard of living.

Greater stress in the growth of the standard of living must be laid on the growth of wages and salaries. However, the growth of average wages and salaries cannot be speeded up in the way that enterprises will raise wages regardless of the real economic results. It will be necessary to consistently apply the principle that the development of wages depends on really achieved production which will find its social utilization. The methods of influencing the development of wages will have to be in this sense elaborated. In keeping with the growth of wages in production, it is at the same time necessary to ensure the growth

a 63

of wages in education, health services and other non-productive branches.

The present system of retail prices is markedly divorced from the costs of production, gives an incorrect orientation to the structure of personal consumption of the population including the consumption of food and in its consequences reduces the possible degree of satisfying their requirements. Under these conditions it is indispensable to be more energetic in removing existing disproportions in prices so as to create prerequisites for a faster growth of the standard of living. The solution of these questions will require opposite movements of prices of individual products and their groups - the prices of some articles will have to be raised and others will have to be reduced. Rational price relations cannot be fixed and proclaimed by a State authority, it is necessary to enable market forces to influence their creation. This naturally involves a certain risk that the changes of price relations will take place along with a certain growth of the level of prices; this risk results from the fact that in the situation we have taken over from the directive system of management overall demand is greater than supply. While opening up the required scope to internal price movements, the central bodies must therefore regulate general economic relations in a way preventing an excessive growth of the price level and ensuring the growth of real wages by at least 2.5 - 3 per cent per year.

It is not possible in the nearest future to substantially raise claims for appropriations from social funds, since this could not be done without substantially weakening remunerations for work. However, in the spirit of the resolution adopted by the plenary meeting of the Central Committee of the Communist Party of Czechoslovakia in December 1967, it is possible to solve the most urgent problems of social policy, such as the raising of low pensions, the extension of paid maternity leave and aid to families with children. It is also possible to outline the principle that social pensions will grow in keeping with the growth of the cost-of living. The Central Committee demands from State bodies to ensure the removal of obstacles which weaken the interest of citizens to permanently continue active work after qualifying for old age pensions. We also want to examine the justification of certain measures carried out in connection with the reorganization of the social security system in 1964 /for example the taxation of pensions and the possibility of its gradual removal, the introduction of a higher basic qualifying for students' scholarships etc./. We consider it necessary to raise the social security allowances of those who participated in the national struggle for the liberation. We shall also elaborate the conception and the further course of improving the wage tax system so that it might be possible after 1970 to solve more justly the taxation of women, mothers and persons who have brought up children, and to further strengthen measures promoting a more favourable population development.

An important component determining the standard of living and the style of life is the care for the health of the people. In our society, we have introduced a number of measures in health care which capitalism was unable to solve. However, there are still many untopped possibilities in this sphere, both in the organization of health care and of spa services as well as in the working conditions of doctors and health personnel. The Central Committee appeals to Communists in the health service and to other health workers to submit their initiative proposals designed to solve the problems which unnecessarily embitter citizens and health workers and which are the result of bureaucratic methods in medical care.

From the point of view of preventive care designed to strengthen the health of the people, particularly children and youth, and of effective use of spare time, we consider it indispensable to duly appreciate the social importance of all forms of physical and para-military training and recreation; we are in this respect expecting a principled stand from the government and the educational administration as well as initiative from social organizations.

An important qualitative aspect of the standard of living will be the general introduction of a five-day working week for which it is necessary to create technological, organizational, economic and political conditions in order to enable its operation already at the end of 1968.

It is a serious shortcoming that the programme of housing construction was not carried out in the past years. We at present regard the solution of housing construction as the altogether decisive question of the standard of living. We consider it necessary to concentrate forces in this sphere and to secure also the necessary support of the Government and of State bodies for substantially raising, the annual number of flats built by building organizations and for utilizing the initiative of the population in building family houses. At the same time, it is necessary to work out a conception of a long-term housing policy corresponding with the changing social conditions, which would gain the confidence and support of the population, promote the interest of citizens in building and modernizing flats and which would also influence the development of the material basis of the building industry and its capacity. For a transitional period it will be also expedient to endeavour to employ building organizations and manpower of other countries and concentrate construction to places where the need is most urgent.

It is characteristic of the bureaucratic and centralist tendencies, applied over and over again in our life in the past that one of the places most affected by insensibility towards people is the centre of our Republic, Prague.

The capital city, with its experienced and highly qualified cadres of workers, technicians, scientists, artists, organizers of our construction and which comprises an immense wealth of monuments and cultural values, has paid dearly for sectarianism in economy and politics, for the low standard of responsible officials. Its facilities and amenities are not in keeping with its social functions, growing tourism and the requirements of the life of its inhabitants. It is indisputably necessary to speed up housing construction in the capital and, in addition, to concentrate efforts on at least some of the other problems which annoy the people in Prague most: municipal and suburban transport, as well as cleanliness in the city. It is necessary to solve similarly the problems of the capital city of Slovakia-Bratislava.To see to it that as many children as possible from these cities may be able to spend their holidays outside the capital in view of the present inadequate possibilities of recreation in Prague.

The Central Committee is of the opinion that despite the faster growth of the standard of living, the present results and these measures do not by far meet existing needs. Nor do they correspond to our real economic possibilities; however, the low effectiveness of our economy is creating barriers which in the process of the further satisfaction of personal and social needs can be overcome only by efforts to mobilize the reserves and to develop resources in production. The elimination of the shortcomings in economy will require time. But we are convinced that the consistent implementation of the economic reform and the activation of all Communists and non-party members will enable our country to embark upon the road of a fast, modern development of the economy.

By rational utilization of the resources in Slovakia to the prosperity of the Republic

The economy of the Czechoslovak Socialist Republic is the integration of two national economies which makes it possible to multiply the economic potential of our entire society. This is conditioned by rational utilization of the resources and reserves of the growth of both our national political regions in the interest of an effective development of the Czechoslovak national economy as well as by the creation of a social and economic balance between the various regions. The new constitutional set up must definitely rely on the integration basis and further integration tendencies in the economy of the entire State.

The past development of Slovakia within the unified Czechoslovak economy was marked by major changes in the economic and living standard. Slovakia has become an advanced industrially developed agricultural part of the Republic. For the further development of the integrated Czechoslovak economy it is not decisive to make partial individual adjustments but to fundamentally elaborate the rational integration of the national political regions in the economic complex of the entire State.

However, the undeniable achievements were accompanied by the emergence of serious problems. Slovakia's share in the creation of the national income increased from 14.2 per cent in 1948 to 24.4 per cent in 1965, it is not adequate to the possibilities of growth which exist in Slovakia. /Favourable geographic position, qualitative changes in the fund of manpower, possibilities of space concentration,new basis of chemistry, metallurgy, fuels and power, agriculture, natural resources./

68 a

The processes of creating a balanced social and
conomic level between Slovakia and the Czech lands are
haracterized by their internal contradictions. An undeni-
ble success of the Party policy is the elimination of social and economic backwardness and the decrease of relative
er capita differences. However, the faster rate of growth
as not sufficient for reducing absolute differences. The
rocess of creating a balanced level was not based on the
onception of national economic effectiveness of the deve-
opment of the Czechoslovak economy.

The existing problems are caused mainly by the fact
hat the extensive economic growth of the Czechoslovak So-
ialist Republic was markedly enforced also in the economic
evelopment of Slovakia. The potential source of growth was
ot used rationally, both in industry and in agriculture.
he tertiary sphere, particularly the build-up of the scien-
ific, research and development bases, has lagged greatly
ehind. Slovakia's development was not sufficiently coor-
inated, it proceeded along departmental lines, without in-
ernal integration relations of modern economic entities.

The intensive development of Slovakia's economy is
onditioned by a complex of measures connected with the so-
ution of short-term factual problems, with the clarifica-
ion of conceptual questions of long-term development, with
he effective operation of the new system of management
nd with the definition of the competence and authority of
he Slovak national bodies.

The measures designed to speed up Slovakia's econ-
ic development up to 1970 constitute the starting-point
or a fundamental change in Slovakia's integration into the
rocess of transition of the Czechoslovak economy to the
oad of intensive growth. At the same time it is necessary
o seek possibilities of solving acute problems: employ-
ent, the lagging behind of micro-regions with special re-

gard to those which are inhabited by Hungarian and Ukrainian fellow-citizens, specific problems of the standard of living, particularly the housing problem etc.

It is of decisive importance for Slovakia's long term economic development to raise substantially Slovakia's participation in the creation and the utilization of the national income and to solve the task of creating a balanced economic level essentially by 1980.

This necessitates faster economic development in Slovakia than is the national average. The prerequisite of this is to give strong support to progressive structural changes, to intensify agricultural production and the interconnected processing industry; to develop the tertiary sector in all spheres; to purposefully concentrate production and the infra-structure.

The development of Slovakia is taking place within the new system of management. However, this system in its present form has not created scope for the development policy of national political regions. Past adjustments of the plan and of economic instruments are not sufficient. It is therefore necessary to elaborate the system of management in such a way as to ensure that also territorial and national aspects of development become an equal organic component of the system of management of the entire national economy.

THE DEVELOPMENT OF SCIENCE, EDUCATION AND CULTURE

At the present stage we must base the development of ur society to a much greater extent on the progress and pplication of science, education and culture, It will be ecessary that their wealth is used fully and completely to he benefit of socialism and that our people should understand the complicated claims connected with creative work in hese spheres.

The importance of Science in our Society is Growing

Socialism originates, lasts and wins by the connection of the working movement with science. There is no reationship of subordination and compromise between these orces. The more resolute and impartial is the advancement f science, the more is it in harmony ith the interests of ocialism; the greater are the achievements of the working eople, the bigger is the scope opened up to science. In he relationship to the development and application of science in the life of socialist society is reflected how much he working people are aware of their historical tasks, to hat extent they really enforce them. Socialism stands and alls with science, just as it stands and falls with the ower of the working people.

Just now, at the beginning of the scientific-technoogical revolution in the world, the social position of cience is changing considerably. Its application in the ntire life of society is becoming the basic condition for he intensive development of the economy,care for man and his living environment, culture of the society and growth of the personality, modern methods of management and administration, the development of relations between people and the solving of various problems raised by the current period. It is in the field of science and technology where the victory of socialism over capitalism is decided in long-term perspective.

Therefore the Party regards it as one of its primary tasks to provide an ever greater scope for the promotion of creative scientific work and for a timely and more efficient application of its results in social practice.

Relatively complete foundations of basic, applied research and development unprecedented in extent and importance, have been built up in this country together with the construction of socialism. A number of qualified scientific workers have grown up, who made an important contribution by their achievements to building up this country and whose qualification is recognized all over the world. In spite of this the opportunities offered by socialism for the development of science and especially for the application of its results to the benefit of society are, for the time being, far from being fully used which is also because of the still existing branch barriers between science, technological development and production. The inflexibility of the system of management by directives, connected with the low-level qualification of managing personnel is the reason for this; in the sphere of research the reasons are mainly differences in the level of applied research institutes, caused by lack of scientifically trained staff.

To solve the existing state we shall continue making substantial improvements particularly in the material conditions of our basic research so that in the decisive branches it could remain permanently at a world level. The development of science must at the same time proceed from the real possibilities of Czechoslovakia as a middle-size country, which can ensure top-level scientific research only by efficient specialization and concentration of energy in connection with extensive international cooperation and exploitation of the results of world science as such. Therefore it is also necessary to develop the system of the evaluation of scientific workers in such a way that selected progressive, scientific and socially important directions of research be supported more fully by a system of moral and material incentives.

If the social sciences are really to become an official instrument of scientific self-cognition of socialist society, it is necessary to respect the principles of their internal life and to ensure such a position and conditions for them as would enable them to achieve high scientific standards. By means of its bodies the Party will take the initiative in encouraging the development of social sciences and contributing towards their orientation to important social problems; but it does not interfere with the very process of creative scientific work and in this respect relies on the initiative and social responsibility of scientists themselves.

In addition to creating favourable conditions for the very development of science it is an urgent task to strive for surmounting all the obstacles between science on the one hand and social practice on the other. Even though the full and more consistent application of the new system of management is expected to bring the fundamental solution, we shall help this process also by new measures at the level of central management. The Party will especially support the development of feasible stimuli for the application of the results of science in production and other social practice and for a rapid improvement of the qualification structure of slowly developing applied research institutes. At the same time we shall also support a more profound examination of the social function of science, especially the problem of its effectiveness and the relationship between science and economy in Czechoslovak conditions.

The development of socialist society is at the same time a process of constant increase of the social involvement and responsibility of science and its application in the management and shaping of the entire life of society. We shall strive on a broader scale than hitherto for scientific staff to take part in the work of representative bodies and in the activities of other bodies of social management; we shall intensify the active participation of scientific institutions and scientific workers in drawing up proposals for political and economic measures. We shall encourage the application of scientific workers in social management and the system of education on the broadest possible scale and create favourable social and economic conditions for their activity in these fields. We shall prepare without delay the introduction of a binding system of scientific expertise and opponency on important proposals. This will contribute towards qualified decisions at all levels of management.

Quality of education - the aim of our educational system

The progress of the socialist society is conditioned by the growth in education of the people. This is a precondition for solving initial tasks of the scientific-technological revolution, promoting the relations and institutions of socialist democracy and further asserting the cultural and humanistic character of socialism and the development and employment of every man in it.

Therefore we regard further progress of education as a primary task. In this respect we proceed from the traditions of the education of our nations and from the good results by which the socialist stage of development has improved our school system, especially by its broad democratization and materialization of the principles of co-education. It is still necessary to surmount the consequences of past shortcomings, when the quantitative development of education was frequently achieved at the expense of the quality of teaching. Neither was sufficient care given to the qualitative training of teachers. The frequent reorganization in the past did not contribute to the desirable improvement of the standard of education. On the contrary, this was the reason why, in many respects, it was lagging behind the existing needs and future demands. Therefore it is a foremost task today to concentrate the main attention and strength towards a purposeful improvement of the standard, exaction and value of education and especially towards improving and raising the standard of general education of people, towards expanding the base for a more efficient choice and education of talents, and towards modernizing the content, forms and means of education.

The dynamic development of our economy and of the whole society requires an end of the underevaluation of education and of the needs of schools and teachers; it requires that a much bigger proportion be set aside from social resources for the development of education. We shall ensure that educational bodies in cooperation with the broad masses prudently materialize projects which will enable our economy to fully keep pace with the dynamics of the development of science and technology and with the needs of the time. We consider the following tasks as the most urgent ones:

a/ to work out a draft hypothesis on the long-term development of the educational system, which will make it possible to stabilise the development of the educational system at all levels, to solve its personnel and material

a 75

base in advance so as to gradually eliminate the unevenness in the development of education in individual regions of the country.

To prepare a new concept in harmony with the long-term project of basic polytechnic education, which would be based on the logical grasping of the subject, to take advantage of the independence and initiative of students and make it possible to fully apply the principle of differentiation according to interests and talents; to solve the urgent problems of secondary general education schools by extending the base and time of secondary general education, thus to improve preparations for later university studies while providing conditions for those secondary school students who will not study at universities to take up practical jobs.

To form and to gradually introduce a system of additional education of young people who start working at 15 years. To increase the thoroughness of the preparation of young skilled workers in harmony with the technological and structural changes in our economy by improving the theoretical, specialised and general education of young apprentices. To take advantage to a greater extent of the resources of plants and enterprises for the construction and equipment of apprentice centres in the sense of the new system of management of the national economy and in justified cases also to grant state subsidies. Not to allow a further decrease of material investments in these establishments. The same criteria should also be applied by National Committees in the construction and equipment of apprentice schools.

b/ To create material and personnel conditions at secondary schools and universities for all young people, who fulfil the necessary requirements and proved it by their results during preceding education, to be enrolled for studies. Therefore the system of enrollment at secondary schools and universities should be made more flexible. Administrative methods should be replaced by economic and moral stimuli, a sufficient amount of information and improvement of educational advice, which will help regulate sensitively the influx of students to particular branches and bring closer the abilities and interests of individuals and the needs of society. Meanwhile secondary and university education should not be understood only as training for a certain profession, but as a means of improving the extent of education, the cultural level of man and his ability to solve new situations in the production process as well as in the economic, social and qualification structure of society. This requires simultaneously an increase in the social responsibility of economic, cultural and political institutions and of every individual for the application of education in practice.

c/ At universities, democratic principles and methods should be consistently applied in their management. The prerequisites of scientific work, unity of teaching and research should be continually strengthened, the authority and autonomy of university scientific councils should be increased. Universities should be given preference regarding modern equipment, the possibilities of scientific work should be improved, all-round cooperation between research, universities and secondary schools should be intensified, expensive equipment should be taken advantage of jointly by research institutes and universities. Universities should be given broader access to foreign literature and more opportunities of study and training visits abroad in view of their pedagogical and scientific work, while understanding correctly the importance of acquiring knowledge for the development of science and flexibly applying the principles of profitability of foreign currency resources.

d/ The structural changes in the national economy will

also require re-training and complementing of the general or specialised education of adults. Therefore it will be necessary that schools, enterprises, social organisations and mass information media /press, radio, television/ co-operate in order to improve and intensify the system of education for adults.

e/ The complexity of education management should be safeguarded by legal arrangements so as to raise the role of school administration. In this connection it will be desirable to ascertain the effectiveness of university law so as to strengthen the democratic relations in the internal and external management and the social position of universities. The authority of Slovak National Council bodies in education in Slovakia should be applied fully in view of the importance of education as a basic element of national culture.

f/ Equal study and development conditions should be consistently ensured for young people of all nationalities. An end should be put to the belittling approach towards solving problems of nationality education, and legal and institutional preconditions should be created to allow the nationalities to have something to say on the specific issues of nationality education.

The Party appreciates the work of our teachers in educating the young generation. Teachers belong above all to school and young people and their work must not be disturbed by anything. Educational work is of nation- and society- wide importance. Therefore the social position of teachers must be safeguarded in the first place by the respective state bodies and National Committees. Efforts to provide conditions essential for their work must also correspond to this. This means to ensure a high standard of the training of teachers, development of wage relations of teachers and other school staff so as to be in harmony with the growth of the real wages of workers in other branches, and also to solve other urgent material needs of teachers so they can perform their responsible profession with full concentration. In projects and the materialization of school capital construction, it is essential to ensure its complex character including flats for teachers. The Party regards this as part of its policy to increase the prestige, authority and social importance of the educationalists of the young generation.

The Humanistic Mission of Culture

The development of culture in the broadest sense is one of the basic conditions of dynamic and harmonious development of socialist society. The culture of socialist Czechoslovakia consists of independent and equal Czech and Slovak cultures, together with the cultures of the other nationalities. The arts and culture are not a mere decoration of economic and political life, but they are vital for the socialist system. If culture lags behind, it retards the progress of policy and economy, democracy and freedom, development of man and human relations. Care for culture, material and spiritual, is not only the concern of the cultural front, but it must become an affair of the entire society.

It was an important tradition of the Communist Party from the start that it was able to unite the best men of culture and art around itself. This is proved not only by the socialist orientation of our pre-war artistic vanguard, but also by the fact that most of the cultural intelligentsia were standing on the left or were in the ranks of the Party after the liberation in 1945. Later, especially in the early fifties, certain representative of culture were discriminated, some were subjected to unjustified political

a 79

repression and the cultural policy of the Party was also demand.

The documents of the 13th Congress should have been a starting point of a new cultural policy, which would proceed from the best traditions of the past and from much positive experience acquired after 1956 and after the 12th Congress of the Communist Party of Czechoslovakia. However, the surviving bureaucratic attitudes and old methods of management prevented the impetuses of the Congress from developing. The contradictions between the proclaimed and practiced policies were creating a conflict tension and restricting the involvement and development of socialist culture. The Central Committee will investigate all the reasons for these conflicts and will create favourable conditions to normalize the situation.

We reject administrative and bureaucratic methods of implementing cultural policy, we dissociate ourselves from them and we shall oppose them. Artistic work must not be subjected to censorship. We have full confidence in men of culture and we expect their responsibility, understanding and support. We appreciate how the workers in culture helped force through and create the humanistic and democratic character of socialism and how actively they participated in eliminating the retarding factors of its development.

It is necessary to overcome a narrowed understanding of the social and human function of culture and art, overestimation of their ideological and political role and underestimation of their basic general cultural and aesthetic tasks in the transformation of man and his world.

The Party will guard and safeguard both the freedom of artistic work and the right to make works of art accessible.

To socially administer culture means, first of all, to create favourable conditions for its development. Disputes,

80

a

which will naturally arise, will be solved by discussion and democratic decisions. Independent decisions of cultural workers in the spheres of their activity must also be an expression of the necessary autonomy of culture and art. They must be indispensable partners for state bodies. We are convinced that communist intellectuals and all other leading workers in the sphere of culture and art are capable of cooperating in the formation of, and carrying out responsibly and independently, the policy of the Party in state, social, cultural and group-interest institutions, that they are a guarantee of the socialist, humanistic orientation of our culture.

Of course, the social effect of culture does not occur outside the political context. We shall ensure that the freedom of different views, guaranteed by the Constitution, is fully respected. However, the Communist Party cannot give up its inspiring role, its efforts that art, too, should efficiently help form socialist man in the struggle for the transformation of the world. The Party will apply consistently its political programme, it will stimulate the development of Marxist thinking.

Socialist culture is one of the primary agents of the penetration of socialist and humanistic ideas in the world. It helps unite the humanistic streams of world culture. It has the capacity of bringing closer the socialist nations and of strengthening the cooperation and fraternal relations of nations and nationalities. Culture is a traditionally important value for our nations, by the means of which we have always proved our vitality and individuality to the world. But the interpretation of the national traditions of the culture of the Czechs and Slovaks was one-sided in many respects, whole important periods were artificially omitted from it. We give our full backing to the humanistic traditions of national cultures and we shall support all efforts to endorse this heritage in the present psychology of Czechs and Slovaks.

We are supporters of both internationalism and national specificity of culture. We think it inevitable to take efficient measures without delay so that culture in Slovakia has the same conditions and possibilities as those in Bohemia, so that disproportions do not grow, but disappear. The equal position of national cultures also requires an equal position of national institutions. The competence of national bodies in Slovakia includes the management of the decisive instruments of national culture, such as radio, television, film, scientific institutes, artists' unions, book publishing, care for historical monuments, etc. It is necessary to secure the representation of Slovak national culture abroad; to increase the exchange of information and cultural values between the Czech and Slovak nations; to ensure the cultural life of the Slovaks in the Czech lands and of the Czechs in Slovakia in their native tongue.

Similar principles must be applied also towards the cultures of all the nationalities in Czechoslovakia, while realising that they are specific cultures and not Czech and Slovak culture translated into another language. The culture of nationalities is an organic part of Czechoslovak socialist culture, but it is also in context with the general culture of its own nation, with which it is inseparably linked. Material conditions and personnel problems of the further development of national cultures must be guaranteed institutionally, scientific and cultural institutions and offices must be established with a view to nationality needs. The decisive role and care for the material base of national cultures pertains to state bodies, National Committees, together with the cultural unions of the various nationalities.

We shall take care not only of cultural work, but also of the system of communication of cultural values, we

82 a

shall strive for the active participation of citizens in the development of socialist culture and in their cultural education, in the closest possible cooperation and complex influence of mass and local culture. We consider it urgent to examine the reasons of the catastrophic shortcomings of cultural and aesthetic education and to take measures to rectify them; - to create sufficient material, organisations and other conditions of cultural activity, to loosen the organisational forms; - to allow the establishment of various cultural and hobby groups as well as their regional and national associations; - to complete an efficient network of cultural establishments with an active participation of National Committees, enterprises, social and group-interest organisations; - to purposefully build up new important regional cultural centres in addition to the capitals.

The entire sphere of culture must be decently and responsibly secured economically in view of its importance, and protected from the uncontrolled nature of the market and from commercialism. We shall recommend, in the spirit of the 13th Congress resolution, that the government should complete without delay the planned solution of the entire complex of culture economy. The planned expenditure on culture must be stabilised and must increase progressively in harmony with the trend of the national income. We shall also support voluntary combination of the means of industrial and agricultural enterprises, national committees and social organisations for culture. The means invested in culture can become an important instrument of its development, if he, who uses them, becomes a modern socialist customer.

We regard the following problems as the most urgent ones, dependent upon new distribution of the means for culture on a national scale: to guarantee material care for the creators of important cultural values; - to eliminate discrepancies in the royalties, wages, incomes and taxes system in culture; - to cover the whole territory of the

a 83

Republic with a good-quality radio and television signal as soon as possible, to open the second television programme in 1970; - to overcome without delay the disastrous state of polygraphy; - to secure more polygraphic paper in desirable assortment for the press and publishing houses; - to improve care of historical objects of art and save handicraft among others things by making way for co-operative or private enterprise in this sphere.

The planned expenditure on culture must be concentrated in culture directing bodies which must distribute it to cultural institutions. To increase the economic independence and responsibility of cultural establishments, enterprises and groups is a prerequisite of the functioning economy of culture. Independent control will lead towards a more rational exploitation of means and possibilities, towards increasing the spirit of enterprise.

The International Status and Foreign Policy of the Czechoslovak Socialist Republic

We shall be putting the Action Programme into practice during a complicated international situation and its further development will influence the realisation of certain important principles of the programme. On the other hand, the process of the revival of socialism in Czechoslovakia will make it possible for our Republic to influence this international development more actively. We stand resolutely on the side of progress, democracy and socialism in the struggle of the socialist and democratic forces against the aggressive attempts of world imperialism. It is from this point of view that we determine our attitude to the most acute international problems of the present, and our share in the world-wide struggle against the forces of imperialist reaction.

Proceeding from the real relationship of internatio-

84

nal forces and from the awareness that Czechoslovakia is an active component of the revolutionary process in the world, she will formulate her own attitude towards the fundamental problems of world policy.

The basic orientation of Czechoslovak foreign policy was born and verified at the time of the struggle for national liberation and in the process of the socialist reconstruction of this country - it is in alliance and cooperation with the Soviet Union and the other socialist states. We shall strive for friendly relations with our allies - the countries of the world socialist community - to continue, on the basis of mutual respect, to intensify sovereignty and equality, and international solidarity. In this sense we shall contribute more actively and with a more elaborated concept to the joint activities of the Council of Mutual Economic Aid and the Warsaw Treaty.

In the relationship to the developing countries, socialist Czechoslovakia will be contributing to the strengthening of the anti-imperialist front and supporting within its power and possibilities all the nations opposing imperialism, colonialism, neo-colonialism and striving for the strengthening of their sovereignty and national independence and for economic development. Therefore we shall continue supporting the courageous struggle of the Vietnamese people against American aggression. We shall also be enforcing a political settlement of the Middle East crisis.

We shall actively pursue the policy of peaceful coexistence towards advanced capitalist countries. Our geographical position, as well as the needs and capacities of an industrial country require that we should carry out a more active European policy aimed at the promotion of mutually advantageous relations with all states and international organisations and at safeguarding collective security of the European continent. We shall consistently proceed from

a 85

the existence of two German states, from the fact that the German Democratic Republic, as the first socialist state on German territory, is an important peace element in Europe, from the necessity of giving support to the realistic forces in the German Federal Republic, while resisting neo-nazi and revanchist tendencies in that country. The Czechoslovak people want to live in peace with all nations. They want to develop good relations and cooperate with all states in the interests of strengthening international peace and security as well as mutual confidence in the economic, cultural, scientific and technological fields. We shall also take more active advantage than we have done so far of our Republic's membership in international organisations, especially in the United Nations and its agencies.

Our science, culture and art can strengthen and increase much more the international authority of socialist Czechoslovakia in the world. Czechoslovak foreign policy must provide conditions and extend the scope for the international application of our culture abroad. A broad application of our science and art abroad helps to prove efficiently the advantages of socialism and the possibilities of an active policy of peaceful co-existence.

Our foreign policy did not make use of all the opportunities for active work, it did not take the initiative in advancing its own views on many important international problems. The Central Committee of the Communist Party of Czechoslovakia, the National Assembly, the Government and the respective ministry must overcome these shortcomings without delay and consistently ensure that our foreign policy should express fully both the national and international interests of socialist Czechoslovakia.

A full development of the international role of socialist Czechoslovakia is inseparable from the education of citizens in the spirit of internationalism, which com-

86 a

prises both the grasping of common interests and aims of the world progressive forces and understanding of specific national needs. This is linked with the necessity of making prompt and detailed information on international problems and the course of our foreign policy available to the public and thus creating conditions for an active participation of Czechoslovak citizens in the shaping of foreign political attitudes.

The Communist Party of Czechoslovakia will be more active in the sphere of the international communist and workers´ movement. We shall put special emphasis on friendly ties, mutual consultations and exchange of experiences with the Communist Party of the Soviet Union, with the communist and workers´ parties of the socialist community, with all theother fraternal communist parties.

The Communist Party of Czechoslovakia will continue taking an active part in the struggle for the unity of the international communist movement, for strengthening the action cooperation of communist parties with all the progressive forces while regarding a resolute struggle against the aggressive policy of American imperialism as the most important task. The Communist Party of Czechoslovakia will take full advantage of its specific possibilities of establishing contacts with the socialist, peaceful and democratic forces in the capitalist and developing countries.It will contribute to expanding the forms of cooperation and coordinating the work of communist parties, while attaching great importance to international party consultative meetings. From this point of view it welcomes and supports the outcomes of the Consultative Meeting of Communist and Workers´ Parties in Budapest. With dozens of fraternal parties the Communist Party of Czechoslovakia supports the proposal for convening an international communist consultative meeting in Moscow late in 1968.

Comrades,

We are submitting to you quite frankly all the main ideas which guided us and which we want to adhere to at the present time. Everyone will understand that the proposals comprised in this Action Programme are far-reaching and their realisation will profoundly influence the life of this country. We are not changing our fundamental orientation; in the spirit of our traditions and former decisions we want to develop to the utmost in this country an advanced socialist society, rid of class antagonisms, economically, technologically and culturally, highly advanced, socially and nationally just, democratically organized, with a qualified management, by the wealth of its resources giving the possibility of dignified human life, comradely relations of mutual cooperation among people and free scope for the development of the human personality. We want to start building up a new intensely democratic model of a socialist society, which would fully correspond to Czechoslovak conditions. But our own experiences and Marxist scientific cognition lead us jointly to the conclusion that these aims cannot be achieved along the old paths while using means, which have long been obsolete and harsh methods, which are always dragging us back. We declare with full responsibility that our society has entered a difficult period when we can no longer rely on traditional schemes. We cannot squeeze life into patterns, no matter how well-intended. It is now also up to us to make our way through unknown conditions, to experiment, to give the socialist development a new look, while leaning upon creative Marxist thinking and the experiences of the international workers movement, relying on the true understanding of the conditions of the socialist development of Czechoslovakia as a country which assumes responsibility to the international communist movement for improving and taking advantage of the relatively advanced material base, unusually high standards of education and culture of the people and undeniable democratic traditions to the benefit of socialism and communism. No one could forgive us were we to waste this chance, were we to give up our opportunities.

We are not taking the outlined measures to make any concessions from our ideals - let alone to our opponents. On the contrary: we are convinced that they will help us to get rid of the burden which for years provided many advantages for the opponent by restricting, reducing and paralysing the efficiency of the socialist idea, the attractiveness of the socialist example. We want to set new penetrating forces of socialist life in motion in this country to give them the possibility of a much more efficient confrontation of the social systems and world outlooks and allowing a fuller application of the advantages of socialism.

Our Action Programme comprises tasks, intentions and aims for the immediate future, up to the 14th Party Congress. We are aware that many of the shortcomings and difficulties which have accumulated over recent years cannot be fully overcome in a short time. However, the fulfilment of this programme can open up the way to solving other, more complicated and important problems of the organisation and dynamic development of our socialist society in directions which could be only indicated until now; in the coming years, we want to start working out a long-term programme, which would give form and elaborate in detail the concept of the over-all development of our socialist society in the stage we are entering, make clear the conditions and open up prospects of its communist future. After everything we have lived through over the past years we are obliged to give a reply to all our workers and ourselves as to how the Party imagines its aims can be achieved, how it wants to materialise the expectations and desires which are being invested by workers in their life and in their participation in the communist movement. We believe that our Marxist science has gathered and will gather now and in future such an amount of strength as to enable it to prepare responsibly scientific preconditions for such programme.

a 89

We are not concealing the fact that difficult moments and extraordinarily exacting and responsible work face us in the coming months and years. For the fulfilment of the forthcoming progressive tasks it will be necessary to unite as many citizens of our Republic as possible, all who are concerned with the welfare of this country, with its peace efforts, with a flourishing socialism. Confidence, mutual understanding and harmonious work of all who really want to devote their energy to this great human experiment will be needed. But the work and initiative of every communist, every worker will be needed above all. We want to responsibly, consistently and without reservations make room for this, remove all the barriers which stood in its way, set the creative capacities of our man, all the physical and moral capacities of society in motion. We want to create conditions so that every honest citizen, who concerns himself with the cause of socialism, the cause of our nations, should feel that he is the very designer of the fate of this country, his homeland, that he is needed, that he is reckoned with. Therefore let the Action Programme become a programme of the revival of socialist efforts in this country. There is no force which could resist the people who know what they want and how to pursue their aim.

The Central Committee of the Communist Party of Czechoslovakia

3

The document which follows should be read as a blueprint for the implementation of the Action Program. As such, it deals less with the decision to initiate change than with the decision to insure that the process of change is presided over by the Czechoslovak Communist Party.

When read in this context, the message of the document seems fairly obvious. It is, in brief, that the initiation of change carries with it the risk of failure as well as the risk of extinction—that in both cases it is the Party's responsibility to see to it that neither danger ever materializes, that at present the Party is ill-equipped to fulfill this responsibility, and that accordingly it must prepare itself for the difficult days ahead.

THE INTERNAL AUDIENCE

This message is conveyed to the internal audience in a pattern of challenge and response. Within the framework of that pattern the document considers the internal development of the CCP in terms of its consequences for the past, present and future development of Czechoslovakia in what amounts to an apparent effort to establish the need for, and define the scope of, internal Party reform.

The emphasis throughout is, as might be expected, on individual and institutional shortcomings. As in the documents already discussed, the Party emerges as the repository of "truth," a repository which—although admittedly presided over at times by less than perfect individuals—nevertheless retains the capacity to inspire and lead the people of Czechoslovakia in the development of a society which, if not perfect, will be as close to perfection as is humanly possible.

Just as the Action Program sought to intimidate and inspire, so too is it with this document. For those who would minimize the need for internal reform, there are the familiar references to the evils of the past coupled with pointed reminders that as far as the present leadership is concerned the responsibility for these errors rests squarely on the shoulders of those who formerly presided over the Party. Thus a distinction is made between the leadership on the one hand and the rank and file members on the other. Although neither escapes the brunt of the criticism, the presumption is that in a Party organized around the principle of democratic centralism, primary responsibility for conditions within that Party as well as for conditions throughout the society belongs to the leadership elements.

In this way the problems of the past are defined as essentially problems of poor leadership. To be sure, the fault is shared by the members and by the constraints of operational necessity. Having already replaced the former leaders, Dubcek and his supporters must now deal with their sources of strength within the membership. This, however, poses a difficult problem. A thoroughgoing shakeup of the Party, assuming they were capable of carrying it out, would be, under the circumstances, both internally disruptive and, as viewed by other members of the bloc, externally harmful. The only solution, therefore, is to win these elements over or, if that is not possible, to neutralize their effectiveness. In part, this is accomplished by assigning the blame for past errors to the former leaders of the CCP. In part, it is accomplished by criticism which is directed against the membership itself. Finally, it is accomplished on the one hand, by pointing out the advances of the past and, on the other, by recognizing that some of the difficulties were related to the conditions under which the Party had to operate. In this way, elements who might reject the authority of the new leadership are warned of the dangers which attach to continued opposition and obstructionism. They are at the same time assured of "forgiveness" if they "confess" the errors of their ways.

Such a solution, unless accompanied by organizational changes, is likely to be of only limited utility. As the document suggests, this fact was not lost on the members of the Central Committee or, at least, on those members who supported the changes outlined in the Action Program. For reasons of internal necessity and external reality, the reorganization of the CCP could not appear to be a direct attack on those elements who probably still supported the policies of Novotny. Internally, these elements undoubtedly cut across Czech-Slovak lines. A purge directed against them would have only served to fragment the Party at a critical period in its history—a period in which unity of effort would be essential to a continued mastery of the process of change. Externally such a move would have only served to further alarm members of the bloc who were already concerned about the course of developments within Czechoslovakia.

An alternative solution to this problem lay in relating the need for internal reform to the capability of the CCP to respond to the challenge of change. In this way dissident elements could be effectively isolated and, perhaps even more importantly, the leadership could at the same time develop an organizational structure which would be responsive both to the demands of Party leaders and to the demands of Party programs.

As I understand this document, it was precisely this solution which was finally adopted. Thus, for example, the proposed organizational changes are characterized here as a necessary prerequisite for dealing effectively with problems of the present as well as those which are likely to occur in the future. In part, the justifications provided are probably quite valid. Presiding as it were over a Party which had traditionally rewarded loyalty and faithful service and had discouraged individual initiative and competence, the leadership of the CCP undoubtedly felt that internal reform was essential if the proposals outlined in the Action Program were to be effectively implemented. This would appear to be particularly true with respect to the call for an improvement in the relationships between the Party and other segments of Czech society. After all, institutional arrangements and practices which were created for the purpose of maintaining a rigid imposition of Party rule, could not be expected to function as effectively when it came to guiding the development of Czech society. The requisites for presiding over change were, in short, somewhat different from those needed to preside over the status quo.

To an equal, if not greater, extent, however, the call for reform seems to have been guided by the necessities of exercising power in a system where legitimacy resides in a party rather than a government, and where, as a result, the struggle for power is characterized by a minimum of institutional constraints. Again, let me emphasize that I am not suggesting that Dubcek and his followers were concerned with nothing more than consolidating their own positions of authority within the CCP. Although this was probably a major consideration, the call for reform outlined in this document was undoubtedly also motivated by the desire to maintain effective control over the process of change and a recognition that this could only be accomplished by eliminating internal weaknesses of the Party while at the same time improving its capabilities for dealing with other groups in the society.

What I am suggesting is that here, as in other Communist political systems, the two are inter-related. For the Party to effectively control the Action Program, Dubcek would have to effectively control the Party. While the ouster of Novotny paved the way for the implementation of the first of these objectives, the reforms proposed in this document were undoubtedly viewed as a contribution to the second.

If this is correct, then the message set forth here should be interpreted both as a gesture of confidence in the ability of the CCP to preside over the process of change and a concession to the realities of gaining and maintaining power in Czechoslovakia. In the first instance, the intended audience is the "masses" as well as those identified as anti-socialist elements. To them, the call for internal reform represents a determination on the part of the CCP to organize and direct the process of change. In the second instance the intended audience is the membership of the CCP. To them, the call for internal reform represents a determination on the part of Dubcek and his supporters to organize and direct the activities of the CCP.

THE EXTERNAL AUDIENCE

The message is presented to the Soviet Union, members of the bloc, and other "fraternal parties" in essentially the same fashion, although there are, of course, the usual assurances of continued solidarity with the "socialist camp." Seen in the light of the subsequent developments, it raises the question of whether the message was actually received and, if so, why the decision was taken to intervene. There are, it seems to me, at least two possible explanations. On the one hand, the message could have been misinterpreted—that is to say, the Soviet Union and other members of the bloc could have taken these documents as simply another indication of what appeared to be a growing tendency on the part of the CCP to further compromise its already shaky position as the dominant force in Czech society. There are certainly suggestions of this view in the statements published by the Soviet Union during the months preceding the intervention. Considered against the background of events then taking place within Czechoslovakia, such a misinterpretation would be understandable.

The second explanation, and one that I find more plausible, is that the message contained in this document came through as intended. I find it difficult to believe, for example, that men accustomed to the manipulation of power in a similar context would not be able to understand the dual meaning of this call to reform. What I do not find difficult to believe is that the Soviet Union and its Allies had strong misgivings about Dubcek's ability to manage both the consolidation of internal Party control and the regulation of external change at one and the same time. Recognizing, as I suspect they did, the interrelationship of the one to the other, they must have had even greater misgivings about the future of the CCP. For unless Dubcek could maintain effective control over the Party, it was highly unlikely that he could, no matter how well-intentioned, maintain effective control over the implementation of the Action Program. Failing in that, it was almost certain that the initiation of change would become less and less the exclusive prerogative of the CCP, and more and more a responsibility shared with other groups in Czech society. To extend the thesis developed in the introductory comments to the internal arena, so too would the obligation for accommodation. I will return to this question in my concluding remarks. For now let me only suggest that the events which both preceded and followed the release of the statements contained in this document must have confirmed their worst suspicions.

In the non-Communist world, the message appears to have been completely misinterpreted—understandably so, I might add. Unaccustomed as we are to the vagaries of manipulating power in a Communist political system, it is easy to read this document as another indication of Dubcek's liberal instincts at work. The confusion is further compounded by the fact that the proposals advanced here do seem to constitute a genuine attempt to transform a party dedicated to the maintenance of authoritarian rule into a party which is capable of initiating and directing change. Bound as most of us have been to certain preconceptions regarding the operations of these parties, it is difficult to separate the search for flexibility from the search for "freedom." It is even more difficult to associate the pursuit of individual power with the pursuit of political, social, and economic development. Thus the tendency is to regard the call for Party reform either as a sign of liberal trends at work or as a propaganda effort designed to hide an intramural struggle for personal power.

As I have suggested above, the message of this document is, or at least appears to be, consistent with neither interpretation. On the contrary, the aim of these reforms seems to have been that the CCP would preside over the initiation of change and that Alexander Dubcek and those around him would preside over the CCP. This is not to suggest either the illusion of change or to imply a condition of acute megalomania. It is to argue that Dubcek, committed as he seems to have been to the initiation of change and trained as he obviously was in the exercise of power within the context of a Communist political system, undoubtedly recognized that the danger of failure, like the danger of extinction, could only be avoided if those making the decisions also controlled their implementation.

Based on that understanding, he appears to have set out to create a Party that would not only be better able to manage the complexities of change but would be able to do so under the direction of those in the Party who had formulated the Action Program and who were therefore presumably most interested in its successful implementation.

CONCLUSION

In the preceding analysis I have tried to indicate what I regard to be the message of this document. If I have interpreted the contents correctly, then it would appear that the reforms proposed here were intended to insure the continued primacy of the CCP as the dominant force in Czechoslovakia. It would also appear that the intention of these proposals was to insure that the dominance of the Party would be consistent with the successful implementation of the Action Program and whatever other changes would be introduced in the years to come. Finally, and in a related sense, the intent seems to have been to insure that the future of the Party and the future of the reforms would be in the hands of those in the CCP who were genuinely committed to both objectives.

FROM THE MEETING OF THE CENTRAL COMMITTEE OF THE COMMUNIST PARTY OF CZECHOSLOVAKIA /May 29 - June 1 1968/

CONTENTS

FROM THE REPORT DELIVERED BY A.DUBČEK

AT THE PLENARY MEETING OF THE CENTRAL COMMITTEE OF THE COMMUNIST PARTY OF CZECHOSLOVAKIA ON MAY 29 1968

Dear Comrades,

In view of the development of the situation, we propose to today´s plenary meeting of the Central Committee that it decides about the further tactical course of the Party in the present intense social process, and especially about making arrangements for the next extraordinary Party Congress.

In preparing today´s plenum, we proceeded from the results of the regional conferences, from the evaluation of the written reports about the development of the political situation which we demanded from all district Party committees as well as from resolutions and standpoints of basic organisations which are still being received by the Central Committee of the Communist Party of Czechoslovakia (CPCz) in great numbers.

When preparing the plenary meeting, we also arranged a number of nation-wide conferences; a conference of leading secretaries of district and regional Party committees, a meeting of chairmen of Party organisations from the largest industrial enterprises, as well as of village organizations, a conference of Communist journalists, of workers active in the ideological sphere and others. We also proceeded from an independent evaluation of the decisive political questions in the Presidium.

a 3

In the Party Central Committee, we hold the identical view that the most important task facing this meeting of the Central Committee is for the whole Party to move unitedly, in an organized and purposeful way over to the offensive, to more resolutely take the lead in the social process in the forthcoming new stage, by its conclusions and measures and its bold and active work. The time has come to fulfil the expectations and hopes of the people by practical deeds and at the same time to publicly and resolutely react to all attempts to obstruct our road ahead.

This fundamental task of the Party determines our present approach to the whole complex of problems posed by the new stage of the socialist process of regeneration.

The central point of the offensive course will be the preparation of the Party Congress which must become the basis for the unification and the political drive of the Party in the next few months.

In the eight weeks since the April plenum the social process has accelerated. While in the period immediately after January there was an essentially uniform stream, it now begins to become gradually differentiated. Various specific interests are appearing and individual political tendencies are more sharply crystallizing.

The differentiation of society is reflected also within the Party in the diversity of views on the evaluation of the present situation, its causes and the further course of the Party. There are fears - as can be seen from resolutions of Party organs and organizations - as to whether the Party is not giving up its positions, whether it does not resign its leading role and give free scope to rightist, non-socialist forces. On the other hand, there are fears lest the Party should slow down the process of democratization.

4

a

If we want to arrive at a correct view, we must not see only extremes and absolutize partial phenomena.

The fundamental characteristic of the present day is determined by the positive social process initiated in January. Since the April plneum, which in principle characterized the situation existing at that time correctly, it has been possible to strengthen certain elements of political consolidation. The regional conferences created conditions for activating the Party. The ideas of the Action Programme and of the Government statement have met with widespread support even though efforts to make them the basis of the everyday political and organizational activities of Party bodies, organizations and all Communists are still not always successful. We have resolutely started, along Party and State lines, to rectify unlawful acts and deformations. We are also changing the methods and the style of Party work. We have not only worked out clear programme principles of the future course in the main spheres but we have also created the most important organizational and institutional prerequisites for pushing them through.

The most valuable capital for the Party is the fact that after the January plenum it was able to restore confidence in our policy. This is proved by positive socialist activities of even those people who in the past stood aside from political life and to whom the January plenum has given new hope and trust in socialism. We realize that their confidence in the Party is conditioned by the way in which we shall be able to fill it by concrete deeds.

The contradictions and conflicts which quite naturally appear in the present process and which frequently become even dramatically acute are neither the product nor the consequence of the policy we started in January. They are in the first place the fruit of the long social crisis which had been

a 5

growing over many years, which accumulated a whole number of unsatisfied needs and unsolved problems to which the previous policy not only did not react but which, on the contrary, it gradually worsened by its methods although attention had been drawn to this by many voices in the Party since the 12th Congre and, more intensely, since the 13th Party Congress. In January, we opened up scope for their solution. This cannot naturally proceed without contradictions and a certain degree of elemental development. The present difficulties therefore originate in the burden of social contradictions, mistakes and deformations which crystallized especially in the past few years, under conditions of concentrated personal power, in a situation of extreme crisis.

This historical view is necessary in the interest of truth and also in order that we may not only understand the necessity of the January plenum and its conclusions but that we may also see in proper perspective the basic causes of the difficulties in the present political development.

We naturally do not shirk a critical analysis of our work after January. We know about the weaknesses in our work. But it should be recalled that under the former system of work in the Party it was impossible for us to prepare a ready-made programme of the further course in advance, and that there was no other possibility than to shape it on the march. It was even less possible for us to prepare conditions for organizational work in advance. At the same time, developments have made it necessary and continue to make it necessary for us to re-examine and revalue things which had been shaping and accumulating over many years and perhaps decades and which had remained unsolved, and to defend them in public discussion.

The many years of administrative regime and administrative methods of work have also paralyzed the action capacity of the Party. The Party as a whole was therefore unable to re-

6 a

act with sufficient speed to the rapid change in the political conditions of work, to the need to wage an open political struggle for confidence. Many Party organizations were pushed into the defensive under the pressure of the exposed deformations of the 'fifties. The wave of elemental criticism and the exposure of past deformations have even shaken certain links of the State and economic apparatus.

Were we not to get this development under control, were we not to give it purposive leadership and a system, it could happen that it might become hardly bearable for the present social and political power structure and that it could lead to a certain conflict.

The past few weeks have also seen the emergence of certain other phenomena we are following with anxiety, since they could hamper the socialist process of regeneration. We drew attention to them already at the plenary meeting in April.

However, since that time the situation has changed insofar that anti-Communist tendencies have intensified and certain elements are trying to go over to more active forms of activity. This danger which today constitutes the main threat to the further development of the process of democratization, has been realized by the decisive part of the Party and is also being realized by ever wider sections of the progressive public.

The activation of right-wing forces leads also to a certain activation of sectarian tendencies which are trying to solve the situation by fundamentally incorrect methods which could also promote the emergence of undesirable tension and conflicts.

Comrades, in what do we see these negative features of development? Firstly in the one-sided onslaught which is constantly developing and intensifying with the aim of discredit-

a 7

ing the Party as a whole. I am referring to the large number of small, sometimes indirect and sometimes also directly and purposively conceived political tendencies and manifestations which in their total represent such a stream of one-sided criticism we had to politically evaluate because, in its consequences, it could have a destructive influence on the Party, it could blunt its action capacity and unity and create an unfavourable atmosphere directed against socialist development.

I am not referring to the justified criticism of various deformations which is being raised by people with honest views. neither to the justified criticism of actual persons, but to efforts to morally discredit the whole Party which objectively tend to create the view that the Party has no right to play a leading role in our society. Even if this is a temporary, one-sided reaction of a certain part of public opinion to certain shortcomings of the past, we cannot ignore the political danger that these tendencies and manifestations could be abused.

If this stream of unobjective criticism were to grow and if it were to remain without our answer,it could lead to a disparagement of the past work of Communists and of all those who honestly ensured postwar reconstruction, socialist revolutionary changes, the establishment of cooperatives, nationalization and eventually also the February events; it could lead to a disparagement of all who contributed to the past achievements of socialist construction.

We must realize that such one-sidedness is in its consequences very harmful.

We have no reason to let ourselves be provoked into changing the political course adopted in January. However, we must not give room to unsocialist or even anti-revolutionary forces. This is why we are focussing the attention of the Party on these questions in time.

8 a

It is extremely important for our course to evaluate the real forces and possibilities of these tendencies.

The socialist Republic has been in existence for only twenty-three years. Among us, there live remnants of the former exploiting classes and their political exponents. Old ideological influences and their bearers still survive. We live in a divided world in which the class struggle has not ceased to exist. These facts do not determine the character of our social development. They do exist however, and we cannot fail to take them into account,especially in the present intense social process.

This is why we must closely follow the political and ideological activation of the remnants of the defeated bourgeois classes, of bankrupt pre-February right-wing politicians and so on.We can see how, here and there, they are trying to create ideological and political preconditions for their activities. Attempts are also being made to create a legal basis for their activities in certain organizations which are now elementally emerging, especially in the K 231, which includes also people rightly sentenced for anti-State activities.

Increased interest is being also displayed by hostile emigré circles. The interest of enemy espionage services in events taking place in Czechoslovakia has been also intensifying recently. Various enemy news agencies are spreading false information, half-truths and conjectures by which they are trying to disrupt mutual relations between the socialist countries, the unity of the Party, and to disorientate Party members and the general public.

It is true that, for the time being, the internal anti-Communist forces are showing restraint. They are even ready to maintain that they support the process of regeneration.In this, they apply the tactics of achieving their aims by degrees. If we consider what a profound contradiction there exists between their aims and the real interests of society, we can rightly say that the extremist, marginal forces cannot of themselves seriously threaten our Party and socialism. The reality of their danger,however,lies in the fact that they are trying to create themselves a basis in an atmosphere of anti-Communism and anti-Sovietism, in supporting various elemental and disintegrating tendencies which would threaten the structure of our society. We must realize that in the present period of the struggle between the two antagonistic class ideologies, anti-Sovietism is the greatest vogue among the various sorts of anti-Communism.

We must naturally differentiate, distinguish between individual tendencies, between disorientation and deliberate intention.At the same time, however, it is necessary to demand consistent observance of valid legal regulations, valid law, and ensure that no propaganda be made and support be given to the activities of organizations which do not have legal authorization. We need as quickly as possible the Act on Assembly in order that the present period of activities of various organizations without a legal basis, without duties towards the State and the principles of the National Front may rapidly end.

Through our policy we must endeavour to overcome the doubts and mistrust of people, endeavour to win over the widest sections of socialist and democratically-minded citizens for joint work and we must not permit sectarianism and a commanding attitude in relations with them. At the same time, however, we shall resolutely and publicly expose all anti-Communist tendencies, politically isolate their bearers and intentions which represent the greatest danger for undisturbed socialist development and the process of socialist regeneration. The measures of the Central Committee which are directed against attacks on the Communist Party are not being taken against but in the interests of furthering the process of democratization. Relying

10 a

on the people the Communists have opened scope for the development of socialist democracy. This is why the Party continues to be the decisive force and the guarantee of this movement.

We shall use the Party's full authority to defend honest and honorable members and officials of the Party, national committees and the State apparatus who are not unfrequently exposed to unjustified an unjust attacks. I should like to say that the Party fully supports honest officials, that we consider it our duty to defend the results of their honest work. This in no way prevents resolute and concrete rectification wherever necessary, wherever the principles and norms of our socialist laws were violated.

All this is a natural and inseparable part of the policy we developed in January.

We consider the main road to combatting right-wing anti-Communist forces to be a positive policy of the Party which will unite all positive, pro-socialist forces of society for creative work in developing our society. The basic course for us is a policy which will be fully supported and recognized as its own by the working people, the working class, co-operative farmers and the intelligentsia. The leadership of the Party is fully aware that without the working class the foundations of socialism cannot be successfully defended in case of an active open stand by anti-Communist right-wing forces. We shall be guided by this in the policy of the Party.

Besides fears of a right-wing danger there are also fears of the conservative forces in the Party, of a return to the state of affairs which existed before January 1968. This danger lies in the surviving stereotype of past thinking, in the persistence of bureaucratic methods and ways.

Although their bearers voice recognition of the correctness of the new policy, they have not yet discarded old think-

a 11

ing and evaluate social development in such a way that they support nervousness and mistrust in the policy of the leadership of the Party and readily give the worst labels to each deviation from the old routine, to each more original socialist initiative. Some of them even develop purposive activities aimed against the policy of the Party. I recall for example the attempts made to distribute slanderous leaflets in the Party as well as among the public, leaflets which demagogically slander the policy of the Party and try to bring about a split between the workers and the Party, between Party members and the leadership as well as within the leadership itself.

Such views and attitudes naturally threaten the action capacity of the Party and could discredit the Party in the eyes of broad sections of the people who are rightly linking their hope for a new Party policy with the elimination of the old sectarian and dogmatic methods of work. It is therefore necessary to take resolute action also against these activities. Any attempt to revive sectarianism, dogmatism and pre-January conditions in general, even in the name of fighting anti-Communism, would greatly damage the Party and its policy and would objectively play into the hands of anti-Communist tendencies.

It is clear, from all I have said, that our present development includes intertwining tendencies of the most varied character. We must therefore have a very well-conceived, bold and prudent policy which must take all these factors into consideration. We cannot give truth to views which do not take into account political facts and the contradictory character of the transitional period, and which one-sidedly absolutize or underestimate the danger of these or those tendencies.

As so frequently happens in politics, both extremes eventually join in their objective effect and prevent progressive devdopment which is and must continue to be our primary concern. We must not and shall not stop half-way.

If I were to sum up the results of the development since the January plenum, I would say that its essential feature is the fact that social progress has entered a new phase. The present polarization of views in the Party and in society reflects the contradictions arising out of the need to cope with this transition. While immediately after January it was necessary to form new bodies, to fight against rigidity, to shape and popularize the new policy, this policy now begins to be tested in practice. If we are to succeed, we must consolidate the process of democratization, define clear aims and methods of their implementation in a way resulting in the development of socialism, in the consolidation and not in the weakening of the positions of socialism. An unconstrained process would give scope for the growth of extremist tendencies, which in their effect are strengthening each other, and would in its consequences lead to clashes which in their consequences could endanger the development of socialism in our country. This would not be only a defeat for the progressive forces of the Party but it would also disappoint the hopes of the forces of the international workers' movement. We have assumed a responsibility from which we cannot retreat. We must therefore draw the necessary conclusions from the new situation.

The offensive political onset of the Party makes it necessary to lay down a clear tactical and political course for the immediate future. From what positions do we proceed?

First of all, we must not waste the confidence given to the policy of the Party after the January plenum by the broad sections of the people. This makes it necessary to consistently unite the healthy forces of the Party for putting into practice the Action Programme, to markedly focus the attention of the Party on the social-political problems of the working class and the broad masses of the people, to activate the policy of the National Front on a consistently socialist basis, and to speed up preparations for the constitutional arrangement and for the extraordinary Party Congress.

It is just by this active course that we must avert the growth of elemental and disintegrating forces.

In other words, we cannot permit the destruction of the existing political power structure before we gradually and deliberately replace it by a new one. We must gradually change it. Not destruction, but a qualitative transformation and development of the socialist system - this is the main thing at present. We must discriminate between the aims we want to achieve and the transition to these aims through which we are now passing and which must proceed gradually, in stages. We must also very accurately define and frankly explain certain necessary conditions which we must at present respect and without which this transition cannot be made.

This does not mean to abandon the final goal. But it would be threatened if we wanted to anticipate developments, if we wanted to achieve premature solutions to problems which cannot, under existing conditions, be solved, if we were to formulate demands people would not understand. We must clearly and convincingly tell the broadest masses for what we stand, for what we are fighting, for what we are striving, and at the same time make it clear to them what we are defending, what we cannot renounce under any circumstances if we want to preserve and augment the positive values which form the basis of socialist society.

Which, then, are the main tasks we must solve?

First of all, we must consistently dissociate ourselves - the Party as a whole - from past deformations. We must dissociate ourselves especially from the crimes of the 'fifties for which responsibility rests with certain groups in the leadership of the Party who slipped out of the control of the Party, placing themselves above the Party and Communists, just as above the society and above the laws of the State, groups of people who relinquished and besmirched the programmatic Communist ideals of the Party and the democratic and socialist ideals of the whole society.

Let us ask ourselves: what prevents Communists from actively pushing through the policy of the Party, from reacting in a really polemical and convincing way to various incorrect and untrue accusations, to views they cannot and do not accept because they are frequently clear manifestations of right-wing or anti-Communist tendencies?

To a certain extent, this is because of unpreparedness, a small ability to get adapted to the conditions of real political fight to win the confidence of the people. Other factors are certainly also shortcomings in the political and organizational activities of the Party. But there is also a deeper cause. It is signalized at Party meetings and conferences, in hundreds of resolutions and letters being sent to the Central Committee. Communists demand that the Party should clearly and consistently dissociate itself from all deformations of the past, that it should part with those who are concretely mainly responsible for these deformations. They demand that the Party gives clear and convincing guarantees that there is no going back to the old, bureaucratic methods of management and even less to the deformations which so tragically affected the 'fifties.

Have we actually given such guarantees? In certain things we undoubtedly have. In the past four months, we have clearly dissociated ourselves in the leadership of the Party from the methods which were typical of the state of affairs before January. But I nevetheless believe that the shortage

a 15

of time, the complexity and contradictory character of the situation under which we are working as well as other circumstances are having the effect that the dividing line between the things which must be justifiably criticized in the practice of the Party, and our sincere effort for a new approach to problems,is not always sufficiently clear to Communists, and to the working people. We have fundamentally changed the composition of the bodies of the Central Committee and its leadership but Communists and non-Party members draw attention to the fact that the supreme Party body still includes certain comrades who have lost the confidence of Communists and of the entire public. This only increases pressure on the Central Committee and serves as a pretext for disparaging its work.

We have adopted the Action Programme in which the new general line of the policy of the Party began to take shape but the necessary tempo was not always maintained in implementing many measures which must and can be taken immediately. In addition, it appears as if we had in this connection forgotten the rudiments of propaganda: we are even largely unable to convey and explain things we have already done. This applies to all links of Party management and media of influencing.Important steps of the Central Committee, the National Assembly, the Government and other institutions remain sometimes unnoticed and the mood of public opinion is frequently determined by highly doubtful sensations which are not dictated by a responsible political approach to the interests and needs of society but rather by efforts to be original at any price. Members of the Party as well as the public then ask themselves why there is no harmony in this respect.

For instance, we adopted a clear attitude in the Action Programme on the abolition of censorship. However, the adoption of the respective legal measures is proceeding slowly. The same applies to preparations for the law on assembly and so. This is giving rise to an atmopshere which makes it possible, by

16 a

the establishment of "clubs in defence of freedom of the press", to create doubts as if the Party were changing its attitude, and the public is thus being disorientated. We believe that such initiative is unjustified.

How can the Party dissociate itself from the faults of the past? How can all people be given guarantees that the way from today's state of affairs leads neither to conditions existing before January nor to those from before February 1948 and even less to those before 1938 but that the road leads only ahead, to a higher stage of socialist development? How can we positively develop the policy on which we decided at the January plenum and by adopting the Action Programme?

The most important task is to adapt the Party so that it may as a whole stand at the head of social development, to be able to fulfil its leading role under the new conditions.

The consistent regeneration of the Party makes it necessary especially in view of certain new circumstances, to speedily convene the extraordinary 14th Party Congress. Without this, no definite guarantee can be created within the Party for the consistent implementation of the new policy. We therefore propose to convene the Party Congress for September 9th, 1968.

We are convinced that the Congress will reaffirm the course which was adopted in January and that it will create the pre-requisites for developing it into a new political line. It is necessary to evaluate the political development since the 13th Party Congress and after the January meeting of the Central Committee of the Communist Party of Czechoslovakia and to lay down the political and tactical course of the Party for the immediate future. We must unite the Party for consistently implementing our policy of further socialist development of the society whose starting-point is the Action Programme and whose basic line must be discussed and approved by the 14th

a 17

extraordinary Congress. In view of urgent demands to speed up the realization of the new constitutional arrangement, the Congress must approve the principles of the Party course in solving this question, and work out the principles of the Party structure under the conditions of a federative arrangement of the State. Another task facing the Congress will be the adoption of new Party Statutes and the election of a new Central Committee which, with full authority, will improve and defend the unity and action capacity of the Party and stand at the head of a uniform and organized course of the Party in implementing the Congress decisions.

The tasks should be relfected in the following programme of the Congress:

1. Report on the activity of the Party and the development of society since the 13th Congress of the Communist Party of Czechoslovakia and the principal tasks of the Party in the immediate future.
2. Report of the Central Control and Auditing Commission.
3. Draft of the political directives for the constitutional arrangement of the Czechoslovak Socialist Republic, for the structure of State bodies and the Party structure under conditions of the federative arrangement of the State.
4. Draft of the new Statutes of the Communist Party of Czechoslovakia.
5. Election of the Central Committee of the Communist Party of Czechoslovakia and of the Central Control and Auditing Commission.

Membership meetings for the election of delegates, as well as district and regional conferences, should be held in the period from June to August. The Presidium of the Central Committee will submit the respective proposals at the next meeting.

18 a

Why did we decide to speed up the convocation of the Congress? Our earlier considerations concerning the date for convening the extraordinary Congress were based upon the need - - on which we placed great emphasis - that we should have as much time as possible for a really good and all-round elaboration of these questions. We also intended to prepare an economic-political directive for the Congress. In view of new circumstances we agreed in the Presidium to drop this idea. We made the fixing of the date of the Congress dependent on the level of the elaboration of the Congress materials. According to preliminary information, it is possible to prepare the materials intended for the Congress within a short time although we shall not have the originally anticipated time for intra-Party and public discussion.

The regional conferences came to the conclusion that the Congress should not solve only measures concerning cadres but also concrete issues appertaining to the Congress. The regional conferences also demanded that the Congress should be held as soon as possible. They substantiated this standpoint especially by the demand that the comrades who have lost confidence should leave the Central Committee without any delay. Clear standpoints were voiced especially with regard to comrade Novotný.

In deciding about the Congress, the Presidium of the Central Committee also took into consideration the fact that the past few weeks were characterized by a considerable acceleration of political movement introducing qualitatively new elements. Demands for convening the extraordinary Congress as soon as possible not only continue but are growing stronger. The tasks facing the Central Committee are constantly increasing. It is necessary to make decisions on vitally important questions concerning the future of our country. It is necessary to take concrete measures to strengthen the unity of the

Party, to unify its active forces, to strengthen its unity in action. However, in contrast to these tasks the authority of the Central Committee is ever more declining and consequently this also applies to its ability to solve these questions with authority, to lead the Party in this complicated situation.The election of a new Central Committee is therefore the natural and democratic method, corresponding to the Statutes of the Party, for solving these questions.

The conference of chairmen of basic organizations, who in addition to this informed the Central Committee of certain negative tendencies in the development of Party work, has shown that a situation is arising in which the question of speeding up the holding of the Party Congress has become extremely urgent. These voices and all circumstances must be taken into consideration. There are also other questions which are pressing for time. This applies, in particular, to the constitutional arrangement which cannot be implemented without discussing its principles at the Congress.

As can be seen from the whole preceding analysis, the fundamental question which has to be resolved is to strengthen the authority and the influence of the Party in society. Without solving this question, it would be illusory to believe that there will be no further growth of the pressure of extremist tendencies which could lead to attacks on the socialist power in our country. We therefore arrived at the conclusion that without an extraordinary Congress the Party today will not unite quickly enough and be able to fulfil its tasks.This is why even such an extraordinary measure as we propose - to prepare the Congress within three summer months - is a question of fundamental importance for the development of the whole internal political situation.

It must be also taken into account that autumn will see the beginning of a new wave of social activity.

The Congress could be prepared to greater advantage and more thoroughly according to the originally planned time-table but the complex of new circumstances, which we must take into account, forces us even at the cost of reducing the time available for holding pre-Congress membership meetings, district and regional conferences, to convene the Congress at a much earlier date. We therefore propose to the Central Committee that the Congress be held as early as September. Its preparation and proceedings could become instrumental in unifying the Party on the basis of a new policy, in stimulating an offensive onset of Communists.

Preparations of the elections of the Central Committee and of the Central Control and Auditing Commission as regards cadres will make it necessary to consistently democratize the method of selecting delegates for the conferences and new members of the Central Committee in order that it may express the social composition of the Party and enable the choice of the most able representatives of the Party, who enjoy high authority and full confidence among Party members and non-Party people. Despite the shortage of time we shall organize preparations for the Congress so as to enable the participation in it of the whole Party and, as regards problems concerning the society as a whole, the participation of the general public.

An especially important role and consequently also responsibility in preparing the Congress falls to Communists in the press, radio and television which, in modern times, are becoming a very important instrument of exerting political influence. The Central Committee seriously reckons with the work of Communists in this sphere and invites them to responsible work also in the preparations for the 14th extraordinary Party Congress. They should pay special attention to organizational work which is partly suppressed in the entire Party and which should be more strongly supported by these media as well. Communists from these places of work should prudently respond to certain critical comments which are being made at present in connection with their work and should purposefully contribute towards strengthening the self-confidence, certainty and action unity of Party members, Party bodies and organizations contribute towards the growth of strength and confidence in the further successes of the Party.

The Presidium of the Central Committee realizes that the preparation of the Congress within such a short period will place extraordinary demands on the whole Party, on all Party organizations, on district and regional committees, as well as on Communists active in the theoretical sphere who will take part in preparations for the Congress. It therefore expresses the conviction that, aware of the importance of the mission of the Congress, they will devote such care to its preparation as will enable its successful work and the attainment of the desired results.

The preparation of the Congress, which will become the central point in the present life of the Party, will enable us to solve a whole chain of tasks facing us today in the field of Party work. This applies especially to the consolidation of the unity of the Party on the basis of the Action Programme. A uniform voice and united deeds which we now need so urgently have nothing in common with what we condemned in January and in April.

I want to emphasize that for the future we are not at all concerned with false "unity" which is blind obedience in executing directives from "above". We expect there will be clashes of views and efforts to find the best solution. However, the seriousness of the situation and the principles of Party structure make it necessary that after the adoption of decisions and conclusions Party members should unite their efforts to secure their implementation. The role of the Party in society

22 a

makes it necessary for us to unite on the basic principles of the tactical course of the Party and to uniformly apply them in keeping with democratic centralism.

Organizational Party work must be based on the Action Programme. All regional and district committees and committees of basic organizations must elaborate it within the scope of their activities into their own programme of political work and must set themselves concrete political aims for which they will enlist the support of the people and with whom they will jointly strive for its realization.

When we emphasize the political-organizational work of the Party, we have in mind especially the forming of close ties between Communists and non-Communists in order that the whole Party, all Communists, workers, farmers, the intelligentsia, in brief, the absolute majority of the working people may participate in shaping the policy of the Party and in its being put into practice. Our policy will be successful only if it expresses the interests of the people as far as possible, if it is intelligible to them, in brief, if it is their policy.

This makes it urgently necessary to extend and intensify our policy in the outward direction. In this sense we must return in methods and forms of Party work to the period of before February 1948. If our political work is to fulfil a purpose, if our discussions are to fulfil a purpose, we must go out from the secretariats, conferences and Party meetings, out among the working people, to factories and villages, to the press, radio and television. We must over and again publicly explain for what we stand, what is our programme, what are our aims, how they can be achieved and what obstacles stand in the way, what we shall oppose. Under the new conditions, a great deal depends upon the assertion of the leading role of the Party, upon the work of Communists in social and other non-Party bodies and organizations.

a 23

It is from these points of view that we must develop and also "regenerate" a well-conceived ideological education and in a certain sense also a re-education of Party members. Ideological work must be at present stimulating, it must be part of the vigorous struggle for the Party policy.

Preparations for the Congress will also be an opportunity for admitting new Party members. We can say that the influx into the Party has even in this complicated period a rising tendency. The Party has in the post-January period gained great capital among young people who are not indifferent to the future of the Republic and of socialism. This must be taken into account and young people must be given every care on the part of the Party. In admitting new members to the Party, it is necessary to concentrate especially on young people to whom the present Party policy is opening the road.

In order to improve the work of the Party and in the interest of a thorough preparation of the Congress it is necessary to reorganize the forces of the apparatus in keeping with the needs of the present policy. The apparatus of the Central Committee and other Party bodies must be much more closely linked with the work of the members, especially through various commissions, including temporary commissions, in which Communists from the various spheres will take part in managing Party work in these spheres. We say quite unequivocally that indiscriminate attacks on the Party apparatus do not pursue honest aims. We reject them and will counter them. The Party cannot do without good work of the apparatus. In intensifying its work, we shall place emphasis on making the apparatus serve Communists and Party bodies effectively in the implementation of the policy of the Party.

I should like to say once more quite clearly; the purpose of our work - and this must be a distinct feature of the pre-Congress period - is to strengthen the political management of society by the Communist Party. This includes the rejection of all attempts to discredit the Party as a whole, attempts to create mistrust in the Party and to deny it the moral and political right to lead our society.

The Party has been leading our society since February 1948 as the leading political force. It therefore assumes responsibility for the successes in socialist construction as well as for shortcomings. It has self-critically drawn attention to past mistakes and is resolutely ridding itself of them.

However, in the interest of truth we must emphasize that responsibility for the deformations is not borne by the Party as a whole. Rank-and-file members and functionaries did not know about the reprisals of the 'fifties. Direct responsibility for them rests with concrete culprits of the Security Force, as well as in judicial, State and Party bodies. Some Communists in this period became victims of the deformations. Most Communists have gradually and increasingly realized their harmful character and have taken up the risk of fighting against them. The Communists were the initiators of the current regeneration of socialism. This gives them the moral and the political right to strive for the leading role in the further development of socialism in this country.

Denial of these facts and efforts to discredit the Party as a whole are considered by the Party as concrete anti-Communist, anti-socialist and essentially anti-popular tendencies. In very many cases the Party has already carried out consistent rehabilitation and continues to rehabilitate all Communists and non-Communists who were in the past unlawfully affected. The Party is determined to purge itself of those who are responsible for past deformations. We resolutely declare that we reject an atmosphere of hysteria, as well as the creation of indiscriminate distrust in Party, judicial, security and State officials. We say quite frankly - and this is also con-

a 25

tained in the Government statement - that the revolutionary measures which affected the bourgeois class, regardless of whether they were economic or political and state power measures after February 1948, will not be the object of any revision.

The Communist Party of Czechoslovakia is today the only political force in this country with a scientific socialist programme. It is the main guarantee of good relations between the Czechoslovak Socialist Republic and other socialist countries and consequently also the guarantee of a stable international position of our Republic. It is the unifying force of both our nations - Czechs and Slovaks. It associates hundreds of thousand of workers, land workers and brainworkers, who enjoy respect and esteem among their fellow-workers. Its ranks include the overwhelming majority of the best creative forces of society - scientists, technicians and artists. Its members are people who have earned their authority by their fight against capitalism and Nazi occupation, people who were the initiators and organizers of the present process of regeneration of socialism and of the development of socialist democracy. Its cadres form the predominant part of the administrative and managerial structure of our society. All this creates an historical reality, a situation under which there is no other way ahead for really democratic and socialist development without undesirable upheavals and without unleashing a struggle for power, than the road along which the Communist Party of Czechoslovakia as the strongest organized political force in this country will lead the further process of development. It will naturally lead this process along the new roads and methods outlined in the Action Programme of the Party and which will be discussed as a new Party line by the extraordinary 14th Congress.

We should like to emphasize that we highly esteem the self-sacrificing and meritorious work of the old Communist guard

26

a

We want to continue along its revolutionary tradition of self-sacrificing, devoted and selfless service to the Party and the people which we regard as the revolutionary heritage of the Communist Party of Czechoslovakia. It is just these Communists, used to varied and manysided political work, who legitimately and sharply condemned the incorrect pre-January methods of Party work.

Just at this time, when unity of the Party is required as the basic guarantee of our new policy, we regard sporadic views wanting to "revise" the historical step of the unification of the two Marxist workers' parties as very harmful. The Party will resolutely counter them.

Another important factor in implementing the Action Programme is the policy in the sphere of the reconstruction of the socialist state and within it the first place is taken by the problem of constitutional arrangement. We have decided to draw all consequences from the slogan of self-assertion of nations and to go over to ensuring a full equality of Czechs and Slovaks, while guaranteeing adequate rights to nationality groups. The symmetric constitutional arrangement will enable the national missions and peculiarities of the Czech and Slovak nations to assert themselves more fully and at the same time will create a firmer basis for their mutual cooperation. Not only the Slovak, but also the Czech nation will be able in the future to better appreciate its peculiarities and conditions, formulate more precisely its national tasks and its place among the nations of Europe and the world. In the federative model of the Czechoslovak state the autonomous Czech and Slovak bodies are asserting themselves not only in the organism of the State, but also in mass organizations.

This gives rise to very important tasks. Some of which are being solved already, while the solving of others is just beginning. In the spirit of the Action Programme and the Go-

a

vernment Statement and at the initiative of the Presidium of the Central Committee of the Communist Party of Czechoslovakia, a committee for preparing the federalization of the Czechoslovak Socialist Republic and a government commission of specialists for preparing the bill on federation have been set up. The work on drafting the principles of the federalization law is being organized so as to get it ready for submission to the National Assembly on the 50th anniversary of the foundation of the Republic. This constitutional law must outline the structure of the new Czech, Slovak and all-State representative bodies. It would then be followed by the reconstruction of State bodies and the preparation of elections.

Federalization creates a wide scope for the self-assertion of each of our nations. At the same time, however, it will be the task of the centre and the national bodies to see that the importance of the economy as an integrating factor and binding agent of Czechoslovak mutuality and united statehood be respected in the federation. The Federal Government must have instruments in its hands with which it will assert its role in the development of the Czechoslovak national economy.

We have submitted a proposal recommending that the Government, in cooperation with the National Assembly, sets up a representative commission for the preparation of Czech national bodies. The task of this commission will be to express the Czech national interests in the process of solving these problems in relation with all-State bodies, to act as a partner of the Slovak national bodies and to help make it understood among the public in the Czech lands that the federative regulation is in keeping with both the Czech and Slovak national interests.

The federative regulation of the State demands corresponding changes in the structure of the bodies of the CPCz. This is why we consider it necessary to set up a commission composed of representatives of regional Party organizations from the Czech lands. The task of the commission will be to cooperate in drafting the principles on the organizational construction of the CPCz under conditions of the federation, so as to create pre-conditions for the fulfillment of the tasks which face the Party in the Czech lands, while ensuring the international unity of the Party.

For the time being there is not enough material to enable us to take a stand on the solution envisaged. However, we must realize that the CPCz will have to play the important role of an integrating force in the new federal regulation. We shall have to take care that in solving questions previously neglected the principles of socialist internationalism and objective integration tendencies be fully respected. The draft proposals will be submitted to the Party Congress for decision.

Now only briefly about the other questions. After January we finished in the Party with substituting the activity of the State and of economic bodies. This is why the political responsibility of communists working in these bodies is sharply rising; it is necessary that they contribute with their initiative to the fast, practical implementation of the objectives advanced by the Action Programme, that they help us perceptibly to move ahead with solving mainly those problems on which the attention of the public is being centred. In this sense it is really so that today the Party, the Communists, must literally daily achieve in the centre and in individual posts successes even though only in minor things, which will prove the consistency in implementing the Action Programme.

The new stage of development requires a speeding up on a new base of the consolidation of the State apparatus, certain elements of which have slackened their activity in the past few weeks. Special attention must be devoted to national committees to prevent the postponement of the elections from leading to a passive wait-and-see attitude. The result of the elections is now already being decided.

The plan of legislative work for ensuring a speedy approval of laws which embody the results of the democratization process and give it a firm order, strengthening the authority of law, is ready.

We consider of exceptional importance the consolidation of the bodies of defence and the defence of our socialist state.

The deformations of the past period affected also the Army. This is why not only the analysis of the mistakes and shortcomings has been started, but fundamental measures have been made in the Command of the Army, so as to attain a qualitatively higher combat efficiency of the armed forces.

There has been much talk recently about the People's Militia. We have said many times before and repeat it again that the People's Militia has an undeniable place in our society, in the system of the armed forces. With the whole authority of the Party we shall oppose attacks against its existence, in which we see one of the guarantees of the socialist character of our society.

In the spirit of the Action Programme we shall support the strengthening of the bodies of the security apparatus. The Central Committee is proceeding from the fact that it is necessary to emphatically dissociate from all that in the past led to profound aberrations, and to ensure full political and legal guarantees of legality.

The point is to ensure that the process now started might continue successfully, that the principles of the Action Programme should be realized also in this sphere. A consistent reconstruction of these bodies and their purging of all persons responsible for the aberrations is a condition for their effective activity.

30 a

Every state, just as ours, needs an effective organism for the defence of its interests against forces violating it. This is why we cannot agree with a general abuse of the Security Force, the Army, the Justice, and their workers, who loyal to their country are truly guarding its interests.

The criticism of the shortcomings in the sphere of prosecution and justice was also justified. On the other hand, however, there have been all sorts of incorrect generalizations which could provoke mistrust in the valid law order. This is why it is necessary to lend support to political, cadre and legislative measures which will give guarantees that the mistakes of the past years be not repeated in this sphere. This also enables tendencies undermining the confidence of these bodies to be opposed.

Another fundamental demand conditioning the successful development of the socialist regeneration process is that it must help an all- round development of the life of our society. It cannot lead to anarchy, exposing the national property to risks, but must help such organization and specialized management of the national economy which would enable the solving of problems preventing an economic growth and the rise of the living standard. The close links between the democratization process in the political sphere with economic life in our country is evident. From the problem, when the political sphere was tying the economic dynamics we are going over to the necessity of thinking out how to correctly direct the emerging initiative in the political sphere into positive results in the sphere of economy.

I think it is necessary to underline the principle that no lasting progress of society can be achieved without a decisive progress in economy. Otherwise it is not possible to make use of the advantages of socialist democracy for a real development of the personality, for a self-assertion of people and for such human development that would be a humane challenge for real competition in social progress ensuring the people a full and happy life.

I am pointing this out lest we should lose sight of certain strategic aspects and economic perspectives now that we are exposed to a great pressure of economic problems. At the same time, however, we must be sober realists and must not fail to see the present economic situation as it really is, and in keeping with the problems and needs this implies to develop our efforts.

This year, too, the economic situation is characterized by the continuance of controversial tendencies. On the one hand, there is a fast growth in industrial, agricultural and building production. It may be presumed that even this year we shall achieve a relatively high increment of the national income. On the other hand certain negative tendencies continue to arise and make themselves felt in our economy, which deprecate the positive production results, due to shortcomings in the composition of the supply of products, quality, technical and economic standard of production, piling stocks of unsalable goods or ineffective exports reflected negatively in the balance of payments.

The result is the growth of inflationary pressure and worsening of the economic imbalance.

We are aware of the conflicting character of this economic trend started in the past years, and we do not want to consider separate tendencies and draw exaggerated conclusions, whether pessimistic or optimistic. In any case it is necessary to develop the economic reform in a thorough, well premeditated way so that it might increase the economic pressure on the rational activity of enterprises and all economic subjects. I have in mind the urgent task of systematically strengthening

32

the forming economic policy which would lead to a reliable economic consolidation.

Since we do not retreat from the basic sense of the socialist revolution, we are obliged to oppose that the negative consequences of these necessary measures should fall on the shoulders of the workers and the working people as a whole, and we must ensure that the working people too should have an opportunity of participating in solving these questions, so as to find a way which would not damage the worker and the working people and at the same time would ensure the necessary effectiveness of the whole national economy.

I should like to stress that great reserves still exist in our national economy which provide conditions for achieving a fast economic consolidation. When this will be done depends upon the people, upon those who control the economy, and upon all the working people. In this respect we must create all conditions necessary in the sphere of political leadership.

Permit me now to say a few words on the work of the press, radio and television. On different occasions we have appraised their exceptional merit in clarifying the present happenings and the development of socialist democracy.

We have also said that we continue to count with their work in shaping and implementing the policy, and that we expect from them assistance in pushing through the basic tencencies of our development while respecting the present state of public opinion. We also expect that they will not speed up the rate in an uncontrolled way, and table now problems without considering the order of urgency, which might lead to disorganization in solving the tasks of the democratization process.

However, it is also necessary to give thought as to why the work of the press, radio and television provoked such sharp criticism at the Party working session and in our society over the past one-and-a-half months, Party members and other workers could, in many cases, not find a reply to the question why there is not sufficient harmony between the standpoint of the Central Committee and the work of mass communication media, which of late have presented exceedingly one-sided views.

I think that some of the journalists did not see the objective consequences of their influence upon the society. The one-sided underlining of mistakes and shortcomings influenced public opinion to the effect that there arose a feeling of uncertainty and mistrust among part of the people towards our policy. Public opinion was often being more influenced by drawing attention to the problems of the 'fifties than to helping solve the tasks of the Action Programme, to positively overcoming mistakes of the past. A feeling of dissatisfaction was also provoked by the fact that the Party press and also Communists in television, the radio and in journalism are unable to react quickly to covert and overt anti-socialist attacks, which are aimed at the Party from the outside.

If communist and socialist-minded journalists want to support the regeneration of socialist democracy, they must take into consideration the real political situation which changes quickly, and the objective influence of their activity. They cannot proceed only from their subjective wishes. Unconsidered, even though well-meant appearances harm it objectively and play into the hands of both rightist opposition elements and dogmatic forces.

At present, mainly proceeding from the Action Programme, we believe that the main task of communication media is their positive work, their creative and organizational role, which not only will not disrupt the consolidation process, but will help to strengthen it, will create an atmosphere of political confidence and provide concrete critical analyses of the obstacles impeding the realization of a positive policy.

In this sense it is necessary to give the means of communication all round assistance and draw conclusions also for ourselves in learning to count more with the possibilities of these means, with their importance for increasing the effectiveness of the Party policy.

We shall continue to call working meetings of communist journalists so that also communists in this sphere might participate in the creation and realization of Party policy.

I think that the demand for an active share in the implementation of the new and creative policy of the Party is a worthy demand and is fully in keeping with the mission of our journalists and publicists.

The Party has the right to ask of communist journalists to develop and defend the basic values of socialism.

In the foreign political sphere we expect that the mass information media will not affect negatively Czechoslovak State interests, that the editorial staff will see that there is no interference in the affairs of other socialist countries, and that they will react with consideration and in a matter-of-fact way to eventual expressions of anxiety or critisism of our development on the part of other countries.

The legislation prepared embodies freedom of speech, abolition of preliminary censorship. This, however, cannot be confused with the right to express subjective views before millions of spectators, listeners or readers, without sufficiently considering their social influence.

The government is responsible for State information media -- ČTK , the radio and television.

The Presidium of the Central Committee has devoted considerable attention to this sphere, because the influence of the press, radio and television assumes really great importance in the political development. In the Presidium we dealt in detail the work of the Rudé Pravo in the presence of the paper´s editorial functionaries. We stressed that the Rudé Právo is the organ of the Central Committee and discussed the programme of measures to increase the effectiveness of its work. We approved that as soon as possible a Party political weekly should be issued to be devoted to analyses and commentaries of political development. We want to make of Nová Mysl a theoretical Marxist journal which would provide a platform for dialogue and polemics of Marxism with other indeological streams.

In other press too we must strive for increased responsibility and authority of the publisher and editors. We shall rely on communists in editorial offices and on the work of the National Front, whose components should exert influence on its press bodies in the spirit of its policy.

It seems that of late, during the past few days, sensations and one-sided negativism is dying down. A more serious tone begins to prevail. These are the first signs that communists in these places of work are aware of the critical notes which are being addressed to them by Party members and other working people.

We have rejected the conception which degraded journalists to passive interpreters of the policy of the Party. We believe that the Party press should mediate an exchange of suggestions between the leadership and Party members, between the Party and society. However another extreme would be if individual communists in newspapers considered themselves as autonomous makers of Party policy. Even in this respect it is necessary to advance the Leninist principles of broad joint creation of the Party policy, but also of action unity in implementing the adopted resolutions. On our part this presumes a more regular, more frequent and consistent cooperation with this group of communists.

The process of the development of socialist democracy in our country continues to be the subject of increased interest in the world. It is the centre of attention especially of communist and workers' parties.

We, of course, are in the first place interested in the attitude taken by the fraternal parties of socialist countries. It is a fact that their representatives, whom we met, express support and understanding for our party, support for the Party Central Committee, in its effort to build an advanced socialist society, but in these talks and sometimes in public they do not conceal their anxiety over certain anti-socialist, anti-communist and anti-Soviet tendencies which have emerged in the course of the regeneration process.

The countering of anti-communist expressions, of undermining our alliance and good relations with the Soviet Union and the socialist countries, of attacks on the international aspects of the policy of our Party, form an inseparable part of our policy, together with the combatting of past aberrations.

If we want to strengthen our friendly relations and prevent various misunderstandings, it is necessary to make it quite clear that we are not pressenting our policy as a model and an example to others, that we shall not judge the policy of other socialist countries according to our needs and that we cannot award good or bad marks. We have reserved the right to arrange our internal affairs according to our conditions and traditions. We do not deny this right to others and neither do we interfer by publishing various aspects concerning the internal affairs of other socialist countries.

We must on no account play into the hands of bourgeois propaganda, directed to splitting the unity of socialist countries and creating an atmosphere of mistrust by spreading not only distorted interpretations of certain different views, but even explicitly provocative reports, for example, about prepared military intervention by the socialist states against Czechoslovakia, or by grossly distorted statements of our leading comrades, by quoting these statements out of context and so on. I do not know what good purpose is served by our news service taking over slanderous reports and information of bourgeois propaganda and giving them publicity without comment.

It is necessary to reassure our public that all meetings with representatives of the Communist Party of the Soviet Union and the government of the Soviet Union have been proceeding and continue to proceed on principles of equality and non-interference in internal affairs. As internationalists we are in the first place fully aware of our own repponsibility for the development of the situation in this country, for the work of the Communist Party of Czechoslovakia in guiding the socialist development. I should like to repeat that the Soviet comrades are showing great readiness to help us solve our economic difficulties.

I can assure you of relations of full mutual confidence between the Presidium of the Central Committee of the Communist Party of the Soviet Union and the Presidium of the CPCz Central Committee, the Natioal Assembly and the Government of the Republic.

We must still more often and in more detail inform the fraternal parties of our development, meet them and seek ways for further concrete cooperation. We do not think that we are and will be able to reach an ideal and complete unity in all questions of the development in the individual socialist countries, because while respecting international experiences and interests it is necessary to see also the peculiarities and specific conditions under which the different communist parties work. Certain differences objectively exist and will continue to exist between us and other socialist countries, in the political practice of building a socialist society, especially as we shall proceed from

38 a

certain peculiarities which are characteristic for this or that country and the work of the communist parties in them.

We are convinced, however, that our cooperation with the fraternal Communist Party of the Soviet Union and the socialist countries will proceed on principles of mutual understanding and mutual asistance.

We are doing everything to promote cooperation with countries with which we are linked by bonds of alliance and common interests of the defence and socialist progress. In June joint staff exercises of the Warsaw Treaty armies will be held in Czechoslovakia as previously agreed.

The policy of our Party is and will remain international, as it corresponds to the basic principles of a Marxist-Leninist party, the most vital even fateful interests of both our nations. Defending the friendship and alliance with the Soviet Union and other socialist countries is not only a matter of communists, but of all citizens of this country who have not forgotten Munich, who do not lightheartedly want to endanger the basic condition of the existence of our country, its inviolability and independence. As we know the value of our friendly relations and bonds of alliance with the Soviet Union and other socialist countries, we would like our allies also to see that we repay like with like, that also our relations to them are of a lasting character.

The alliance with the socialist countries, our allegiance to the Warsaw Treaty does not prevent an active and flexible development of cooperation and relations with all other countries in keeping with our political, economic and cultural interests. In this lies the basic element of our active foreign policy, which we want to pursue seriously and responsibly.

In the first place this means to add to a gradual creation of a system of European collective security. The cardinal question is the German issue. For us and for the whole ef Europe it is a matter of historical importance that in one part of Germany, the German Democratic Republic, there exists today a socialist state, built on the principles of friendship and peaceful coexistence with the other European countries, a state which recognizes the realities of the outcome of the Second World War and which has our full support.

We also favour good neighbourly and friendly relations with the German Federal Republic. If, however, there exist causes for concern, provoked not only by the growth of neo-Nazi forces, but also by the fact that the German Federal Republic has still not decided to recognize the existing frontiers in Europe, to recognize the German Democratic Republic and the invalidity of the Munich agreement from the very beginning, then it is these very facts that stand in the way of normalizing mutual relations.

The international attitude of our Party expresses also the share in the preparations of the international meeting of communist and workers' parties to be convened in Moscow on November 25, 1968.

In this connection I should like to stress appreciation of the fact that the participating countries have reached unity on basic issues. This naturally does not solve everything. Much effort many consultations and discussions will be necessary if the meeting is to bring the expected result.

Our party considers two things as decisive. First: a political document should be worked out, and concrete measures adopted which would lead to a real activation of the international communist movement in the combatting of imperialism, and the striving for peace, socialism and democracy.

Second: the meeting should contribute to the utmost towards invigorating the action unity of the international communist movement and towards inspiring the development of extensive cooperation with all other anti-imperialist forces in the world.

We fully understand the difficulties involved in this task. However, in the spirit of our international traditions and according to our capacity, we want to contribute to the unity, action capacity and authority of the entire movement.

Comrades, permit me to sum up the main tasks confronting the Party in the nearest future.

1. The development since the plenum in January is in keeping with the needs of the regeneration of socialism. The content of our policy must therefore be a consistent implementation of the Action Programme of the Party. By their initiative and honest work in solving the problems of the society, the communists want to persuade all citizens of the correctness of their course, that they are capable and entitled to lead the society. Therein lies the main content of the struggle against a possible danger of creating an anti-Party and anti-socialist opposition.
2. A condition of the success of our policy is to enhance the authority of the Party and strengthen its leading role. This is not possible without dissociating the Party in all respects from past aberrations of socialism. To strengthen the Party, its unity and action capacity we shall centre on the preparations of an extraordinary, the 14th Congress of the Party, to be held in September 1968, so that the Congress might be an impetus for political activity in the whole country; we shall develop political and organizational activity, work in social organizations, mainly in the trade union movement. We shall resolutely oppose sectariamism and dogmatism. We shall strive to win over for the Party socialistically minded citizens, especially progressive youth.

We consider the strengthening of Party unity as a necessary precondition of its leading role, while observing the principles of intra-Party democracy. We shall insist on the consistent rehabilitation of those un-

a 41

justly affected. We shall not however retreat from the results of socialist revolution, we shall back up all honest members and functionaries of the Party, workers of national committees and state bodies against scandalizing.

3. We see the prime task in creating conditions for an active participation of the working class, which is the leading force of our society, in implementing the present social changes. The Party policy must express the interests and needs of the workers and strive to strengthen their influence on the management of society. Proceeding from the Action Programme, we shall make proposals for setting up workers' bodies in enterprises. With our policy we shall express the interests of farmers, the intelligentsia and primarily of the youth.

4. We shall implement consistently the policy of the National Front. We shall lay stress on its socialist content and help in uniting all honest forces for concerted work - members of all social groups and their social organizations, political parties, all citizens. We exclude the possibility that forces standing in opposition to its socialist programme might organize legally outside the National Front. In the interest of the development of socialist democracy and in the interest of preserving the socialist attainments of our people we shall put up a resolute political challenge to efforts formulating opposition, anticommunist forces in any form.

5. We shall strengthen the socialist legal order as the basis of democratic life. We shall insist that legal amendments ensuring the development of socialist democracy be approved as soon as possible. We shall support the authority of bodies of the socialist state: national committees, the Czechoslovak People's Army,

42

a

the Security Force and Justice. We consider the People's Militia, which arose as a result of the victory over reaction after February 1948, as an important achievement of the working chass and the workers, and we categorically reject attempts to weaken them.

6. The Central Committee asks communists in the press, the radio and television to help concentrate all forces of the society on the positive tasks of the Action Programme and to actively defend and develop the policy of the Party and the National Front and reply to anti-communist and anti-socialist voices.

7. We shall strive to speed up the preparations for the federative regulation of the Republic. Along with changes in the structure of representative and State bodies we shall draft a proposal on the reorganization of the bodies of the Communist Party of Czechoslovakia in the future federative state.

8. We shall defend the interests and needs of our nations, cultivate national traditions, fulfil all international duties and commitments. In the spirit of proletarian internationalism and mutual equality we want to strengthen in every way possible the fraternal links and bonds of alliance with the socialist countries, primarily with the Soviet Union.

When deliberating on the further advance of the Party we realize that it must be essentially based on the working class becoming in practice the main creative economic, social and political force in our country, on its occupying the key position in socialist society. The Party must draw a lesson from the fact that many critical voices and comments of workers were hardly ever heeded in the preceding period.

a 43

It is, therefore, our prime duty to study the real needs and interests of the working class. This is the leading force and the vanguard of society, the most numerous social category. We must approach the needs of the workers with full responsibility and, at the same time reveal the political meaning of the demagogy which is being developed around the concept of working class by various false "friends of the workers and friends of the people", whether they come from left or right.

One of the key problems of the working class policy is the creation of organizational norms for a direct participation of workers in the management of society. I shall speak on the extension of forms of the political influence of the working class on the management of society in connection with the policy of the National Front.

It is very urgent, however, to prepare concrete proposals for the implementation of that part of the Action Programme which suggests formation of collective bodies of democratic administration of enterprises. However, this still calls for discussion, not only among experts, but also in Party and trade union organizations, in works, discussion of workers and other working people.

We assume, being aware of the high standard of our working class in whose memory the activity and the tradition of revolutionary works councils of 1945 to 1948 is still vivid, that this step towards democratization will result in a strengthening of cooperation between the working people and the bodies responsible for management of the enterprise, that the relationship between the workers, economists and technicians will continue to improve, that their initiative will be spurred and the management of enterprises will become more efficient thanks to the support they will find in enterprise councils as elected organs of the working people.

We are of the opinion that this is the real way towards setting many economic, social and political problems inside the works which are very pressing and which the old system was basically unable to tackle. The enterprise itself will remain the property of the society, it will not be owned by the collective of the works. A suitable way must be found to safeguard institutionally the interests of the society and the State in establishing the working people's councils in enterprises.

The establishment of enterprise councils does not exclude, in fact it presupposes, an increased importance of the role played by trade unions as a distinctive form of social activization of workers and of all working people of our socialist society. It may now clearly be observed that already the trade unions are changing into an organization which intends to express, represent, and enforce in an unambiguous way, the real social needs of the working people.

This calls for a political character to be imprinted on the trade unions. If the trade unions are to represent and defend social interests, if they are to be an important political force of socialist democracy, they should once again become an organization which, even if based on direct partial interests of individual groups, must reach the stage of grasping and expressing these needs from the point of view of society as a whole. They should once more become that important political force in the National Front which they were before February, 1948. We, communists, will give all-out support to this political and economic standing of the trade unions in our system.

Thus a new political activity of the workers will spring from, take shape and expand in the trade unions and will spread from here to the political life of our country. This was the tradition of the revolutionary trade unions from 1945 when they represented the main political support of the Party.

The communists in the trade unions will make a point of defending concrete economic and social claims of the working people in works and of ensuring that the trade unions as representatives of an all-society organization of workers and working people express their all-society interests, oppose one-sidedness and narrow-mindedness, send highly qualified people to enterprise councils, and raise the level of political-mindedness of the working people, bring partial interests of individual collectives into harmony with the general interests of the working class and of our socialist society.

This dual role of the trade unions, in representing the interests of the working people against State power and in correctly enforcing partial and society-wide interests of the working people against enterprise management, this, in our opinion, is the new role of the trade unions in the system of socialist democracy. This role will necessarily result in making the trade unions a platform for the forming of a new political-awareness and of a new political activity of the working class without which the progress of our socialist democracy is hard to imagine.

The importance of this new role of the trade unions is emphasized especially in connection with some spontaneous social pressures and one-sided claims. We should stress all the more now the principle of "each person a manager at his place of work." The trade unions are an irreplaceable part of the social mechanism which must help us solve the controversies mainly in the economic field, as well as in the political sphere, too, without any upheavals.

The post-January developments opened new prospects also for cooperative farmers to become a real part of political life, to have a more productive say in the development of socialist society. At the congress of agricultural cooperatives and especially in the Action Programme we expressed our basic conception of agricultural policy. Then we were witnesses to discussions, debates and all sorts of views on the way of organizing farmers and agricultural workers generally. The time is now ripe, in our opinion, to close the discussions and to act: to give definite shape to the proposals and submit them to the agricultural public.

I think that we, communists, who initiated the idea of building up an agricultural organization in the spirit of post-war traditions, should now use the same initiative in helping to set it up as special-interest organization of cooperative farmers. It is going to be an organization with individual membership of cooperative farmers, a union of cooperative farmers opening its ranks also to individual private farmers, an organization that would give expression to the main social interests of people working in socialist agriculture who are not organized in trade unions. The organization would take up all the positive aspects of the farming folk's contribution towards the development of socialist society in the past years. That is to say, and this was also expressed in the standpoint of the Presidium of the Central Committee, not only to defend individual interests of cooperative farmers regarding their wages and so on, but also to represent the cooperative farmers politically in the National Front with all the rights pertaining to their political representation in society, and to take an active part in tackling the problems of the life of our countryside.

Another key point of our march forward is a consistent implementation of the policy of the National Front.

We want to set up such a system of political relations in society, such a political system, in which our Party will share decision-making and power with non-communists, in which the Party will not become directly identical with the monopoly of the State power centre.

At the same time it would be a distortion of facts to state that the Party does not express the interests of society. Its leading position in society is based primarily on the

a 47

fact that it represents the most progressive and perspective social interests. The problem is that the range of interests expressed by the political direction of our State and society should be as broad and concrete as possible. This is the most profound sense of our present efforts at developing the National Front policy which is and should be pivoted on a policy aiming at an intensification of socialist democracy, a democracy providing ample room for active participation of all people in socialist construction. However, it would be a misunderstanding to think that the essence of democracy consists in mechanically transferring the formal democracy of bourgeois parliamentarism into socialist society.

The present process of development is essentially a process of the revival of socialism. To speak only of a process of democratization without this clear-cut socialist content would equal a distortion of the underlying efforts of our Party to develop socialist democracy.

The new face of the socialist democracy we want to form will differ from a formal democracy in at least two respects:

First of all it will have to settle the problem which no bourgeois democracy has so far tackled or even formulated: how the working people themselves, workers and technicians in production and working collectives in other fields, can and should have a say in the management and administration of society. How to make sure that no system of various procedural forms and by-passing can carry out State policy without reference to or even against the interests of workers and working people. It is well known that this is not only possible under formal democracy, but actually made use of by the bourgeoisie as part of their programme.

Socialist democracy cannot develop as a system in which policies are decided by political parties alone. Our

48

a

experience from 1945 to 1948 brings sufficient proof that such a "party" in political life is detrimental to the interests of the working people. Our democracy must therefore provide also for the right of the working people to take a direct share in the power of the State, to have their representatives in elected bodies: through the trade unions, through an organization of farming people, organizations of youth, women's organizations, and the like. The Communist Party is of the opinion that these organizations are equal political pertners in the National Front. We shall defend the idea that even people who are not members of any political party should have a factual opportunity of participating directly in policy-making in a socialist state. The National Front cannot ever be changed into a mere coalition of political parties. The chief political organizations mentioned shou should get an appropriate position in the National Front.

The National Front will certainly clearly define as soon as possible, the programme of its socialist basis, the violation or rejection of which will be incompatible with membership in the National Front.

The Communist Party of Czechoslovakia will submit its proposals suggesting that such a basis be constituted by the acceptance of a socialist, class ownership system of social relations and activity supporting their development. Further conditions are, activity complying with the Constitution of the Czechoslovak Socialist Republic, rejection of activities against the people's interest, of anti-communist, fascist- and similar nature, inciting nationalist or racial controversies; any activity aimed against the foundations of the State and national independence, as expressed by the alliance with the Soviet Union and the socialist countries is impermissible; it is further essential to respect the principle that the Marxist conception of the construction of socialism forms the programme basis of the development of our society and that the leading political position of the Communist Party of Czechoslovakia is a historical fact.

a 49

The common platform should include a declaration that the National Front has endorsed the contents of the Action Programme and of the government statement.

As regards parliamentary elections, they will probably take place in the first half of next year and will refer to bodies extablished under the new constitutional pattern of the State.

All of these problems will be subjects of debate in the National Front so as to reach binding agreements.

The basic difference between bourgeois parliamentarism and socialist democracy is that the relation between political parties, which preserve the basis of the National Front, must be a relation of partnership and cooperation, not one of struggle for redividing power in the State, which is characteristic for a bourgeois political system. This does not mean to eliminate political autonomy, to eliminate controversies and mutual opponency inside the National Front. The clashing of views must be based on a common socialist programme. This programme is guaranteed by the leading role of the Communist Party of Czechoslovakia, as there is no other real programme of the building up of socialism but the Marxist one based upon scientific cognition and the most progressive social interests.

We exclude the possibility that socialist democracy would develop in our country at the present time by forming an opposition political party which would be outside the National Front, as this would result in a revival of a struggle for power. Our Party will oppose such tendencies with all its means as they would, under existing conditions and independently of the wishes of those who advocate such ideas, lead finally to an attempt at undermining the position of the Communist Party of Czechoslovakia in society and ultimately even of the socialist development.

Therefore we are radically opposed to the setting up of any opposition party that would be outside the policy of the National Front. This is the principle we adopted as early as 1945.

In the new conception of the National Front there will be room enough for controversies, clashes of views and for mutual opponency of various forces inside the National Front.

These principles will also be the basis of our standpoint in formulating new laws, especially the electoral law and the law of association and assembly. We shall maintain the principle that the organizations that want to carry on political activities, want a share in the elections and a share in State power, must be organizations of the National Front, and cannot stand in opposition to its programme.

o o o

It is not only communists who want to gain favour with the young people of our Republic. We must do all we can to win them over for our policy. That means to work with the youth and open the gates of the Party to them. With the Action Programme as our foundation we should work out a comprehensive programme for the young generation which would open prospects of their fuller assertion. The care of the Government of the future builders of our socialist Republic is one of the key duties of communist policy in the Government. We should, therefore, consider the ways and means to be used by the State, Government and its policy in order to exercise a greater influence on the youth.

As regards a youth organization, the Central Committee Presidium lends support to all the efforts tending to achieve an agreement and unification of all the various organizations of young people, in accordance with their individual interests, in an organization of the federative type. We favour a unified organization of young people, the unity of youth. This is the agency through which the youth may achieve a greater influence in the National Front, on the policy of our country, in elected bodies. They can win the support of the Government and State authorities in realizing common interests of all the young generation and its individual groupings. An atomization of the movement can only harm the common interests of the youth.

- - - - -

52

a

RESOLUTION ON THE PRESENT SITUATION AND THE FURTHER COURSE OF THE PARTY

After the plenary session in April of the Central Committee of the Communist Party of Czechoslovakia, at which the action programme of the Party was approved, the government programme drawn up, the new government formed, and a new (Party) presidium and secretariat elected, a new stage of the development, initiated by the plenary session of the Party Central Committee in January, has begun, Newly elected Party bodies have started working in regions and districts. The Party Central Committee considers the most important task of this stage to be full exertion of positive effort aimed at fulfilling the Action Programme, to ensure the offensive of the whole Party towards carrying out its unified political line so that the confidence of the people, won over for the Party policy by the plenum in January, is strengthened and further augmented.

We cannot be fully satisfied with the development of our internal political situation since the April plenum, because not all its objectives have been always achieved to the full. Along with certain attempts to support the consolidation process, fears have also been arising within the Party and among the general public as regards the further development of socialist democracy in our country. On the one hand, fears are being voiced that the process of developing socialist democracy might give rise to anarchist tendencies and create scope for endangering the very foundations

a 53

of socialism, for attempted attacks of anti-socialist and downright anti-communist forces. On the other hand, fears are also being expressed lest the development does not get stuck half way, and lest attempts be made to revert to the state existing before January 1968.

The Party Central Committee notes that negative tendencies in our internal political development, justifying the fears of both kinds, actually exist. The Central Committee considers it the main condition of further successful development of socialist democracy in Czechoslovakia for the Party to strengthen its political authority in a determined way, and to win over for the support of its new policy working class, cooperative farmers, youth, intelligentsia and wide strata of the working people, to remain within the actual conditions of the present stage, and not to ourstrip the development which is realistically possible.

The Party considers it of decisive importance in the present stage to shape, strengthen and develop unity of the communists on the basis of the new policy line, as laid down by the Action Programme, and to create all necessary safeguards in the Party leadership for clear-cut and consistent carrying out of this policy. The Party will execute its policy so as to make the broad masses of the working people, especially workers, sure that in Czechoslovakia there will be no return to class, ownership, social and political conditions as they existed before the victory of the working people in February 1948, that the political leadership of the society by the Communist Party will be strengthened by the new methods and will be more effective, based upon mass support of the people. This will above all require the Party to dissociate itself, clearly and in a way comprehensible for the broadest masses of the working people, from the deformations of the past, and to formulate a fundamental stand of the Party on contemporary problems and questions which have recently been the subject of various speculations, that have often been one-sidedly distorted, give rise to apprehension, and spread distrust among the working people in the leadership of the Party and its policy. The Party Central Committee considers it a serious shortcoming that so far, the Party, social and State bodies and organizations, as well as the mass communications media which shape public opinion (press, radio, television) have been making only few and insufficient efforts to make the new policy of the Party known, in an intelligible, positive way, to wide masses of the working people, especially to workers, and that they have been taking little care to make their voice and their views more pronouncedly heard in our whole public and political life. This creates a favourable atmosphere for the spreading of distrust and uncertainty, for the possibility of exacerbating disputes and conflicts which by their consequences would tend to disorganize our life, and might also encourage the hopes of anti-communist forces that they might gain something from the development of the process of socialist democratization.

In the present situation, the Party considers it to be the main issue to ensure that the socialist character of power and social order could not be endangered from either side - neither by rightist, anti-communist tendencies, nor by conservative forces which would welcome a return to pre-January 1968 conditions, which were incapable of ensuring the development of socialism.

The foundation, on which we stand firmly, is the Action Programme of the Party. The political line of the Action Programme must be discussed by the Party Congress, which alone can set up in a democratic way such central bodies which will fully guarantee consistent implementation of the new policy. This alone can repel the attacks against the Party, fostered by doubts as to whether the Party will be able to dissociate itself absolutely from the past mistakes and deformations, by mistrust in the unity of the Party and its leadership. The new form of socialism, to which the Action

a 55

programme shows the way, has not yet been shaped, and necessitates solving not only a number of practical problems, but also a number of theoretical questions concerning the programme. This final objective of the course which has been adopted must be viewed apart from the conditions and possibilities of individual stages of the transition from the past to the ultimate goal. The concrete policy of the Party must at all times proceed from the conditions existing in every stage of this transition, which is a realistic possibility. It is, therefore, harmful for the policy of the Party when some comrades do not realize this necessity, and confuse the final objectives with concrete, practical tasks of the present stage.

To ensure a uniform, politically effective course of the Party in the present political situation, at the time when the Party Congress is being prepared, the Party Central Committee considers it necessary that all communists, at any sector of their social work - in factories and in agriculture, in political work and in journalistic work, in their influencing of public opinion - should uniformly observe the following main principles of the political course of the Party:

1. To ensure political leadership of the society by the Communist Party, and to effectively repel all attempts aimed at discrediting the Party as a whole, attempts to create distrust in the Party and to deny it the moral and political right to lead our society, to be the decisive political force of socialist power.

The Party has led our society since February 1948, and thus claims as its own the achievements of socialist construction, and admits responsibility for the deformations which distorted the socialist ideal. Some communists have themselves been victims of the deformations and crimes of the 1950s, for which quite specific individuals and groups in the Party leadership are responsible. The communists were at the same time initiators of the fight against these deformat-

56 a

ions, and the culmination of the fight into the results of the January plenum of the Party Central Committee and into the Action Programme of the Party gives them full moral and political right to strive for the leadership role in Czechoslovakia during the further development of socialism.

To deny these facts, to try to discredit the Party as a whole and to fight against its being the decisive political force of socialist power - those in the opinion of the Party are the concrete anti-communist and anti-socialist tendencies which exist at present. The Party has already carried out rehabilitaiton in a number of cases, and is at present engaged in consistently rehabilitating all those communists and non-communists who had been unjustly victimized in the past. To raise doubts about this means causing distrust in the Party. The Party is determined to purge itself of those who are responsible for the past deformations, and will see to it that all those found guilty will be punished, without regard to their position. The Party will, however, proceed according to legal and Party norms so that the guilt and responsibility of everyone could be justly determined. The Party is quite resolutely opposed to all attempts to create an atmosphere of hysteria and all-inclusive distrust in Party and state functionaries by means inconsistent with just and legal procedures, and which could be politically beneficial only to anti-communist forces and their designs. The revolutionary measures which affected the bourgeois class after February 1948 - regardless of whether they were political, economic or state power measures - will not be the subject of any "revision".

The Party Central Committe proceeds from the fact that consistent regeneration of the Party needs convening an extraordinary 14th Party Congress at the beginning of September 1968, because without this,all guarantees of consistent implementation of the new policy could not be provided. The Party Congress will:

a

a) discuss the development after the 13th Party Congress, and especially after the January plenum of the Communist Party Central Committee, assess the main tendencies in the development of society and the Party; on this basis, it will lay down the political line of the Party for the next period, including the political line of the Party for the solution of the constitutional (federative) structure of Czechoslovakia, and will lay down the political line of the Party for the development of the whole political system (especially the structure of representative bodies as organs of state power, and elections to these bodies),

b) discuss the results which will have been achieved as regards the rehabilitation of unjustly victimized comrades, and the responsibility of the old political leadership for the unlawful acts;

c) adopt new statutes of the Communist Party of Czechoslovakia, which will express in detail the principles of intra-Party democracy and methods of Party work;

d) elect a new Central Committee of the Communist Party, and new central inspection and auditing commission.

The Party Central Committee considers it necessary to ensure the preparation of the agenda of the extraordinary 14th Party Congress very speedily and at the same time in a responsible way. All this work, and the process of electing delegates to the Congress, should be organized so that the extraordinary 14th Party Congress could be held at the beginning of September, and that the outset of the development of political activity in the autumn (congresses and conferences of all National Front organizations, legislation on federalization, celebrations of the 50th anniversary of the birth of the Republic) could begin by an offensive of the Communist Party as the leading political force in the country.

At the beginning of 1969, the new constitutional relations in federalized Czechoslovakia would be expressed by a

58 a

constitutional law, the structure of representative bodies would be adopted, and a new election law passed, according to which elections to the representative bodies of the State, on all levels, would be held.

The Party Central Committee considers the views, sporadically cropping up, that the Party should dissociate itself from the past shortcomings and create final, firm guarantees for the new policy in another way than by convening speedily the extraordinary 14th Party Congress, to be wrong. This applies especially to those infrequent views which in essence call for a split of the Party, and for the establishment of some other Marxist workers party - regardless as to whether they are based on instigations of certain individuals describing themselves as "progressive communists", or, to the contrary, whether they are being instigated by those social democrats who want to "revise" the historic step of 1948, when the two Marxist workers' parties merged. These views are considered by the Party Central Committee, at a time when the unity of the Party is of prime importance as a fundamental safeguard of the new policy, as attempts whose political character is, in the last analysis, downright anti-communist.

The Communist Party of Czechoslovakia is the only political force in this country which has a scientific, socialist programme. It is the main guarantee of good relations between Czechoslovakia and the other socialist states, and thus also the guarantee of a stable international position of our Republic. It is a unifying force of both our nations - Czechs and Slovaks. It associates hundreds of thousands of workers, farmers and members of professions who enjoy the personal respect and esteem of people in their proximity; within the ranks of the Party the overwhelming majority is comprised of the best creative forces of our society - scientists, technicians, artists. There are also such Party members who have gained their authority by their participation in the fight against capitalism and Nazi occupation, there are people

a 59

in the Party who were initiators and organizers of the present process of regeneration of socialism and the development of socialist democracy. The Party cadres form the decisive part of the administrative and managing structure of our society. All that creates, as a historic reality, a situation in which there is no other way for a really democratic, socialist development without conflicts, without undesirable upheavals, without unleashing a struggle for power (and thus for the very socialist character of power) than the way, along which the Communist Party of Czechoslovakia, as the strongest organized political force in this country, will lead the whole development process - by those new means and methods, however, which are clearly outlined by the Action Programme of the Party, and which will be laid down by the Party Congress.

The Party Central Committee declares that if anti-communist elements should try to attack this historic reality, and if they should try to lead astray the development of our nations, the Party will mobilize all forces of our people and of the socialist state, and will repel and suppress such an adventurous attempt. That would, however, considerably endanger the whole development to date, and would also endanger the implementation of the line of the Party Action Programme: the Communist Party will therefore strive by all available means to prevent such a situation from arising in our development.

The Party Central Committee is of the opinion that anti-communist forces, as such, are numerically weak in Czechoslovakia: they are the small remnants of the former members of exploiting classes still living, a handful of still living political representatives of the reactionary, right-wing pre-February politics, unless they have already renounced their political ambitions; this is but a handful of enemies, who sold themselves to foreign imperialist forces, who were justly punished by the state in the past, and who in certain cases, having served their just sentences, did not change their real

60

a

designs, and the like. These anti-communist forces have indeed their supporters abroad, but they could gain major political influence only if they succeeded in taking advantage of dissatisfaction and in creating chaos, disorganization and situations of conflict. In order to prevent this from happening, it is necessary to ensure that:

- our policy expresses the interest of workers and farmers, and that it solves the problems which affect them. The support of the working class is of prime importance for the policy of the Party: it is on the attitude of the workers that the character and possibilities of developing socialist democracy above all depend;

- sectarian mistakes are not repeated in the Party policy towards the intelligentsia and youth, and that consequently conflict situations do not arise; the intelligentsia and youth must be won over to actively support the Party;

- non-communists are given the opportunity to participate, with full rights, in the government and management of the society, and that the National Front policy is consistently implemented;

- all vestiges of sectarian, bureaucratic and directive methods in the Party and society are overcome: it is not possible to enforce political leadership by old, administratively authoritarian ways, and to restrict by these means the freedom of expression of different views and interests, socialist in character (freedom of the press and so forth).

The Party Central Committee instructs all Party bodies and organizations, as well as all communists, to direct their efforts - in accord with all of the above principles, and in a united organized way - towards strengthening the political guiding influence of the Party, especially at present, when our society is engaged in preparations of the Party Congress;

a 61

the Central Committee calls on all honest and socialist-minded organizations and citizens to extend the communists help and assistance in their efforts.

2. Our democracy is socialist in character. It strives for the development of socialism, for freedom of workers and all working people. To speak today only about the "regeneration" process and about democratization without this clear content means to distort the essence of the present stage of development.

The development of political democracy, and civil rights and freedoms, belongs inseparably to the development of socialism. Actual possibilities of a free life of workers and all working people stem, however, from conditions provided by the stage of development of the economy. Our whole socialist democracy must ensure the development of social wealth, the development of production, progressive development of our economic and civilization base in the direction which will make it possible for people to enjoy in future all fruits of the scientific and technical revolution.

Socialist democracy does not deny the workers their traditional rights of defending their own interests, including the right to strike. The Communists declare openly, however, that those slogans urging the workers to seek the main problem of their freedom in, for example, the right to strike, and to seek their freedom in adopting a stand against the technical intelligentsia, against the necessary expert management of large-scale production (slogan inciting the workers against the "technocrats") - all that is demagogism, which does not further the real interests of the working class.

The technical intelligentsia represents an inseparable part of socialist producers, and together with the workers, it is a decisive force for the development of socialism and the perspective of the scientific and technical revolution.

62 a

The Party Central Committee also notes critically that the explicit appeal of the Action Programme - to set up democratic bodies for the management of socialist enterprise and other places of work - is being carried out slowly, insufficiently and hesitatingly. State and economic bodies, as well as the trade unions, have not yet fully taken this to be their task. The Party Central Committee considers it a political necessity to solve these questions, concurrently with the questions concerning the status of enterprises and their associations, to make the problems the subject of discussions not only in management bodies, but also directly among the workers and all working people. The Party is for a consistent, speedy solution of problems of democratic forms of management in the socialist sector (workers' councils or similar bodies), carried out so that the planned assignments are nor affected, that no disorganization of interconnections in the economy takes place, and that working discipline and authority of the executive management does not deteriorate. That would endanger the functioning of the economy, and thus also the establishment of realistic prerequisites for a higher standard of living of the people.

The problems of democratic, self-administrative forms of management should be solved, as outlined above, so that the new system of management might become operational already this year. This will have established one of the fundamental features of our democratization development, guaranteeing that the development of socialist democracy is not a return to a formal political democracy of bourgeois type.

The socialist character of democracy as a democracy for the workers and other working people must be expressed in the content and methods of the whole economic policy in our society. We already know today that not even in socialism shall we be able to avoid the effects of several inevitable consequences of commodity production and of the market, especially the pressure of economic profitability and profits as a

63

the "engine" of the economic and technical progress. If we did not permit these pressures to be felt, we would not be able to ensure meeting the requirements of the working people on a permanent basis and to an increasing degree.

At the same time, however, certain short-term interests of workers and working people (their groups, various professions or various territorial divisions) may in this situation get into conflict with long-term perspective requirements of the economic development. In this connection, the Party Central Cemmittee declares plainly: the necessary changes in our economy - e.g. the changes in the structure of the national economy, the closing down of ineffective enterprises and withdraw. of state subsidies to unprofitable production) which is a form that makes workers and employees of enterprises with better economic results partly pay for the losses of less profitable ones), movement of prices according to market laws and so on - all that must be solved by the policy of a socialist state so that the working people, whose immediate interests and social security are tied to these, in principle unsound economic features, would be given democratic possibility of participation in decision-making concerning these questions. Without an agreement, without finding ways of meeting social interests and at the same time not harming the immediate interests of workers as they are harmed by the capitalist ways of solving similar problems, we would be departing from the principles of socialism. The Communist Party will promote perspective economic requirements of the society as a whole, but the methods of solution must be in keeping with these principles of socialist democracy for workers and the working people.

This applies to a number of specific questions, e.g. to the problems connected with the prospects of development of our mountainous areas, development problems of backward areas, the border regions, and so forth.

3) The new political system must be consistent with the development of socialism; it cannot be a return to a merely formal political democracy.

The Party proceeds from the principle that contrary to the formal political democracy, as known also to bourgeois parliamentarism, in which a system of various procedural forms and tricks makes it ultimately possible to pursue a state policy even against the vital interests of the workers and the majority of the working people, socialist democracy must ensure that nothing like this can be done: state policy must correctly bring into accord, express and ensure the meeting of the interests of workers, farmers and intellectuals of all strata and groups of socialist society. Since our political system in the preceding period did not meet these requirements properly, the Communist Party is starting to reform the whole system of political democracy. To ensure that a real development of socialism is the outcome, the Communist Party will pursue the line of the Action Programme with the following aims in sight:

a) All forces standing on the base of the socialist system should participate in the building of an advanced socialist society, and thus also in state power and administration. It is necessary to establish real guarantees against consequences resulting from monopoly of directive, undemocratic decision-making in politics, which prevents the various socialist interests, needs and views of various groups and strata of society from being expressed in a democratic way, and to achieve unity through democratic agreements, which prevents them from formulating their common interests as a political line.

b) It is, therefore, necessary to build a unifying political platform, within the framework of which the individual elements of our society will democratically seek solutions even to conflicting interests, approaches and views so that the result might benefit the building of socialism. We see such platform in the National Front. So that it can fulfil this role, it will be necessary to ensure the following in its development:

a 65

- the establishment of an association of the main political organizations, whose purpose is direct political activity, and the separation from this association (the membership in the National Front in the broad sense of the term being retained), as the second component part of the National Front, of organizations expressing specific, but not the fundamental social and politcal interests (organizations such as the Czechoslovak Red Cross, Cezchoslovak Fire Service Organization, more specialized group-interest organizations, group-interest unions, clubs and the like;

- the association of the main political organizations should in no case be restricted to an association (coalition) of political parties; the trade unions, organizations of cooperative farmers, intelligentsia, youth, women, the Union of Anti-Fascist Fighters, the Czechoslovak-Soviet Friendship Society, nationality interest groups etc. should be accorded representation with full rights, while striving at the same time for the interests of e.g. the intelligentsia or youth to be represented by an organization of a "roof" character (federation etc.), not by separate organizations.

- for the membership in the association of the main political organizations, a certain statute should be worked out in the National Front by mutual agreement of its representative elements of their mutual relations and activities, their position in political life, their relations to the State and so on, as well as certain - binding for all member organizations - principles of political programme, whose infringement would rule out the possibility of participation in political power and State administration. It will be necessary to express in these principles certain fundamental (and at the same time constitutional) features of our socialist society, against which no political force can at the present stage of development legally pursue any political activities, as it would endanger the socialist character of the social development: consent with socialist class and

66 a

ownership structure of social relations, not to permit political activity which is anti-communist, fascist-minded, inciting nationality or racial disputes and discrimination, as well as political activity which would impair the alliance with the Soviet Union and the socialist states as the basis of our State and national independence.

c) the Party is for co-government of all elements standing on the basis of this clearly formulated political programme framework of the National Front, but at the present stage of development, it rejects on principle the establishment of an opposition political organization (party) outside the National Front, because this would, under the existing conditions, necessarily mean legalizing the formation of political forces directed against the socialist political programme within the broadest meaning of the National Front platform.

The Party Central Committee considers it necessary to create already in June 1968, in agreement with the main political organizations of the National Front, a clear organizational and political programme base for the activities of the National Front, with which the whole National Front would come before our public. By its initiative proposals the Party Central Committee will ensure that these questions will be discussed in the National Front within an appropriate time. In the National Front, the Party will fight relentlessly against attempts to "party-ize" our public life, and will promote full possibilities for the main social, generation, nationality and other interests of people, who need not be members of any political party, to manifest themselves directly as a politically influential force in the National Front and in the State. Especially the trade unions must become a political force in our democracy, as an organization of the strongest social element in our society - the workers; political questions concerning the whole development of our political system must not remain outside the

a 67

scope of attention of the trade unions; they must, on the contrary, strive by their policy for guarantees enabling free expression of the interests of the workers and the other working people. Of similar importance is also the speedy establishment of another social political organization - the Union of Cooperative Farmers, whose representation with full rights in the National Front will be supported by the Party.

These principles will also be the base for the Party's stand on the drafting of new laws, especially the law on the freedom of assembly and organization (which should be passed early in summer) and the electoral law.

As regards the guarantees of socialist character, the Party Central Committee will submit to the Party Congress certain proposals concerning the development of our democratic representative state bodies so as to ensure the greatest possible direct influence of the interests of the working people on the decision-making on State affairs. This might be served, for example, by the concept, which in addition to elected bodies of generally political character (to which candidates nominated by National Front organizations would be elected on a territorial division system) - provides for certain auxiliary, corrective bodies (with fixed authority), to which representatives of the working people could be elected according to places of employment, without any party key. In these bodies (chambers), working people from the industries, agriculture and the sphere of social services (health, education, culture) would be directly represented by elected deputies.

An inseparable part of the development of our political system is the federalization of Czechoslovakia, based on consistent application of the principle of equal rights of the Czechs and Slovaks, and ensuring national development to all other nationalities in our Republic. The Party

68 a

Central Committee considers it politically necessary that preparations for the federalization of the country do not proceed only along the line of specialized government bodies, and that political initiative does not rest mainly on Slovak national bodies. The interests of both nations are involved, and the political aspect of these questions must also be dealt with in the Czech lands. The Party Central Committee will, therefore, set up a collective Party organ, consisting of delegations of Czech and Moravian regional Party bodies, which will be instructed to analyze - in conjunction with the preparations of the Party Congress - and to initiatively deal with political questions, both as regards the attitude of the communists in Bohemia and Moravia to constitutional questions, as well as from the point of view of the future organizational set-up of the Party in the federative Republic. The Party Central Committee also recommends setting up by the government and the National Assembly, i.e. also on state level, a preparatory political body representative of Czech and Moravian regions.

The means of mass influence upon the shaping of public opinion and political attitudes of people - the press, radio and television - are also a part of the political system. In the resolution adopted by its plenary session in April the Party Central Committee appreciated fully the positive role played by these media at the time of the Party's inception of its new policy after the Central Committee plenum in January. Those communist journalists, who are discharging the duties of their difficult mission in a responsible way, will continue to be supported by the Party, which will oppose all attacks directed against them, frequently by both rightist and anti-communist forces, as are also communists in other fields of work.

In the present political situation, the Party Central Committee sees the main role of the mass communication media in the necessity of their positive political influence: the

a 69

communists in this sector must strive to adopt such a course which would not impair the positive political line of the Communist Party programme and the present political line of the Party on individual problems as expressed by this resolution, but which will help implement it. The political influence of these media must ultimately result in shaping a political atmosphere conducive to confidence in the present process of developing socialist democracy, and specifically help to recognize the objectives and plans of the Action Programme, to show how they can be realized and to critically and factually draw attention to obstacles impeding the positive policy of the Party in the new period.

The press, radio and television workers have social means in their hands, and social bodies have the right to ask and to ensure in practice that the influence of these means upon the political actitude of the people be not directed against positive efforts of the socialist society and their organization. The communists working in the mass media are responsible to the whole Party that no moods of distrust in the Party and its new positive programme will be spread through the media, and that the main interest of public opinion will not be drawn to questions which impede, make difficult and sometimes even impossible an initiative start of the Party towards the fulfilment of the Action Programme. Especially during the period of preparations for the Party Congress, is it necessary to ensure such political influence of the mass communication media as outlined above, to draw the attention of all citizens to new, positive proposals and to prevent the solution of intra-Party questions from becoming a means of pressure of forces often even anti-communist in character.

The Party Central Committee considers as quite justified the demand to pass legislative measures already in June which would give expression to the conclusion of the Action

Programme on the abolition of preliminary censorship, and would thus, preclude the appearance of moods conducive to distrust on the part of the press, radio and television workers in the validity of the principles of the Party Action Programme. The Party Central Committee also considers it necessary for the communist journalists and publicists to be not only systematically informed of the political and tactical line of the Party, but also to have - just as communist activists in other sectors - real possibility of participating in shaping the Party policy within the Party and in accordance with its inner principles. It is, however, not consistent with the principles of the life and work of the Party - especially in the present situation of necessary consolidation of internal political conditions - for individual communists in editorial offices to regard themselves as autonomous architects of a "progressive policy of the Party", and not to respect in their public political influencing millions of people, the political and tactical line of Party bodies, including the Central Committee, and the need of the whole Party to prepare the extraordinary Party Congress according to the principles of intra-Party democracy.

The influence of mass communications media is, in conditions of a modern society, one of the most important forms of political influence upon the society in general. As a part of the political system, this sector must in its development proceed according to the same principles as the development of the system as a whole: it must ensure the strengthening of socialist relations, prevent the formation of scope for excessive disintegration and anarchist tendencies, support constitutionality and legal forms of the development of our political reform, actively counteract the influence of anti-communist tendencies and attempts at discrediting the Communist Party and the positive results of the socialist development in our country to date.

4) To counter attempts at infringements of legal order and disrupting the State apparatus is held by the Party Central Committee to be one of the prime political tasks in the present situation. The development of socialist democracy in this country can proceed successfully only as a process that is fully constitutional and respecting legal order. It is obvious that the existing legal order must be subjected to qualitative changes, specifically indicated by the Party Action Programme. But the principle must be observed that those laws which have not been abolished and replaced, are in force and must be respected. The Party Central Committee considers criticism to be justified which points to hesitancy and indecision as regards such fundamental legislative amendments as those concerning the assembly and press laws, where the vague legal situation leads to nervousness, facilitates the sowing of distrust in the positive programme of the Party and State bodies, and at the same time creates conditions for not always a sound development of social organizations (e.g. the rise of organizations such as the "Club 231"; extensive press publicity of each "initiative from below" even in cases where such organizations actually lack any legal basis, and so on.)

These principles are also served by the efforts aimed at adjusting and improving conditions for the activities of all state bodies, national committees and bodies of State administration. To weaken their function in the present situation would mean to seriously endanger the necessary organized, democratic and legal character of the development of our democracy.

The Party Central Committee is resolutely opposed to attempts seeking to misuse the development of socialist democracy for all-inclusive accusations and the sowing of distrust in such elements of the state power structure as the armed forces, security, the institutions of prosecutors and the courts. The position of the Party, with regard to these bodies, as expressed in the Action Programme, remains fully valid, and will be consistently realized. The process of reconstructing the security forces and the svstem of prosecutors and courts, as well as the process of purging them of people responsible for the past deformations continues, and will be completed. It must not be permitted, however, to raise doubts about the sincerity of these efforts just because a number of the complicated problems cannot be solved overnight, and will take some time.

The Party Central Committee also considers if necessary for all communists to be united in their stand against all attempts to discredit the People's Militia, which came into existence as an instrument of the workers and working people for the defence of the achievements of the socialist revolution; at present, the Party will not change anything in the status of the People's Militia.

5) Our relations to the Soviet Union, the socialist countries and the international communist movement are based upon the principles of internationalism and full respect for special conditions,under which in every country and in every period,a fight is waged for universal,common aims of the communist movement.Our development today is a development corresponding to our present Czechoslovak conditions;it was with the awareness of responsibility before our nations that the Party has taken this road.That is why,however,the Party Central Committee considers it necessary to stress in the present situation that attempts to present our course as a certain obligatory "model" for all socialist countries are wrong in principle as to content, and politically harmful both for us and for the development of our relations to the allied socialist countries.

It is impermissible for communists to forget that distortions and exaggerations of certain decisions up to the spreading of false information about a "danger of military intervention" (e.g. in conjunction with the manoeuvres of units of the Warsaw Treaty armed forces,etc.) are highly detrimental to the whole course of our present policy, and play into the hands of certain circles in the capitalist countries, intent on disrupting the unity of the socialist countries.

The Party Central Committee declares that all negotiations which were and are being held, on Party and government levels, with representatives of the Soviet Union, lead to positive conclusions, and provide possibilities of extending mutual cooperation and assistance which is very important for the solving of some of our topical economic difficulties; the Soviet comrades have shown good will to extend such help to us.

In the past hew years , grave ideological differences have been appearing in the international communist movement in an especially marked way, as regards significant questions concerning further progress. The Communist Party of Czechoslovakia will actively assist in overcoming these differences, and will promote the development of action unity of the international communist movement. The existence of differences among communist parties should not, however, negatively affect their mutual relations. In accord with the Action Programme, we shall explain and defend our standpoint that our internal development is the sovereign affair of Czechoslovakia. We do not interfere with internal political questions of other countries, and we demand the same as regards their relations to our country.

The action unity of the whole Party during the preparations of the Party Congress is an essential condition for the further successful development of socialism and democracy in our country. The Action Programme of the Party is at the

74 a

moment the conceptual basis of this unity. To know, develop and concretize the Action Programme, as an open political document on the basis of which communists in all sectors, in places of residence and work, should set themselves concrete tasks and solve them - that is one of the prime requirements of Party work today. The Party bodies - regional, district and local organizations - must, on the basis of analyses of their specific situation, seek such problems whose solution is of prime importance with them for a further raising of Party authority, for winning and strengthening the confidence of the people in the Party and its concrete policy.

The initiative and the proposals submitted by communists must not only come in time - they must not only be the first, but they must also counteract the cheap, often bargain-type and therefore questionably "popular" demands which irresponsible individuals are putting forward in various sectors. The principle of the new Party policy is to tell people the truth, even the bitter truth about the limited possibilities of our present economic situation. The communists must sound truthful warnings against demagogism, must win the people over by a well-reasoned responsible approach. Let us point our that chaos and want of method, subjectivism in management account substantially for our present difficulties. If democracy were understood to be a chaotic pressure of various unrealistic demands, it would be impossible to improve the living standard of the people, and to meet their other requirements.

The Party Central Committee considers it necessary at present to create an action unity of the Party around such a concept of 5 fundamental problems of today, as formulated in this resolution. In the spirit of the principles of this resolution the communists in all spheres of their political work must:

1/ strive in accord with the Action Programme for the strengthening of the influence of the political leadership of the Party, fight against the possibility of anti-com-

a

munist tendencies asserting themselves, and determine the character of the future development; they must prepare the extraordinary 14th Party Congress as the prime guarantee for the strengthening of Party authority and for inspiring confidence in the consistence of its new policy;

2/ strive to achieve that the working class has its influence in the management and administration of socialist enterprises, and that the economic policy brings short-range interests of the workers and other working people into harmony with perspective requirements of an effective development of the whole national economy;

3/ strive to achieve that the development of our political system is not understood as a return to formal political democracy as it existed before 1948, or even before 1938, but that it becomes - by the concept of the National Front, the concept of the role of the main political organizations of the people, the concept of the role of mass communications media and by the concept of nationality relations - a truly new, higher and socialist stage in the development of the political system;

4/ strive to achieve that legal order is respected, and that our democratic development is a constitutional reform, and not a process in which anarchist tendencies would prevail and the State apparatus of socialist power of the working people would be distrupted;

5/ strive to achieve that our ties of alliance are not impaired with the socialist countries, with the Soviet Union and with the whole international communist movement, and that we have full sovereignty in solving our internal affairs.

The unified course of the whole Party as regards these matters must also be ensured by practical organizational work in the Party. This was, however, one of the weakest spots, from the highest to the lowest Party level, in the period

76 a

following January plenum. Therefore the Party Central Committee considers it necessary to:

a/ rebuild qualitatively the Party apparatus so that it will, under the new condition, above all organizationally ensure the policy of the Party. All-inclusive attacks against the Party apparatus in the present situation would ultimately lead to the weakening of the Party's capacity to act. We shall not "liquidate" the Party apparatus, but we shall rebuild it in an expedient way. The main condition is that the communists working outside the Party apparatus - in State and social bodies and organizations, in various fields of social activity - should be able, given active help of the apparatus, to regularly and collectively assess and solve, from the point of view of Party policy, problems of their political work in any sector. The apparatus in to serve the communists who implement the policy of the Party in society, and not the other way round - to think up assignments for them. Otherwise, the overwhelming part of the communists would be kept away from the process of shaping the policy of the Party. It is, of course, obvious that both the Party apparatus and the communists in individual organizations and in various sectors must be guided by the line and directives laid down by elected Party bodies, in accord with the principles of intra-Party democracy and democratic centralism of Party work.

b/ ensure an improved and fast method of intra-Party information of all Party bodies and communists from top to bottom, so that the communists receive information about specific questions of the Party's political course and line in advance, before they are to adopt the course and tactic in practical work. The practice as it has been developing in the past few months, as if the Party bodies including the Central Committee had no right to inform and direct the Party, and were obliged to make known all their standpoints immediately to the whole public through mass communications

a 77

media, is considered wrong by the Party Central Committee. The Party bodies do not want and will not conduct any closed chamber policy, and conceal anything from the rest of the people. Nevertheless, to formulate political standpoints of the Party on definite matters within the Party, to first of all inform Party members and only then begin to publicly defend the viewpoints and win over others for them - that is a normal political procedure in every organization and in every political party.

The Party Central Committee considers it necessary at present to employ very intensively and on a broad scale such methods of Party work as are prompt calling of meetings of Party activists - from central to district levels - so as to pass on information and instructions (including discussions). This should be done according to need, withour any bureaucratic prescriptions; differentiation should be made as regards the requirements (and questions necessary to answer) in view of the type of organization concerned (industrial, rural, other sectors of public work) and so on. The Party Central Committee will use this course, while organizationally ensuring the political work of the Party after the present plenary session and during the whole period of preparations of the Congress;

c/ actively develop ideological work and political education in the whole Party. It is necessary to ensure, fast and effectively, forms of ideological education and frequently of re-education of the whole Party membership so that the dogmatic ideas, systematically brought into the thinking of communists in the past, do not impede the new directions and methods of the Party's political work. The Party Central Committee will create the prerequisites for this by providing necessary propaganda material (brochures etc.) so as to enable all Party sections, down to branch organizations, to execute this work effectively, especially in conjunction with the campaign marking the 50th anniversary of our Republic.

78

a

It is of decisive importance in the present situation to bring about a fast and effective reversal of the Party policy from the previously predominant orientation inward to Party organizations to an open policy towards the masses of the working people. The aim is to openly and unitedly defend the principles of our present line, and to apply them in the influence of the Party upon the society, upon all working people. This does not rule out, but directly presupposes the possibility of intra-Party discussions; their purpose and outcome must be, however, to reach united views in all Party bodies and individual organizations as to how to implement the common Party policy in the most effective, united way, all within the sphere of their competence. The communists must not avoid newly arising organizations (group-interest organizations, associations and the like); on the contrary, they must join these organizations and win them over for the policy of the Party, see that the ideas of the Action Programme are adopted, and strengthen confidence in the Party and its policy.

The Party Central Committee will do everything to increase confidence in the policy of the Party by consistent realization of the principles of the Action Programme; it will do everything with the help of communists in the National Front and State bodies to repel the attacks of these who want to discredit the Party. The Party Central Committee will cooperate systematically with communists in central communication media, with communists in the National Front and central State bodies in order to ensure that positive plans are actually realized and not blocked, that delays do not occur, and even less attempts to sow distrust, uneasiness, to create an atmosphere of uncertainty, tension and so forth.

Yet if these efforts were not supported by the independent activity and political work of all bodies and organizations of the Party, and of every individual member of the Party, we would not achieve full success. There is no

a

reason for nervousness and panic, but there are reasons for far of further successful progress of our development. We do not fight for power, because we are its decisive force. But we fight for confidence, for increasing confidence, for permanent and stronger support of the masses of non-communists, workers in enterprises, in villages and in all other sectors. We are concerned with having the confidence of workers, farmers, intellectuals, youth , women, the confidence of both our nations and citizens of all nationalities living on the territory of our Republic. Only this confidence will strengthen the strongest political power and the political leadership role of our Party. The result of this fight of the Party for the confidence of the nation depends today, just as in the past when we were still seeking to win the leadership role in the nation, on independence, the activity and initiative of every communist, just as on fundamental political unity of the whole Party.

80

a

THE PROCLAMATION OF THE CENTRAL COMMITTEE

OF THE COMMUNIST PARTY OF CZECHOSLOVAKIA TO MEMBERS OF THE PARTY AND ALL THE PEOPLE

We are turning to all citizens of the Czechoslovak Socialist Republic, to all the sincere patriots to whom the welfare of the Republic and its successful growth is dear. We are doing this after having evaluated at our session the implementation of the Action Programme of the Communist Party of Czechoslovakia and the programme statement of the Government and drawn conclusions from it for the future activity of communists. If this work is to bring permanent success, we appeal to all citizens for active cooperation. We are convinced that this is the only way of developing socialism.

The communists do not want to close themselves up with their initiative in their own ranks and they will accept all suggestions and proposals which will realistically contribute to the socialist progress of the country.

Five months have elapsed since the December and January session of the Central Committee of the CPCz, which opened up the way to a new policy of the Communist Party. In this short period we have done quite a lot of work with you. We want to give you our opinion on how we should proceed, and ask you for further support and initiative.

The development begun on the stimulus and initiative of the Communist Party is bringing positive results. At the same time we must all realize that all the social problems cannot be solved at once, that the current development has its stages. Gradually conditions are being created for an atmosphere of political confidence. In evaluating their common problems, the working class and intelligentsia are finding ways towards a rapprochement. The political weight of co-operative farmers in society is growing.

We are striving for a perfect system of legal guarantees which must gradually safeguard the real legal security of citizens. We have created conditions for freedom of expression, for public criticism, for an open exchange of views. The public is now better informed about both internal and international affairs.

The Party is resolutely settling deformations of the past. Honour is being returned to all who suffered unjustly, and injustice is being rectified. Right and justice will take their course in the life of society. Of course, the justified criticism of the shortcomings in the application of legality must not lead to the general dissemination of want of confidence in state bodies, in the armed forces, the Security Force and justice.

Social organizations are starting to live an independent and active life according to the interests and needs of their members.

We are eliminating political obstacles so that the citizens have equal possibility of asserting themselves according to their abilities and their work regardless of differences of political conviction, nationality or religion.

We have begun to solve in a consistent manner the relationship of the Czech and Slovak nations on an equal, federal basis. We are bringing much more of our own initiative into Czechoslovakia's foreign policy.

The main representatives of the old course, those who lost the confidence of the people, are leaving political life. The country has a new President. The Party has new leadership composed of people who played a decisive role in the turn of its policy. The role of the National Assembly, as a representative of the will of the people and body of social control, has grown. The new government is starting to implement consistently and in a qualified way the government programme. Our people are filled with new hope, our young people with new stamina. The problems accumulated are starting to be solved. At least the most acute social problems are being eliminated in spite of economic difficulties.

We are now entering a new period. The Party will prove the vitality of the new policy by concrete results. The criticism of past shortcomings has hitherto been the centre of attention. The time has now come to concentrate attention and strength upon active work, when it is necessary to provide the socialist society with a firm order and rules which will safeguard the rights and also the fulfilment of duties.

If we do not want to repeat the mistakes of the past we must guard against impatience and nervousness, imprudent steps and hasty improvisations. The aim we are pursuing can be achieved only gradually, in stages. All the tasks cannot be solved at once. We intend to resolutely eliminate everything that has become outdated, but also to wisely make use of all the positive that has been created by the devoted work of the people over the past years.

We want to consistently pursue the road we set out on in January. The communists will ensure that new laws, such as the Press and Association Laws and other legal measures to incorporate in terms of law the principles of the Action Programme in the constitutional rights of citizens, be approved soon.

Work on the new constitutional structure of Czechoslovakia on a federal basis has begun at the initiative of the Party. Our country will become a real home, offering equal rights to the Czech and Slovak nations as well as to all other nationalities, and a guarantee of real unity of the State. The draft on the principles of the new structure will be submitted to the people for consideration on the occasion of the 50th anniversary of the foundation of the Czechoslovak Republic.

The Communists think it their duty to help in developing the activity of the National Front in which all political forces that want to contribute to the patriotic work for a socialist Czechoslovakia can find a place. We are in favour of honest political cooperation based upon a socialist programme with the other political parties. We support the view that the principle to which the National Front has adhered since 1945 that there should be no place in our political life for opposition parties and political forces not included in the National Front, should be maintained.

In the economy, wa shall pursue the line of higher profitability, better ecohomy and such operation which will ensure economic balance, improvement of the standard of living and a stable currency. We intend to initiate the decrease of all unjustified expenditure of the State. We shall take the initiative in making use of all possibilities to more efficiently incorporate the economy into the international division of labour.

We are not promising that new economic growth is possible without hard work, without resolute measures against unprofitable production, bad and slipshod work, as well as against bureaucracy in economic management. Therefore we shall consistently implement the new system of management, and promote the socialist spirit of enterprise on the basis of expanded independence of enterprises.

Our aim will be to create pre-conditions that would ensure a really democratic participation of work teams in making decisions on basic matters concerning their enterprise, by means of enterprise councils.

The extraordinary 14th Congress of the Party, which will take place in September, is to be the start of the development of the political activity of the CPCz as the leading political force in the country. We shall submit the proposal for the future course of the Party and its attitude towards solving the main problems of the development of our society, for consideration to communists and all citizens.

84 a

In the past few months the communists have proved that they have been resolutely pursuing the new road. For this they have been given the support and understanding of the broadest strata of the people. We shall not dissapoint this confidence. We are determined to completely eliminate and put right all that was incorrect in the past years and we believe that wou will support us also in the view that the basic values of socialism achieved by our people over the past 20 years are a necessary pre-condition for successful advancement.

The positive results of the past 20 years, in which our people have done so much self-sacrificing work, must not be rejected. These results cannot even be negated by the serious shortcomings which appeared especially in recent years. It cannot be permitted that the very outcome of the revolution and socialism be jeopardized.

With the same resoluteness with which we expose the distortions and unlawful acts of the past shall we defend the results of the self-sacrificial work of the millions of honest people who made the victory of socialism possible. Communists and members of other parties as well as non-party people worked just as well. Our Party thinks it its duty to defend them against any attempt of deliberate discreditation.

For us, democracy is as inseparable from socialism as is socialism from democracy. We are aware that the sovereign people is the decisive guarantee of present socialist democracy. In the Communist Party of Czechoslovakia our people have a leading political force which has enforced and put into motion present developments. It gives them a realistic programme and takes care of its implementation. In the contemporary divided world much depends upon the firmness of the alliance with our friendly socialist countries, in the first place with the Soviet Union. This is a pre-condition of the independence, sovereignty and security of our conutry. We want to express the conviction that the solidarity of the socialist countries and other democratic forces of the world will be a support for us in our work.

a

Just as we quite frankly say what we are striving for so we want to say what we shall oppose and struggle against. In our opinion it is not good for the common work if some groups of working people present ultimatum-like demands for the satisfaction of their interests which pay no need to the interests of others and which jeopardize common interests and aims. Wilfulness and demagogy must be confronted with socialist discipline and organization. Neither does it help the process of democratization if the existing legislation and laws are violated.

We cannot conceal either that some discredited political forces of the past, which, thinking their opportunity has come again, are trying to take advantage of democratization and to revert the political stage. Attempts to bring about an atmosphere of distrust against the Party and its members are evident in several places. Under the pretext of combatting distortions, attacks are also made on the work done by the working class and all people in the past years.

We do not want to attribute hostile views to anyone without any reason. But independent of subjective intentions the ultimate political aim of such trends is only one - to evoke distrust of communists, distrust of socialism, weaken the ties with our allies, bring the danger of a split and a conflict into our society.

A menace is hidden in these trends, which might not only impede the process initiated in January but which would also be accompanied by the risk of most serious consequences for a peaceful development of the country.

We express deep conviction that the working class and the broad masses of the people will not permit such a development. In the name of socialist democracy, in the name of creative and harmonious work, for the protection of the socialist system guaranteed by the constitution the communists will wage a decisive political fight against everything that harms the people and the Republic. If during the last few months and weeks,

86 a

full of revolutionary events,our people maintained both a sincere sense for the requirements of new roads and a sober sense of reality so right now when the new policy is going into practice they will not allow its implementation to be menaced. Just as there is no return to the pre-January situation, so there is no return to the situation existing before February 1948 and the more so before September 1938! In the defence of socialism, in the defence of the results of May 1945 and February 1938 all working people will find resolute support in the Party! The Party is opening the door to all honest, capable and especially young people who want to work actively in its ranks for the development of socialism in this country.

By the rectification of the shortcomings of recent years the Communist Party is determined to fully restore the famous revolutionary tradition of its past, the tradition of self-sacrificial and unselfish struggle for the interests of the people so well tried in the years of capitalism, at the time of the Munich Pact, in the struggle for national liberation, in the building of a new life in the post-war years and in February 1948.

In the spirit of this tradition we shall erase everything that was distorting the true face of socialism, which is qualified to be the most humane social order in the contemporary world. We see its basic values in the means of production owned by society, in the co-operative life of the village, in the fact that power in the State does not belong to powerful individuals but to the organized people, in the fact that the security of our socialist state is safeguarded by the alliance with the Soviet Union and association with the socialist countries.

The issue is now that socialism in this country should develop by democratic means, that is should be a truly human socialism. We want to accomplish such a work together and to guard it against all internal and external intrigues.

We appeal to all the honest citizens of our State to support the aims of the Communist Party of Czechoslovakia and actively help to implement them.

CENTRAL COMITTEE OF
THE COMMUNIST PARTY OF CZECHOSLOVAKIA

88 a

THE RESOLUTION OF THE CENTRAL COMMITTEE ON THE CONVOCATION OF THE EXTRAORDINARY 14th CONGRESS OF THE COMMUNIST PARTY OF CZECHOSLOVAKIA

The plenary session of the Central Committee of the CPCz, held from May 29th to June 1st 1968 decided in accordance with article 24 of the Statutes of the Party to convene the extraordinary 14th Congress of the CPCz in Prague on September 9th 1968. The Central Committee of the CPCz reached this decision after the evaluation of the situation in the Party which requires that a new political course of the Party be set for the next period and that a new Central Committee be elected which will have full confidence and authority in ensuring a united advance of the Party.

The extraordinary 14th Congress of the CPCz will have the following agenda:

1. Report on the activity of the Party and development of society since the 13th Congress of the CPCz and main tasks of the Party in the approaching period.
   Delivered by: comrade Alexander Dubček
2. Report of the Central Control and Auditing Commission of the CPCz.
   Delivered by: comrade Miloš Jakeš
3. Proposal for the political guideline of the constitutional structure of Czechoslovakia.
   Delivered by: comrade Oldřich Černík
4. Draft of the new Statutes of the CPCz and reorganization of the Party and the principles of Party work in the conditions of the federal structure of the State.
   Delivered by: comrade Alois Indra

89

a

5. Election of the Central Committee of the CPCz and the Central Control and Auditing Commission of the CPCz

6. Resolution.

The election of delegates to the Congress will be done according to Party Statutes at extraordinary regional conferences and extraordinary city conferences of the CPCz in Prague and Bratislava. One delegate with full voting rights is elected for every 1,100 members of the Party. The plenary session of the Central Committee of the CPCz also decided that:

- Meetings of local Party branch organizations be held between June 10th and June 23rd 1968 at which delegates will be elected to extraordinary district conferences of the CPCz

- Extraordinary district conferences of the Party be held on June 29th and 30th 1968; these conferences will elect delegates to extraordinary regional conferences of the CPCz. (The decision on whether two or one-day extraordinary district conferences will be held following an agreement with the Regional Committees of the Communist Party of Czechoslovakia and the Communist Party of Slovakia, should be left to the District Committees of the CPCz and the CPS.)

- Extraordinary regional conferences and extraordinary city conferences in Prague and Bratislava be held on July 6th and 7th or July 13th and 14th 1968. At these conferences delegates to the extraordinary 14th Congress of the CPCz should be elected also by communists from Party branchecs in the army and the Security Force. (The date will be chosen by Regional Committees of the CPCz in agreement with the Central Committee of the CPCz and the Central Committee of the CPS.)

———

90

a

4

Coming as it does at the end of this collection, the document that follows helps to set in perspective not only the recent crisis in Czechoslovakia, but those factors which, either individually or in concert, contributed to that crisis.

Written in response "to the letters of five Communist and workers' parties"—letters which, it should be noted, expressed concern over the course of recent developments in Czechoslovakia as well as over the implications of these developments for the future of the bloc—the document speaks as much to the internal as to the external audience. The message in both cases appears to be the same: that the process of change going on within Czechoslovakia will not be permitted to threaten either the primacy of the CCP or the integrity of the Soviet Bloc and therefore, should be accommodated by all concerned.

THE INTERNAL AUDIENCE

To the internal audience the message is presented in the form of a warning. The warning is directed, in the first instance, to those within Czechoslovakia who seek an end to Communist rule in that country. They are told in no uncertain terms that the CCP is aware of the danger and is prepared to act decisively when and if it becomes necessary to do so. They are also told, albeit implicitly, that the Soviet Union and the other members of the bloc are aware of the danger, and might decide to intervene should the CCP lose control of the situation. The implication, apparently, is that in Czechoslovakia, if not in the United States, "extremism in the defense of liberty" is indeed a "vice."

Turning to those, particularly within the CCP itself, who might wish a return to the period before the January plenum, the letter carries a warning of indictment. They and those who shared their views are assigned responsibility for the ills which characterized Czech society. It was their policies that drove the people and the Party apart; that divided Czech from Slovaks; that contributed to economic chaos and stagnation; that, in short, threatened the survival of the CCP and, by implication, the integrity of the bloc. These same individuals are also warned, although again in a less explicit fashion, that they can expect no help either from the "masses" or from external sources in their opposition to reforms initiated by the Party. The CCP and the "masses" are as one, or so the letter suggests, in their pursuit of a better future under socialism. Because their cause is "just" it will, moreover, meet with the approval of the "socialist camp." The "letters from the five Communist and workers' parties" are thus attributed to a misunderstanding of, rather than genuine opposition to, the policies of the CCP. Accordingly those who would oppose these policies are, in effect, notified that their cause is hopeless and therefore should be abandoned.

Finally, there is the warning to the "masses." It is a warning against excess which might be misconstrued by sources outside of Czechoslovakia as a danger to the continued primacy of the CCP. In this period of uneasiness, there is a need for patience and moderation. The Party, or so the letter suggests, has the situation under control and the Presidium of the Central Committee is now endeavoring to clear up whatever doubt might exist in the minds of other members of the bloc. Consequently, there must be restraint lest these efforts be jeopardized.

THE EXTERNAL AUDIENCE

The presentation of the message to the external audience takes the form of an explanation, if not a lecture. To the Soviet Union, members of the bloc and other "fraternal parties" the Presidium offers a review of events which led up to the decision to initiate change. In its own way, this review is apparently intended to explain not only what had occurred in Czechoslovakia prior to the January plenum, but why the decisions taken since that meeting have been both necessary and correct. The implication is that the concern reflected in "the letters from the five Communist and workers' parties" is simply the result of a lack of information or a breakdown in communication.

It is unlikely, however, that the Presidium actually believed this to be the case. On the contrary, it is quite probable that the members of the Presidium and, for that matter, the entire membership of the CCP, understood only too well the reasons which prompted the "letters."

This impression would appear to be confirmed by those portions of the letter that deal specifically with the course of events since Novotny's ouster as Party leader. Here, as throughout, an attempt is made to explain these events to an apparently confused audience. Yet it is significant that the explanation is, in each instance, related either to the ability of the CCP to maintain effective internal control, or to the relationship of Czechoslovakia to the bloc, or both. The letter emphasizes, for example, the Party's awareness of the dangers that might arise as a result of the liberalization effort; it goes to great lengths, however, to minimize those dangers and to point out that the CCP not only did not agree with the sentiments expressed in the "Statement of 2000 Words," but said so publicly.

The same pattern is followed in "explaining" the "doubts" concerning Czechoslovakia's position within the bloc. Those portions of the letter that deal with the relationship of the Czechoslovak Socialist Republic to the German Democratic Republic (GDR) and, more importantly, to the German Federal Republic (GFR) are preceded by a reminder that not only has Czechoslovakia suffered at the hands of German imperialism and militarism, but that it moved to normalize its relations with the GFR only after other members of the bloc had done so. As for Czech participation in the Warsaw Treaty Organization (WTO), the letter emphasizes the recently concluded treaties of alliance with the Bulgarian People's Republic and the Rumanian Socialist Republic, as well as the fact that Czechoslovakia, after permitting staff exercises of the WTO on its territory, became somewhat concerned about the purpose of these exercises only after delays had occurred in the departure of foreign forces from Czech soil. In explaining its absence from the meeting held in Warsaw on July 14th, the Presidium assumes a posture of injured innocence. The explanation offered stresses the fact that the meeting was held without the knowledge of the CCP which found out about it only through the official press agency CTK. It also stresses the fact that proposals made by the CCP for bilateral talks prior to such a meeting did not imply a desire on the part of the Czechs to isolate themselves from the bloc.

When these references are read together they leave little doubt as to the growing concern of the Soviet Union and other members of the bloc regarding the situation within Czechoslovakia and its possible consequences for the survival of the bloc. The message as stated in the letter appears to be that the CCP is in control of the internal situation, that it intends to retain control, and that, consequently, the concern expressed in the "letters" is unfounded. To underscore this message, the letter concludes with an appeal for support of the CCP by "fraternal parties" and an all-too-obvious reference to the principles that have supposedly governed intra-bloc relations since the Moscow Conference of November, 1957.

To the non-Communist world the message is expressed as a reproval to those who would seek to exploit either the situation within Czechoslovakia or the concern with this situation which has been expressed by other members of the bloc. Thus, we are told that internally the position of the CCP is strong. and that externally it ties with the "socialist camp" are secure. Admittedly, the letter does hold out the prospect of greater cooperation between "socialist" and "non-socialist" countries. Yet, stated as it is in the context of this letter, the offer would seem to be a notification that such cooperation will come slowly, if at all, and that it will have to be on Czech terms.

CONCLUSION

Although the intended message of this letter suggests strength, the reverse appears to be the case. The fact that the letter had to be written at all is sufficient to indicate deep concern on the part of the Soviet Union and other members of the bloc as to the ability of the CCP to manage the process of change. Despite numerous references to "doubts" and "confusion," the Presidium seems to be fully aware of the fact that this concern is based, not as it suggests, on misunderstanding, but rather on a full understanding of the possible implications of the Czech experience for the bloc as a whole as well as for the individual members. Thus, while endeavoring to "explain," the letter also offers assurances of internal stability and continued participation in the bloc. The intervention that began on August 20th would appear to suggest that these assurances were not enough—that the message as read in Moscow conveyed weakness, not strength, and that as a consequence the Soviet Union thought it necessary to move decisively against the Czechs.

STANDPOINT OF THE PRESIDIUM OF THE CENTRAL COMMITTEE OF THE COMMUNIST PARTY OF CZECHO SLOVAKIA TO THE LETTERS OF FIVE COMMUNIST AND WORKERS' PARTIES

STANDPOINT OF THE PRESIDIUM OF THE CENTRAL COMMITTEE OF THE COMMUNIST PARTY OF CZECHOSLOVAKIA TO THE LETTERS OF FIVE COMMUNIST AND WORKERS' PARTIES

The Presidium of the Central Committee of the Communist Party of Czechoslovakia has thoroughly studied the letter received by the Central Committee of our party from the meeting of the representatives of the parties of five socialist countries in Warsaw.

In the letter it is stressed that it is motivated by anxiety about our common cause and about the strengthening of the positions of socialism. Proceeding from this fact and led by the same striving, we wish to express equally frankly also our own attitude on the questions mentioned in the letter.

We are at the same time fully aware that an exchange of letters cannot fully explain such a complex problem as is the subject of attention and our standpoint therefore does not even aim at such ends but, on the contrary, presupposes direct mutual talks between parties.

A number of fears explained in the letter were expressed by ourselves in the resolution of the May plenary session of the Central Committee of the Communist Party of Czechoslovakia. However, we see the causes of the political situation, which is full of contradictions mainly in the accumulation of these contradictions over the years preceding the January plenum of the Central Committee of the Communist Party of Czechoslovakia. These contradictions cannot be satisfactorily solved

a 3a

at once in a short time. In the process of the realization of the political line of the Action Programme of our party it therefore necessarily happens that the wide stream of healthy socialist activity is accompanied by extreme tendencies, that the remnants of anti-socialist forces in our society are also trying to tag along and that at the same time activity is being also developed by the dogmatic-sectarian forces connected with the faulty policy of the time before the January plenum of the Central Committee of the Communist Party of Czechoslovakia. Not even the party itself can in this complex situation remain untouched by internal contradictions accompanying the process of unification along the line of the Action Programme. The negative phenomena of this process also include violation of the principles of democratic centralism in the dealings of some Communists which is mainly the consequence of the fact that, for many long years, the old party leadership applied bureaucratic centralism and suppressed internal party democracy. All this prevents us from always achieving in political work only those results we ourselves would wish.

We do not wish to hide these facts and we do not hide them from our own party and people either.

For this reason the May plenum of the Central Committee also clearly stated that it is necessary to mobilize all forces to prevent a conflicting situation in the country and the endangering of socialist power in the Czechoslovak Socialist Republic. Our party has also unequivocally stated that if any such danger occurred, it would use all means to protect the socialist system. We thus ourselves saw the possibility of such a danger. We understand that the fraternal parties of the socialist countries cannot be indifferent to this either. We do not, however, see any realistic reasons which would justify assertions calling our present situation counter-revolutionary, assertions of an immediate endangering of the basis of the socialist system, or assertions that a change is being prepared in Czechoslovakia in the orientation of our socialist foreign policy and that there is a concrete threat of a separation of our country from the socialist community.

4a a

Our alliance and friendship with the USSR and other socialist countries is deeply rooted in the social system, in the historical traditions and experience of our nations, in their interests, their thoughts and feelings. The liberation from Nazi occupation and the entry onto the path of a new life is for ever connected in the consciousness of our people with the historical victory of the USSR in the Second World War, with respect for the heroes who laid down their lives in this fight.

This is also the basis of the Action Programme of our party, where we proclaim this tradition to be the starting point:

The basic orientation of Czechoslovak foreign policy was born and confirmed at the time of the national liberation struggle and in the process of the socialist reconstruction of our country - it is alliance and cooperation with the Soviet Union and the other socialist states. We shall strive for the friendly relations with our allies - the countries of the world socialist community - to deepen also in future on the basis of mutual esteem, sovereignty and equality, mutual respect and international solidarity. In this sense we shall contribute more actively and with a well-conceived concept towards the common activities of the Council of Mutual Economic Assistance and the Warsaw Treaty.

The letter mentions attacks against the socialist foreign policy, assaults against the alliance and friendship with socialist countries, voices calling for a revision of our common and coordinated policy in relation to the GFR and it is even asserted that attempts at making advances on the part of the authorities of the GFR and revanchists are finding response in the leading circles of our country. We are surprised at such assertions because it is well known that the Czechoslovak Socialist Republic is implementing a consistent socialist foreign policy, whose principles were formulated in the Action Programme of the Communist Party of

a 5 a

Czechoslovakia and the Programme Statement of the Government. These documents, statements made by leading Czechoslovak representatives and also our further actions consistently proceed from the principles of socialist internationalism, alliance and the development of friendly relations with the Soviet Union and the other socialist states.

We are of the opinion that these facts are decisive and not the irresponsible voices of individuals which are sometimes heard in this country.

In view of the bitter historical experiences of our nations with German imperialism and militarism it is inconceivable that any Czechoslovak Government could ignore these experiences and light-mindedly hazard with the fate of our country. This can be done even less by a socialist government and we must reject any suspicion in this direction.

As regards our relations with the GFR, it is universally known that the Czechoslovak Socialist Republic, although it is an immediate neighbour of the GFR, was the last to take certain steps towards a partial regulation of mutual relations, particularly in the economic field, whereas other socialist countries adapted their relations with the GFR to this or that extent much earlier without this having caused any fears.

We at the same time consistently respect and defend the interests of the GDR, our socialist ally, and do everything in our power to strengthen its international position and authority. This is also explicitly proved by all the speeches of leading representatives of our party and the State and the entire period after January 1968.

The agreements and treaties linking the socialist countries are an important factor of mutual cooperation, peace and collective security. The Czechoslovak Socialist Republic fully respects its contractual commitments and further develops the system of treaties with socialist coun-

6 a a

tries which is proved by the new treaties of alliance we have recently concluded with the Bulgarian People's Republic, as well as by the prepared treaty on friendship and cooperation with the Rumanian Socialist Republic.

Like the authors of the letter we shall never agree to the historic achievements of socialism and the security of the nations of our country being threatened and imperialism, by peaceful or forceful means, to break through the socialist system and to change the balance of forces in Europe to its advantage. The main content of our development after January is the actual effort to increase our internal strength and the stability of the socialist system and thus also our bonds of alliance.

The staff exercise of the allied forces of the Warsaw Treaty on the territory of the Czechoslovak Socialist Republic is concrete proof of our faithful fulfilment of our alliance commitments. In order to ensure its successful course we took the necessary measures on our side. Our people as well as members of the Army welcomed the Soviet and other allied troops on the territory of the Czechoslovak Socialist Republic. The highest representatives of the party and the Government documented by their participation, what importance we attach to it and the interest we have in it. Obscurities and some doubts in the minds of our public occurred only after repeated changes of the time of departure of the allied troops from the territory of the Czechoslovak Socialist Republic after the conclusion of the exercise.

The letter of the five parties also deals with some internal political problems of our present. We accept the assurance that the aim of this interest is not to interfere with the 'methods of planning and management of socialist national economy in Czechoslovakia' and with our 'measures aimed at perfecting the structure of the economy, at developing socialist democracy' and that the 'settlement of relations between Czechs and Slovaks on the sound bases of fraternal cooperation within the framework of the Czechoslovak Socialist Republic' are welcomed.

We agree with the opinion that the strength and the firmness of our ties - which are undoubtedly the common vital interest of us all - depend on the inner strength of the socialist system of each of our fraternal countries. We do not doubt that the undermining of the leading role of the Communist Party would carry a threat of the liquidation of socialist society. However, just for this reason, it is essential that we should understand each other correctly on the question on which the strength of the socialist system and the strengthening of the leading role of the Communist Party depends today.

In the Action Programme of our party we set down the following on the basis of our previous experience:

It is at present especially essential for the party to pursue such a policy that would fully merit the leading role in our society. We are convinced that this is under the present situation the condition for the socialist development of the country...

The Communist Party depends on the voluntary support of the people: it does not implement its leading role by ruling over society but by most devotedly serving its free, progressive socialist development. It cannot impel its authority, but must constantly acquire it by its deeds. It cannot enforce its line by orders, but by the work of its members, by veracity of its ideals.

We do not hide the fact - and we stated this plainly at the May plenum of the Central Committee - that in this country there exist today also tendencies to discredit the party, to deny it the moral and political right to lead the society. However, if we put ourselves the question whether it is correct to judge similar phenomena as a threat to the socialist system, as a decline of the leading role of the

8 a a

Communist Party of Czechoslovakia under the pressure of reactionary, counter-revolutionary forces - we come to the conclusion that this is not the case.

The leading role of our party gravely suffered in the past by the deformations of the 'Fifties and a policy of their inconsistent removal by the leadership headed by A.Novotný. On the contrary, he is responsible for the deepening of a number of social contradictions between the Czechs and the Slovaks, between the intelligentsia and the workers, between the young generation and the older generations. The inconsistent solution of the economic problems has left over to us a situation in which we cannot solve a series of justified economic demands of the working people and when the effectiveness of the entire national economy is seriously impaired. Under that leadership, the confidence of the masses in the party was declining and there were expressions of criticism and resistance, but all this was solved by interference from a position of power against justified dissatisfaction against criticism and against attempts to solve social problems consistently in the interests of the party,and of its leading position.

Instead of a gradual and well considered removal of faults, further errors and contradictions accumulated as a result of subjective decision making in the years when it was objectively possible to gradually develop socialist democracy and to apply scientific management, subjective deficiencies sharpened social contradictions and difficulties.

Outwardly it seemed that everything was in order in the Czechoslovak Socialist Republic, it was made to appear that developments were without conflicts, the actual decline in confidence in the party was masked by outward forms of directive party management. Although this regime was presented as being a firm guarantee of the interests of the entire socialist camp, problems were accumulating within whose real solution was suppressed by forceful measures against those advocating new and creative approaches.

a 9a

Any indication of a return to these methods would evoke the resistance of the overhelming majority of party members, the resistance of the working people, the workers, cooperative farmers and the intelligentsia. Precisely by such a step the party would imperil its political leading role and would create a situation which would really lead to a power conflict. This would really threaten the socialist achievements of the people and also our common interests in the anti-imperialist front of the socialist community.

We agree that it is one of the primary tasks of the party to thwart the aims of right-wing and anti-socialist forces. Our party has worked out its tactical political plan for this matter at the May plenum of the Central Committee and is solving these problems according to it. This plan consists of a system of measures which can be successful only if we have the conditions to gradually implement them in the course of several months.

We consider as the condition for success that the realization of the Action Programme and the preparations for the party congress are not endangered by any false step which would cause a power-political conflict in our country. The May plenum of the Central Committee of the Communist Party of Czechoslovakia stated this quite plainly in its resolution:

'Under the present situation the party considers it as the basic problem that it be made impossible to threaten the socialist character of power and the social system from any side - either from the side of right-wing, anti-Communist tendencies, or from the side of conservative forces which would welcome to return to the conditions existing before January 1968 and which were unable to ensure the development of socialism.'

Our party has laid down the following main aims and stages of political work:

10a a

1) To consistently dissociate the party as a whole from the deformations of the past for which concrete persons of the old party leadership are responsible: these concrete people are being justly called to task.

2) To prepare the 14th extraordinary Party Congress, which will evaluate the development and the political situation after the January plenum and will in accordance with the principles of democratic centralism in the Party lay down the binding line for the entire party, adopt a political standpoint on the federative set-up of the Czechoslovak Socialist Republic, approve the new state and elect a new Central Committee so that it has the full authority and confidence of the party and the entire society.

3) After the 14th congress to launch an offensive for solving all the fundamental internal political questions: for the construction of a political system based on the socialist platform of the National Front and social self-administration for the solution of the federative constitutional set-up, for the elections to the representative bodies of the State (federal, national and local) and for preparing the new constitution.

At present we are at the stage of the political fight for the implementation of the line of the May plenum of the Central Committee of the Communist Party of Czechoslovakia. It is a real fight and we therefore are scoring not only victories but we have also setbacks: however, it is never possible to judge the result of the entire fight according to the results of individual battles. Despite this we nevertheless believe that since the May plenum the political situation is being successfully consolidated.

The extraordinary district and regional conferences in the past few days have clearly shown that the party is becoming unified on the line of the Action Programme. Delegates have been elected to the congress and their composition is a guarantee that the future line of the party will

a 11a

not be decided by representatives of extreme views, but the democratically entrusted progressive core of our party. The representatives of the new leadership of the Communist Party of Czechoslovakia which is linked with the line of the Action Programme and the May plenum of the Central Committee were all proposed by the regional conferences for the new Central Committee. A certain stabilization is thus going on in the party and the basic steps for preparing the congress proceeded successfully.

In conformity with the resolution of the plenum of the Central Committee of the Communist Party of Czechoslovakia a politically binding socialist platform of the National Front is being created on the initiative of Communists. On June 15, 1968, all the political components of the National Front adopted a programme statement which clearly accepts the historically won leading position of the Communist Party of Czechoslovakia and which expresses the principles of a socialist system, of an internal and foreign socialist policy. The National Front is just these days discussing the proposal for its statute, which is a binding organization norm ensuring the socialist political orientation of all parties and organizations.

By the law on judicial rehabilitations we are basically solving the painful problem of the illegal repressive measures against innocent people which took place in the past years. This step has clearly helped that the attention of the wide public and also of the media of information no longer concentrates on these questions.

In September, immediately after the party congress, certain new important laws will be discussed: the constitutional law on the National Front which is to confirm the permanent existence of the system of political parties on the forum of the National Front and further the law on the right of assembly and association which will determine legal regulations for the creation and the activities of various

12a a

voluntary organizations, associations, clubs, etc. This will make it possible to effectively counter attempts of anti-Communist forces to gain an organizational basis for public activities.

Communists are also in accordance with the resolution of the May plenum of the Central Committee of the Communist Party of Czechoslovakia solving with initiative important questions of the work of the trade unions and enterprise workers' councils. On the whole, the party managed in connection with these questions to counter political demagogy, which attempted to take advantage of legitimate demands of the workers in order to disorganize our system and to fan an uncontrolled movement in the name of 'workers demands' so as to make the economic and political situation in the country more difficult. At the same time, however, we are solving, according to the means at our disposal, some burning social political problems such as the raising of low pensions and urgent adjustements of wages. The Government is gradually dealing with the fundamental economic problems of the country in order to provide a new impulse for the development of production and so as to make it possible to move over to further improving the living standard of the people.

We have taken the necessary measures to safeguard the security of our state borders, the party fully supports the consolidation of the Army, the security body, prosecutors and the judiciary. The party has also taken a clear stand on the question of the People's Militia whose statewide meeting has given full support to the new leadership of the Communist Party of Czechoslovakia and the Action Programme. The importance of this step was, as is known, directly welcomed by the working people not only in this country, but also in the USSR.

We consider all these steps to be important result in the implementation of the line adopted at the May plenum of the Central Committee of the Communist Party of Czecho-

a 13 a

lovakia important features of the consolidation of political conditions and of the strengthening of the not only declared but the really leading influence of the party in our country.

In spite of this we see and do not want to conceal that we are not fulfilling all conclusions drawn at the May plenary session of the Central Committee of the Communist Party of Czechoslovakia satisfactorily. It happens also at present that now and then there appear at public meetings and in media of information voices and tendencies which bypass the positive endeavours of the party, the state bodies and the National Front.

We consider the solution of this question to be more long-term task and are guided by the resolution of the May plenary session of the Central Committee according to which 'political management cannot be applied by the old, administrative power structures'.The Presidium of the Central Commi of the CPCz, the Government and the National Front unequivocally rejected the appeals of the statement of 'Two Thousand Words', which induce to anarchist acts, to violating the constitutional character of our political reform. It must be noted that, following these negative standpoints, similar acts did not in fact occur in practice anywhere in our country and that the consequences of the appeal 'Two Thousand Words' did not threaten the party, the National Front or the socialist state. A negative feature of our actual conditions are still the campaigns and unjustified slander directed against various functionaries and public officials - including members of the new leadership of the Coomunist Party of Czechoslovakia - which are conducted from extreme positions both right and left. The secretariat of the Central Committee of the Communist Party of Czechoslovakia and leading comrades have in concrete cases come out unequivocally also against these methods.

We know that this situation is made possible by the fact that we have abolished censorship in our country and

14 a a

enacted freedom of expression and of the press. What in tne past was spread only in the form of 'whispered propaganda', etc. can now be expressed in public.

However, if we put ourselves the question whether it is correct to evaluate such phenomena as forfeiture of the leading political role of the Communist Party of Czechoslovakia under the onslaught of reactionary, counter-revolutionary forces - we reach the conclusion that this is not the case. For all this is only part of our present political situation. There is also another, and in our opinion the decisive part of this situation. The growth of the authority of the new, democratic policy of the party in the eyes of the broadest masses of the working people, the growth of the activity of the absolute majority of the population. The abolition of censorship, freedom of expression are supported by the absolute majority of the people of all classes and straty of our society.The Communist Party of Czechoslovakia is trying to prove that it is capable of a different political leadership and management than by means of the condemned bureaucratic-police methods,mainly by the strength of its Marxist-Leninist ideas,of its program, its correct policy supported by all the people.

Our party can prevail in the difficult political struggle only if it is made possible to implement the tactical line of the May plenum of the Central Committee and to settle basic political questions at the extraordinary 14th congress in the spirit of the Action Programme. We therefore consider all pressures trying to impose another course on the party, that is to settle basic questions of policy at another time and elsewhere than at the 14th congress, as the principal danger to the successful consolidation of the leading role of the party in the Czechoslovak Socialist Republic. Such pressure is being brought to bear by domestic extreme forces from the right as well as from conservative dogmatic and sectarian positions, endeavouring for a return to conditions before January 1968.

a 15a

The evaluation of the situation as contained in the ter of the five parties as well as the undoubtedly sincere-meant advice for our further course do not take into account the entire intricacy of the dynamic social movement as it was analyzed by the May plenum of the Central Committee of the Communist Party of Czechoslovakia and the complexity of the conclusions adopted by this plenum. Our policy, if it wants to remain a Marxist-Leninist policy, connot be based exclusively on superficial phenomena which do not always accurately reflect the profound causes of social development but must understand the substance of the development and be guided by it.

The fraternal parties can at present serve the interests of socialism in our country primarily by expressing confidence in the leadership of the CPCz and full support of its policy.

This is why we have proposed, as a prerequisite of successful joint discussions, bilateral meetings of the representatives of our parties so that the joint talks may proceed from deeper mutual consultations and factual information.

We sincerely regret that these proposals put forward by us were not implemented. It is not our fault that the meeting in Warsaw was held without our participation. We discussed the proposals of the five parties for holding this meeting at the Presidium of the Central Committee of the Communist Party of Czechoslovakia twice - on July 8 and 12 - and each time we immediately conveyed our view on the method of preparing this meeting in the way which we considered to be most correct. Unfortunately, our discussion of July 12 was already superfluous because, notwithstanding its outcome, the meeting had already been convened for July 14, as we learned only through ČTK in the afternoon of July 13, at a time when the representatives of the five parties were already on their way to Warsaw.

16 a

a

In no standpoint that we sent to the five parties did we refuse on principle to take part in a joint conference. We only voiced our own view concerning its suitability at the present time and on the method of its preparation so that it may be really factual and based on more profound information about our complex problems. From the contents of the letters of the five parties, sent to us between July 4 and 6, 1968, we actually judge that such information is absolutely vital if talks are not to be held whose success would be threatened in advance by one-sided and sparse information of the great majority of the participants in the conference about the real situation in Czechoslovakia.

This is the purpose of our proposals for preliminary bilateral talks. We were guided not by an effort to isolate ourselves from the community of our parties and countries, but on the contrary, by the effort to contribute to its consolidation and development.

We think that the common cause of socialism is not advanced by holding conferences at which the policy and activity of any fraternal party is judged without the presence of its representatives. We consider as permanently valid the principle expressed in the declaration of the Government of the USSR of October 30, 1956, which says: "The countries of the great community of socialist nations, united by the common ideals of the construction of a socialist society and the principles of proletarian internationalism, can build their mutual relations exclusively on the basis of complete equality, respect of territorial integrity, national independence and sovereignty and mutual non-interference in internal affairs. This principle, as is well known, was confirmed by the conference of representatives of Communist parties in Moscow in November of 1957 and was generally accepted. In all our acivities we want to further strengthen and develop the deep internationalist traditions which, in our view, must include both understanding of the common in-

a 17a

erests and goals of the progressive forces of the world as well as understanding of specific national needs.

We do not want our relationships to further deteriorate and are willing to contribute on our part towards coming down the situation in the interest of socialism and the unity of the socialist countries on our part we shall do nothing that would be at variance with this aim. We expect, however, that the other parties will help these efforts of ours and will show understanding for our situation.

We consider it an important task to be able in the nearest future to hold the bilateral talks we proposed and which would assess, among other things, also the possibilities of a common meeting of the socialist countries and at which it would be possible to agree on its programme and the composition, the place and the time of its convening. We consider it decisive that we agree within the shortest time on positive steps which would ensure the continuation of our hitherto firendly cooperation and which would convincingly demonstrate our common will to develop and strengthen mutual friendly relations. This is in the interest of our common fight against imperialism, for peace and the security of nations, for democracy and socialism.

SUMMARY

The reader who has followed me up to this point will recognize an apparent contradiction in what I have said. In introducing these documents I advanced the thesis that the intervention which occurred on August 20th was prompted by a fear on the part of the Soviet Union and its Warsaw Pact Allies—excluding Rumania, of course—that events in Czechoslovakia had reached the point where they posed a significant threat to the survival of Communist rule in that country and, indirectly, to the survival of the bloc itself. In the subsequent commentaries on each document, I have consistently argued that Dubcek and his supporters had decided that the time had come to initiate change; that having made this decision they further decided that the CCP—and only the CCP—would preside over the process of implementation; and that as a result they and the system would be better off for the effort.

If I am correct in my interpretation of the underlying cause of the intervention and if, moreover, I am also correct in my assessment of the motives which prompted the initiation, and then guided the subsequent implementation of the changes that took place in Czechoslovakia after January 1968, then the question which remains to be answered is how, given the unwillingness of the CCP to permit its position to be threatened, the situation reached a point where the Soviet Union felt that only prompt military action could prevent a political disaster?

There are, of course, a number of possible answers to this question. First, it might be argued that the Soviet Union had simply decided to revert to a process of change and accommodation similar to that which characterized intra-bloc relations during the Stalinist era; that having decided to do so, the Soviets simply seized upon Czechoslovakia as a convenient place to begin the reversal. Such an argument, however, hardly seems plausible in light of the changes that have occurred in the bloc during the period since 1953. Nor does it conform with what we know of the events which both preceded and followed the intervention. Viewed in the context of these events, there can be little doubt that the USSR was genuinely concerned about the liberalization taking place in Czechoslovakia and that having tried unsuccessfully to remedy the situation by the application of more subtle pressures, turned to force only as a last resort.

Secondly, it might be argued that Dubcek and the CCP had decided the time had come to put an end to Communist rule in Czechoslovakia; that having discovered the "error of their ways" they deliberately set about creating a new political order based on the principles of liberal democracy. As I have tried to indicate, such an argument—no matter how comforting to those who view the triumph of democracy as inevitable—simply cannot survive a close reading of these documents.

The answer I am proposing is somewhat more complex. To begin with, it appears to me that, initially at least, neither the Soviet Union nor the Czechs themselves perceived the danger that lay ahead. The Soviet Union, for its part, seems to have accepted the fact that Novotny had blundered badly and that in light of the economic crisis and growing intellectual unrest his ouster was both necessary and desirable. If this is so, then Moscow probably also was prepared to accept change within Czechoslovakia; provided that the change in no way jeopardized either the position of the CCP, or the integrity of the bloc. Dubcek and his supporters within the CCP probably shared these views.

On at least two points, however, there may well have been a divergence of opinion. There was, in the first instance, the question of how much and what kind of change was needed. Given the differing perspectives of the two, it is not unreasonable to assume that whereas the Czechs, because of their intimate knowledge of the situation, were inclined to consider a broad range of reforms, the Soviets, for their part, were probably inclined to a more conservative estimate. Secondly, there was the question of the ability of the CCP to retain the initiative for change. Here too, one can only speculate as to whether the estimates of the two sides varied and, if so, how much. Considering the history of animosity between the Czech and Slovak wings of the Party and the seeming inability of Dubcek to eliminate all of the pro-Novotny elements from positions of authority within the CCP, it is quite likely that Moscow had some reservations about the internal strength of party leadership —reservations which were probably shared, although to a lesser degree, by the leadership itself.

Be that as it may, in the months immediately following the downfall of Novotny both sides appeared to have accepted the need for accommodation. The U.S.S.R., for its part, continued to play up the theme of continuity of leadership in the CCP. The initial reforms were accorded favorable coverage in the Soviet press and Moscow refrained from expressing whatever private misgivings it may have had about the ability of the CCP to preside over the course of developments in Czechoslovakia. The CCP, for its part, moved quickly to correct some of the more oppressive features of the system. At the same time it also cautioned against moving too quickly.

It was during these early months following the change of leadership in Prague that a new element appears to have entered the picture. The CCP, which for so long had felt the animosity of the Czech people, suddenly found itself the center of public acclaim. To say, as Dubcek does, that the popular reaction to the initial reforms and to the promise of more to come was surprising is, I think, an understatement. For a party that had grown used to an atmosphere of public hostility, the response was probably overwhelming.

In any event, the sudden popularity of the CCP seems to have convinced the leadership in Prague that the reforms, rather than constituting a threat to the Party, actually served to strengthen its position vis-a-vis the "masses." This, at least, is the impression conveyed by these documents. From the standpoint of the Soviet Union the growing popularity of the CCP, accompanied as it was by adoption of the Action Program, the promise of even greater liberalization, and expressions of anti-Soviet sentiment, must have been a disquieting development—so disquieting, in fact, that in the period after the adoption of the Action Program the Soviet Union began to express some reservations about the motives of the CCP. As already suggested, their reservations, although initially stated in rather mild terms, grew in intensity as the months passed.

Here, I suspect, is the key to why the reforms got out of control. On the one hand we have the sudden popularity of the CCP which, it would appear, convinced Dubcek and his supporters that their policies were in no way endangering either the position of the Party or the future of the Soviet Bloc. On the other hand, there were the pressures brought to bear by the Soviet Union—pressures which would have made any curtailment of the liberalization process appear to be a bowing of the CCP to the will of Moscow.

The situation can probably best be understood in terms of a specific reform, i.e., the end of press censorship. Initially, the decision to relax controls over the press seems to have met with widespread public approval. It also seems to have been followed by a short period of restrained criticism. In time, however, the criticism became more strident as reflected in the publication of the so-called "Statement of 2000 Words." Confronted with this and other critical statements which appeared in the press during June and July, the CCP must have had second thoughts about the original decision. Yet, its popularity with the people was growing every day. So too, of course, was Soviet opposition to the liberalization. Consequently, since the attacks in the press did not seem to pose a very serious threat to the position of the Party and since, moreover, a reimposition of censorship would have appeared as a concession to the Soviet Union, the CCP did nothing, with the result that the criticism continued.

If this assessment is correct, then it is easy to see how the reforms initiated after the January plenum were permitted to get out of control. The CCP, enamored as it was by its new-found popularity among the "masses," does not seem to have viewed the situation as a threat to its own position. Although the Soviet Union appears to have taken a somewhat different view, by bringing pressure against the CCP it only seemed to further blunt the Party's instinct for survival. The more pressure Moscow applied, the more it must have appeared to the leadership in Prague that a reimposition of controls would be interpreted by the Czech people as subservience to the dictates an external power.

Whether the CCP actually viewed these pressures as an unwarranted intrusion into the internal affairs of a "fraternal country," or whether it simply felt that the pressures were unjustified in light of the improved relationship between the Party and the people, is difficult to say. The point is that once the differences between Prague and Moscow assumed the character of an inter-nation rather than an inter-party dispute, resistance apparently became a matter of "national honor." Consequently, the Party would have found it difficult to impose controls, even if, as seems unlikely, it had felt such controls were necessary.

Under the circumstances, the intervention was all but inevitable. Confronted by a Party that, initially at least, *would* not act to correct what appeared to be a potentially dangerous situation, the Soviet Union and its allies undertook to pressure the CCP into curbing the excesses of the liberalization process. In doing so, however, they only succeeded in creating an even more dangerous situation: one in which the Party *could* not act without being thoroughly discredited in the eyes of the Czech people. In a sense, then, the Soviet Union is correct when it says that it intervened in Czechoslovakia to save the CCP from itself. What Moscow fails to add, however, is that it was pressure from the Soviet Union and other members of the bloc which, in the final analysis, seems to have placed the CCP in such an untenable position.

INDEX